The Sustainable Tall Building

The Sustainable Tall Building: A Design Primer is an accessible and highly illustrated guide, which primes those involved in the design and research of tall buildings to dramatically improve their performance. Using a mixture of original research and analysis, best-practice design thinking and a detailed look at exemplar case studies, author Philip Oldfield takes the reader through the architectural ideas, engineering strategies and cutting-edge technologies that are available to the tall building design team.

The book takes a global perspective, examining high-rise design in different climates, cultures and contexts. It considers common functions such as high-rise housing and offices, to more radical designs such as vertical farming and vertical cemeteries. Innovation is provided by examining not only the environmental performance of tall buildings but also their social sustainability, guiding the reader through strategies to create successful communities at height.

The book starts by critically appraising the sustainability of tall building architecture past and present, before demonstrating innovative ways for future tall buildings to be designed. These include themes such as climatically responsive architecture, siting a tall building in the city, zero-carbon towers, skygardens and community spaces at height, sustainable structural systems and novel façades. In doing so, the book provides essential reading for architects, engineers, consultants, developers, researchers and students engaged with sustainable design and high-rise architecture.

Philip Oldfield is Director of the Architecture Programme at the University of New South Wales Sydney, Australia. Here he convenes the architecture + high-performance technology stream and leads a studio exploring sustainable high-rise design. He researches and writes widely on tall buildings and sustainability and is a British Science Association Media Fellow.

"This book provides a well-illustrated exploration of the broader sustainability issues tall buildings face, from energy performance to social connectivity. Its research and case studies demonstrate how approaching high-rise architecture as the design of urban infrastructure, rather than individual objects, can unlock the potential of this building type to provide a range of public benefits."
—Jeanne Gang, Founding Principal, Studio Gang Architects

"To create high performance tall buildings, designers must better respond to a number of factors – including environmental considerations, lifecycle carbon emissions, efficiency, integration within the community and context etc. Dr Oldfield's book provides a framework for a dialogue on how to do this. It informs and inspires the reader in terms of some of the fundamental considerations necessary when creating sustainable tall buildings through providing details on several key themes for the essential future of skyscrapers, from the creation of zero-energy precincts, to the use of highly efficient structural systems."
—Adrian Smith, Founding Partner, Adrian Smith + Gordon Gill Architecture

"This book challenges claims about tall building sustainability in a balanced and evidenced manner, providing a compelling mix of data, literature and precedent throughout. In doing so, it presents historical and contemporary issues that inform tall building design and performance, both environmentally and socially. It will be an important resource to all of those involved in the design, research and realisation of skyscrapers internationally. High-rise development is not universally appropriate as an urban typology. It should be used only where there is no opportunity for a less urbanistically intrusive solution. If you are building for need rather than ego, this is the book to consult."
—Peter Wynne Rees, Professor of Places & City Planning, University College London (UCL) Faculty of the Built Environment, and City Planning Officer for the City of London from 1985–2014

The Sustainable Tall Building

A Design Primer

Philip Oldfield

Routledge
Taylor & Francis Group

LONDON AND NEW YORK

First published 2019
by Routledge
2 Park Square, Milton Park, Abingdon, Oxon OX14 4RN

and by Routledge
52 Vanderbilt Avenue, New York, NY 10017

Routledge is an imprint of the Taylor & Francis Group, an informa business

British Library Cataloguing-in-Publication Data
A catalogue record for this book is available from the British Library

Library of Congress Cataloging-in-Publication Data
Names: Oldfield, Philip (Philip Francis), author.
Title: The sustainable tall building : a design primer / Philip Oldfield.
Description: New York : Routledge, 2019. | Includes bibliographical references and index. |
Identifiers: LCCN 2018048093 (print) | LCCN 2018048461 (ebook) | ISBN 9781315695686 (eBook) |
    ISBN 9781138905863 (hardback : alk. paper) | ISBN 9781138905948 (pbk. : alk. paper)
Subjects: LCSH: Tall buildings—Design and construction. | Sustainable buildings—Design and construction.
Classification: LCC NA6230 (ebook) | LCC NA6230 .O43 2019 (print) | DDC 720/.483—dc23
LC record available at https://lccn.loc.gov/2018048093

ISBN: 978-1-138-90586-3 (hbk)
ISBN: 978-1-138-90594-8 (pbk)
ISBN: 978-1-315-69568-6 (ebk)

Typeset in Adobe Caslon
by Apex CoVantage, LLC

Printed and bound in the United Kingdom by Bell & Bain Ltd, Glasgow

Contents

Chapter opener image credits

Figures

Tall buildings and the specifics of place

Antony Wood, CTBUH

Though we have seen major advances in the technologies, efficiencies and performance of tall buildings over the past couple of decades, arguably the urban expression of the typical skyscraper has not changed much from the predominant glass-and-steel aesthetic championed by Modernism in the 1950s. The architectural details have become much more refined since then, and certainly both materials and systems perform much better than they did a half century ago, but the rectilinear, air-conditioned, glass-skinned box is still the main template for the majority of tall buildings being developed around the world. Many of these boxes vary with how they meet both ground and sky, but they are part of a globalised expression.

However, a smaller group of ever-more-adventurous sculptural forms have come to the forefront over the past decade or two. But, in both the "box" and the "sculptural" approach, the relationship between the building and its location is predominantly either a commercial one or a visual one. Thus, these buildings are largely divorced from the specifics of the place they inhabit – physically, culturally, environmentally and, often, socially, too. For hundreds of years, the traditional architecture in many cities had to be intrinsically tied into its location – for its materials, its ventilation, its ability to function within a given climate and culture – but this approach was largely rejected in the Modernist belief in a "universal architecture", which transcended mere "context" and worked on a higher philosophical plane.

The consequence of this change was the aesthetic (and arguably, cultural) homogenisation of cities around the world – a force that has gathered pace exponentially over the past two decades, with the easier flow of capital, labour, goods and imagery – that now ensues. Now a "progressive" city is largely defined by its set of skyscraper icons, but the association is largely "synonymous" rather than "indigenous" – the same set of icons would largely become just as synonymous with other cities around the world if they were placed there. The models are thus readily transportable.

This building type has only 130 years of history and has now spread from its North American roots to encompass almost the entire world. So how can a relative typological newcomer be considered in such "indigenous" terms? The answer is that we need to consider the future and how the tall buildings being built today will reflect their culture and setting in 100 or 200 years from now. Many of these buildings will still be around for that time by default; the industry has yet to deconstruct a building over 200 metres in height. Thus, the buildings we are realising today will become the vernacular of a place tomorrow – a huge responsibility.

It is only when a building maximises the potential of its connection with local climate and culture that it can be truly classed as "sustainable" in all facets of that word, including the ecological aspects. Tall buildings are a vital part of the future for creating more sustainable patterns of life – largely through their concentration of people, space, land use, infrastructure and resources – but in many ways they are only several small steps along the huge path they need to traverse to become truly sustainable, and to become positive contributors to the cities they inhabit. There are still far too many question marks hanging over the typology – on ecological, social and cultural grounds.

One of the main challenges for the typology into the future is thus the task of creating tall buildings that are relevant to the specifics of place. To do this, we need tall buildings that maximise their connection to the city, climate and people. The future of our cities, and perhaps our continued survival on this planet, relies on it.

This book captures some of the essential quandaries surrounding tall buildings that remain unsatisfactorily answered today. Within the pages of this book, the reader will find a succinct distillation of the arguments for and against tall buildings, the sustainability of density and the relationship between tall buildings and the cities in which they are built. There is an intense and appropriate questioning of the persistence of the glass curtain wall across vastly different conditions, many of which are inappropriate for the standard, commodified approach. There is also a serious examination of how skyscrapers can better adapt to their environments, and become forces for positive climatic and social change in our urban future. The examples cited overlap significantly with some of the prior research of this author and the Council on Tall Buildings and Urban Habitat, but it is refreshingly presented here as a text that will be usable by students and professionals alike, and uses the visionary contemporary work of both as challenging examples of the way forward. As an architect and professor, I can testify that this is no small feat. I sincerely hope that this book will take its rightful place in the canon of architectural education, and mostly, that you will find it as useful as it is enjoyable.

Dr. Antony Wood, RIBA, PhD

Executive Director, Council on
Tall Buildings and Urban Habitat (CTBUH)

Studio Associate Professor,
Illinois Institute of Technology, Chicago

Visiting Professor of Tall Buildings
Tongji University, Shanghai

The garden city skyscraper

Richard Hassell and Alina Yeo, WOHA Architects

This book is an essential read for all in the built environment industry. It sets out the framework for understanding that sustainability and density go hand in hand in the context of the twenty-first century, where one of the key challenges is to find innovative solutions for living well on an increasingly crowded planet. For those of us within the tropical belt, the problems of the future are not academic or far removed. They are urgent and real. Rapid urbanisation and overcrowding of megacities have caused many green, open and civic spaces to shrink at an unprecedented rate. Taking over these spaces are harsh urban jungles of energy-guzzling buildings and sprawling infrastructure (along with traffic congestion and pollution) that are causing global temperatures to escalate. All of this will lead to inevitable crisis if governments, urban planners, developers and architects fail to urgently rethink the way cities are planned and buildings are designed.

Megacities are already happening; the question is whether megastructures are the solution. We would argue that in some cases they are, provided that they allow for very high densities with high-amenity. To create liveable built environments, designers must address quality-of-life needs, such as green spaces, community spaces and civic spaces within large developments. In that way, the city becomes more hospitable and enjoyable, rather than feeling increased pressure on the same old facilities. Sustainability then, as the author points out, needs to extend beyond the environmental aspects and encompass the social dimension as well. That is because very large structures or tall buildings can often isolate and alienate, unless we cater to human scale and to building communities.

WOHA Architects has been investigating these issues in a series of projects, some of which are mentioned in this book. The Met was the tallest residential building in Bangkok at the time of completion in 2010, standing at 230 metres tall. It comprises six 69-storey breezeway towers in a staggered plan arrangement, which facilitates ventilation, daylight penetration and views from every apartment. Vertical breezeways utilise thermal displacement to generate cooling upward airflow between the towers. Tropical community spaces are located on three elevated ground levels, which span the width of the building to provide a high-amenity aerial environment. The Met offers a new model for high-density tropical housing in dense Asian cities (see also Chapter 4).

The School of the Arts (SOTA) is a prototype of a high-density, high-amenity vertical school in central Singapore, combining an arts school with public performance venues. New elevated ground levels are introduced on the fifth floor where the students assemble and on the recreational rooftop Sky Park where the students play. These social datums, together with intermediate skygardens, form part of the informal learning commons of the school. The entire structure is calibrated as a 'wind machine' that maximises site-wide cross ventilation through breezeways. The academic blocks are also clad with a series of green walls that cut out glare and dust, keep classrooms cool and dampen traffic noise (see also Chapter 6).

Oasia Hotel Downtown is a 200-metre-tall (27-storey) verdant tower in the heart of Singapore's dense Central Business District comprising offices, a hotel and a club. It is a prototype of a naturally ventilated, perforated, indoor-outdoor green tower that is a sustainable alternative to sealed, glazed curtain-wall skyscrapers in the tropics. The tower is layered by four elevated ground levels, each an urban-scale verandah that is sheltered by the one above it. Instead of a fully air-conditioned building, it contains three cross-ventilated breezeway atria framed by L-shaped blocks. Landscaping is used extensively as an architectural surface treatment. This living tower achieves over 1,000% green plot ratio – compensating for the lack of green in buildings on 10 other similar sites and re-introducing biodiversity to the city centre (see also Chapter 5).

One of WOHA's recently completed projects, SkyVille@Dawson, explores the topic of social sustainability in the context of high-rise public housing in Singapore. The development is massive, comprising 960 homes and over 500 carparks. The project is ungated; all common areas are fully open to the public. We found that the traditional form of modern high-rises, with a central core of compressed circulation space, is not conducive for social interaction. To overcome this, we took advantage of Singapore's gentle climate by making spaces within and between the 47-storey tall towers for community interaction, and to serve as breezeways. All circulation spaces in the development are naturally lit and ventilated, and every apartment is cross ventilated.

The central innovation of the project is the public, external, shared spaces interwoven through the cluster of towers from the ground to the roof. Each home is part of a Sky Village comprising 80 homes sharing an elevated community garden terrace. Four vertically stacked Sky Villages across three interconnected blocks result in a total of 12 villages. They are designed to foster interaction and be part of daily life. Every resident passes through, or looks over, this space on the way from the lift to apartment and can greet their fellow villagers,

see children playing and listen to residents chatting. Other community areas include a plaza located along a public linear park flanked by supermarket, coffee shop and retail spaces, and a childcare facility. Community living rooms – large double-volume verandah spaces – at ground level provided with seating areas overlook a park. Pavilions for weddings and funerals, play and fitness areas, courts and lawns are bordered by a 150-metre-long bioswale. The rooftop public Sky Park, which is open 24 hours to the public, incorporates a 400-metre jogging track under pavilions capped by a photovoltaic array. Such a dense and vertical, yet social and sustainable, model would work across the global tropical zone, where populations are exploding.

We are delighted that this book opens the dialogue on rethinking tall building design – a conversation that is vital in the face of climate change and increased pressure on resources. Rather than accepting that building and city typologies are largely established and fixed, it is very important for governments, urban planners, developers and architects to imagine where we need to be in 50 or 100 years, and to start making steps towards that positive and sustainable future with every project.

Richard Hassell
Founding Director

Alina Yeo
Director

WOHA Architects Pte Ltd.

Preface and acknowledgements

Daniel Burnham was one of the earliest skyscraper pioneers of nineteenth-century Chicago. Alongside partner John Root, he designed some of the most iconic tall buildings of the era, evolving the technology and aesthetic of the skyscraper. Yet despite his career taking place far before the 'sustainability movement' we know today, Burnham recognised the consequences of our wastefulness in the creation and operation of buildings and cities:

> Up to our time, strict economy in the use of natural resources has not been practiced, but it must be henceforth, unless we are immoral enough to impair conditions in which our children are to live.
>
> ["The City of the Future
> Under a Democratic Government".
> Royal Institute of British Architects,
> *Town Planning Conference Transactions*,
> London, 1911, p. 368]

Burnham's quote is over a century old, yet it rings truer today than ever before. There is little doubt that one of the biggest challenges of the twenty-first century will be mitigating climate change while accommodating rapid urbanisation; the need to radically reduce our carbon emissions while comfortably and sustainably accommodating billions of new city dwellers in their homes and places of work, education and culture. For many people, the skyscraper has no role to play in meeting these challenges. Instead, the building type is often considered the epitome of our wastefulness, the 'SUV' of the built environment. It is demonised as resource-hungry, in both energy and materials, and as socially unsustainable too, creating dystopias for the poor or isolated penthouses above the city for the uber-wealthy. This book aims to show that this does not have to be the case, and demonstrates how creative design thinking, innovative technologies and careful management and operation can create tall buildings that have the highest environmental performance, and are attractive places to live, work and play.

Personally, I remain fascinated by the design opportunities vertical architecture provides for sustainability, yet frustrated that such opportunities are rarely put into practice. This book aims to bring these to the forefront of the design process by capturing the opportunities and challenges of designing sustainable high-rise from literature, empirical data and international case studies. The book, as the title suggests, is a *design primer* written and organised to prime those involved in the design and research of tall buildings as to the thinking necessary to improve their sustainable performance. However, it does not suggest that the tall building is the best type to tackle the twin challenges of climate change and urbanisation on every site and in every circumstance. Much of the current discourse on sustainable cities seems to pit the tall building against mid-rise forms, with the latter often deemed the best approach. Instead, this work suggests that there is no single solution, and we need to improve the sustainable performance of all typologies in the built environment, from the small to the tall, the suburban to the urban. The focus here is on how we can improve skyscraper design specifically, such that it can play a far more significant role in tackling climate change and meeting our future cities' needs.

The book is split into four sections. Part I introduces the tall building typology, critically appraising its sustainable performance through a number of lenses. It presents the advantages and disadvantages of height, the urban impact of towers on cities and the history of tall buildings' environmental performance. Part II identifies key inspiration for the tall building designer, demonstrating how response to climate, community and emerging vertical programmes can inform sustainable high-rise architecture. More technical opportunities are discussed in Part III, with sustainable structures, embodied carbon and façade design explored in detail. Finally, Part IV completes the book by presenting innovative tall building designs undertaken in graduate architecture studios that were led by myself and colleagues at UNSW Sydney and the University of Nottingham. These ideas represent a new way of looking at tall buildings, transforming the typology into one which embraces sustainability and humanity, just as much as economy.

The research that informs this book first started over 10 years ago, while working on a PhD thesis entitled "Tall Buildings and Sustainability", undertaken both at the University of Nottingham in the UK and on secondment to the Council on Tall Buildings and Urban Habitat (CTBUH) in Chicago. This research explored the links between economic, social and environmental sustainability in high-rise architecture, themes which are built upon throughout this text. It was further developed during a period as Lecturer in Architecture at the University of Nottingham, Faculty of the Built Environment, where I was co-creator and Course Director of the MArch in Sustainable Tall Buildings – the world's only course and qualification at the time focussed on the research and design of high-rise architecture. Finally, the book itself was written in Sydney, Australia, where I am based as Director of Architecture at the Faculty of the Built Environment, University of New South Wales (UNSW). Throughout these years I have been lucky enough to receive the support, guidance and mentorship from so many people who made this text possible, and it is a pleasure to express my gratitude to them here.

Enormous thanks to Antony Wood, Executive Director of the CTBUH, who has acted as an invaluable mentor to me for many years now, and who drives the dissemination of best practice in tall buildings internationally through the many publications, research, events and conferences the CTBUH leads. Antony was also kind enough to write one of the forewords to this publication. Thank you to colleagues both past and present at the CTBUH, University of Nottingham and UNSW, and in particular to David Nicholson-Cole, Dik Jarman and Ivan Ip, who have taught with me directly in tall building design studios. A special thanks to Professor Darren Robinson, whose suggestion it was to write this book in the first place.

And, of course, to the many students who have sat lecture courses, seminars and design studios with me over the past decade. Your energy, creativity and ambition will be essential in tackling the global challenges we face in the future.

Thank you to the huge number of architects, engineers, consultants and photographers who have contributed data, images or feedback. These include 3XN, Acton Ostry Architects, Adrian Smith + Gordon Gill Architecture, AGi Architects, AHR, Mir Ali, Khalid Al Najjar, Architectus, Arup, Iwan Baan, Patrick Bingham-Hall, Büro Ole Scheeren, Henry Cheng, Pollux Chung, CTBUH, Wilson Dau, Nick DeWolf, Diller Scofidio + Renfro, H.G. Esch, Norman Foster, Foster + Partners, Noura Ghabra, Lucas Grecco, Sumit Gupta, Handel Architects, Steven Henry, Ingenhoven Architects, KPMB Architects, Annette Kisling, K. Kopter, Ian Lambot, LSE Cities, Lionel March, Kyoung Sun Moon, More Light More Power, Tansri Muliani, OMA, PLP Architecture, RSH + P, Paul Rafety, Reiser + Umemoto, Sauerbruch Hutton, Schöberl & Pöll GmbH, Schoeck Bauteile GmbH, Seagate Structures, Skidmore Owings & Merrill, Stefano Boeri Architetti, Graham Stirk, Stockwool, Studio Gang Architects, Namgoong Sun, Tange Associates, Dario Trabucco, United Nations, University of British Columbia, U.S. Geological Survey, Vertex Modelling and Wingårdhs Architects. A special thank you to WOHA, whose tropical skyscraper designs are demonstrating more than most the environmental and social potential the tall building can offer. Thanks to Serena Khor at WOHA for her help with images and permissions, and to Richard Hassell and Alina Yeo for an insightful and generous foreword.

I'd also like to thank the editorial team at Taylor & Francis for their support and patience with the manuscript. And I am grateful for the wonderful emotional support of close family and friends.

Finally, the work here, and all that I do, is dedicated to Amanda, Raffaella and Ilaria.

Dr. Philip Oldfield
Sydney, April 2018

About the Council on Tall Buildings and Urban Habitat (CTBUH)

The Council on Tall Buildings and Urban Habitat (CTBUH) is the world's leading resource for professionals focused on the inception, design, construction and operation of tall buildings and future cities. Founded in 1969 and headquartered at Chicago's historic Monroe Building, the CTBUH is a not-for-profit organisation with an Asia Headquarters office at Tongji University, Shanghai; a Research Office at Iuav University, Venice, Italy; and an Academic Office at the Illinois Institute of Technology, Chicago. CTBUH facilitates the exchange of the latest knowledge available on tall buildings around the world through publications, research, events, working groups, web resources and its extensive network of international representatives. The Council's research department is spearheading the investigation of the next generation of tall buildings by aiding original research on sustainability and key development issues. The Council's free database on tall buildings, The Skyscraper Center, is updated daily with detailed information, images, data and news. The CTBUH also developed the international standards for measuring tall building height and is recognised as the arbiter for bestowing such designations as "The World's Tallest Building".

CTBUH Headquarters
The Monroe Building
104 South Michigan Avenue, Suite 620
Chicago, IL 60603, USA
Phone: +1 (312) 283–5599
Email: info@ctbuh.org
www.ctbuh.org
www.skyscrapercenter.com

CTBUH Asia Headquarters
College of Architecture and Urban Planning (CAUP)
Tongji University
1239 Si Ping Road, Yangpu District
Shanghai 200092, China
Phone: +86 21 65982972
Email: china@ctbuh.org

CTBUH Research Office
Iuav University of Venice
Dorsoduro 2006
30123 Venice, Italy
Phone: +39 041 257 1276
Email: research@ctbuh.org

CTBUH Academic Office
S. R. Crown Hall
Illinois Institute of Technology
3360 South State Street
Chicago, IL 60616
Phone: +1 (312) 567 3487
Email: academic@ctbuh.org

世界高层建筑与都市人居学会 (CTBUH)

世界高层建筑与都市人居学会(CTBUH)是专注于高层建筑和未来城市的概念、设计、建设与ff营的全球领先机构。学会是成立于1969年的非营利性组织，总部位于芝加哥的历史建筑门罗大厦，同时在上海同济大学设有亚洲办公室，意大利威尼斯建筑大学设有研究办公室，芝加哥伊利诺伊理工大学设有学术办公室。学会的团队通过出版、研究、活动、工作组、网络资源和其在国际代表中广泛的网络促进全球高层建筑最新资讯的交流。学会的研究部门通过开展在可持续性和关键性发展问题上的原创性研究来引领新一代高层建筑的调查研究。学会建立了免费的高层建筑数据库–摩天大楼中心，对全球高层建筑的细节信息、图片及新闻进行每日即时更新。此外，学会还开发出测量高层建筑高度的国际标准，同时也是授予诸如"世界最高建筑"这样头衔的公认仲裁机构。

CTBUH 总部
门罗大厦620号
美国伊利诺伊州芝加哥南密歇根大道104号 邮编60603
电话: +1 (312) 283–5599
电子邮箱: info@ctbuh.org
www.ctbuh.org
www.skyscrapercenter.com

CTBUH 亚洲总部
同济大学建筑与城市规划学院
中国上海市杨浦区四平路1239号 邮编200092
电话: +86 21 65982972
电子邮件: china@ctbuh.org

CTBUH 研究办公室
威尼斯建筑大学
意大利威尼斯30123，Dorsoduro 2006
电话：+39 041 257 1276
电子邮件：*research@ctbuh.org*

CTBUH学术办公室
伊利诺伊理工大学 S. R. 克朗楼
3360 South State Street
Chicago, IL 60616
电话: +1 (312) 567 3487
电子邮箱: academic@ctbuh.org

PART I

Tall buildings and sustainability

CHAPTER ONE

The sustainable impact of height

Introduction

Is there such a thing as a sustainable tall building? Perhaps a better question is can a tall building *ever* be sustainable? Some architects, engineers, urbanists and environmentalists would suggest the answer is an emphatic no, instead arguing that the very idea of a sustainable high-rise is a contradiction, an oxymoron, an impossibility. Typically, the criticisms of the tall building focus on their perceived high operating energy requirements, reliance on artificial lighting and conditioning, increased material needs, unsuitability for families with children and the negative impact they can have on the surrounding urban realm. Even Ken Yeang,[1] the godfather of the 'bioclimatic skyscraper', suggests the tall building "can never be a truly green building, certainly not in totality" (Richards, 2007, p. 20), due to its greater appetite for energy and resources, as compared to low-rise buildings.

> Right at the outset, we should be clear that the skyscraper is not an ecological building type. In fact, it is one of the most un-ecological building types. The tall building over and above all built typologies uses a third more (and in some instances much more) energy and material resources to build, operate and eventually, to demolish.
>
> [Ken Yeang, from Richards, 2007, p. 20]

To thoroughly explore the sustainability of the skyscraper, we must first define what we mean by a 'tall scraper, we must first define what we mean by a 'tall building'. A problem exists in that there is no definitive definition, and many individual cities and regions have their own classifications. Rotterdam's 'High Building Policy', for example, considers buildings over 70 metres tall (approximately 20 storeys), whereas in Bristol in the UK, any building over 27 metres in height (approximately eight storeys) is considered 'tall' by the local planning system (Bristol City Council, 2005). Although 27 metres may be tall in that context, in the megacities of Asia such a building could only be considered low-rise. Given this ambiguity, the Council on Tall Buildings and Urban Habitat (CTBUH, 2018), the global arbiter for tall building height, considers the definition of a tall building to be a subjective notion which should be measured against one or more of the following three criteria (Figure 1.1):

1 **Height relative to context** – a building which demonstrates tallness in comparison to its urban surroundings, specific to that place
2 **Proportion** – a building which embraces height through its slenderness, thus giving the impression of tallness
3 **Tall building technologies** – a building which contains technologies and/or systems which are a result of its tallness (e.g. vertical transport technologies, structural wind bracing as a product of height, etc.)

This subjective definition encompassing context and technologies, rather than a specific height, is used throughout this book.

1. Height relative to context

2. Proportion

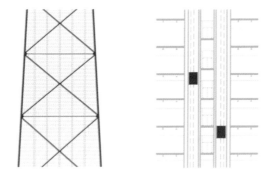

3. Tall building technologies

Figure 1.1   The CTBUH defines 'what is a tall building' subjectively, against three criteria
Source: Council on Tall Buildings and Urban Habitat

We must also define what we mean by sustainability. Perhaps the most recognised definition of sustainable development is that of the Brundtland Report, which defines it as "development that meets the needs of the present without compromising the ability of future generations to meet their own needs" (United Nations General Assembly, 1987, p. 16). This definition has evolved into three 'dimensions' – namely, environmental, social and economic sustainability (Adams, 2006) – also referred to as the 'triple bottom line', or the 'three Ps' of Planet, People and Profit (Collins *et al.*, 2008). These three facets of sustainability are considered equally important, but the environmental performance of the tall building is most often criticised,

particularly given the pressing challenge of overcoming human-induced climate change.

The need for a more sustainable built environment to tackle climate change is widely accepted but worth emphasising here. Anthropogenic CO_2 and other greenhouse gas (GHG) emissions have increased dramatically since pre-industrial times, fuelled by the burning of fossil fuels, industrial processes and deforestation. Current atmospheric concentrations of GHGs are at levels unprecedented in 800,000 years, leading to noticeable changes in our climate (IPCC, 2014). The period from 2011 to 2015, for example, was the warmest on record and saw a variety of extreme weather events, including heatwaves, floods, drought and the loss of polar sea ice (World Meterological Organization, 2015). Such events are often beyond the normal scope of what we are prepared for. For example, following mudslides in California, Eric Peterson, chief of the Santa Barbara County Fire Department, said: "No one could have planned for the size and scope of what a 200-year storm, immediately following our largest wildfire, would bring" (Caron & Stevens, 2018). Unfortunately, it seems this is just the beginning. Unless major changes are made to reduce GHG emissions, global warming will continue throughout the twenty-first century with cataclysmic implications. These could include species extinctions and the loss of ecosystems, sea-level rises and flooding, food and drinkable water shortages and extreme weather events increasing in both frequency and severity (IPCC, 2014).

To overcome these changes, the 2015 United Nations Conference on Climate Change, held in Paris, set in place national and international action and targets. Here 196 countries[2] agreed to develop plans that would limit global temperature increases to below 2°C above pre-industrial levels and to target the more challenging limit of 1.5°C. However, our current plans are not enough to achieve this goal. Research suggests that if we continue to pursue the national targets currently in place to reduce GHG emissions from 2020 onwards, we will still be subject to median global warming of 2.6–3.1°C by 2100 (Rogelj *et al.*, 2016), an increase that would cause vast and dangerous changes to the planet.

If we are to limit global warming to meet and better the targets of the Paris Agreement, significant and radical changes will be needed across all aspects of life. At the forefront of these will be changes to the built environment. As of 2015, buildings accounted for 39% of all global energy-related CO_2 emissions, with 28% due to the energy needed for their day-to-day operations and a further 11% related to emissions from the construction industry (see Figure 1.2). The good news is the energy we use in our buildings is, on average, falling, from 185 kWh/m² in 2000 to 150 kWh/m² in 2015, due to the use of improved building envelopes and more energy-efficient technologies and systems. However, this fall is insufficient to offset the fact that we are constructing more new buildings than ever before, fuelled by population increases and larger homes. The upshot is, despite energy efficiency improving per square metre, the growth of our total building stock is increasing to such an extent that CO_2 emissions from buildings and construction continues to rise as a whole (UN Environment and International Energy Agency, 2017). Projected urbanisation levels and greater access to improved facilities for billions of people could see this trend continue, with building-related GHG emissions doubling or even tripling by 2050, in the exact timeframe they need to be dramatically reduced (Lucon *et al.*, 2014).

Cities will expand rapidly in the twenty-first century to accommodate increased populations. Much of this new development will be high-rise; statistics show that more than three times as many skyscrapers have been constructed in the first 17 years of the twenty-first century, as compared to the entire twentieth century beforehand.[3] This trend is likely to accelerate in the coming years (Figure 1.3). China, for example, is expected to build between 20,000 and 50,000 new skyscrapers to accommodate an extra 350 million urban inhabitants by 2025 (Woetzel, 2009). This equates to between five and 14 new towers *every single day* for a decade – and this in just one country. Although other countries are unlikely to build to quite this extent, all corners of the globe are seeing – and will continue to see – dramatic increases in tall building construction, as urban populations grow. Given this situation, the need for the next generation of tall buildings to contribute to the reduction of GHG emissions is vital. Future towers, like all new buildings, need to be extremely energy and resource-efficient, but also provide vibrant and comfortable communities for people to live, work and play. Although built examples of low-rise housing, schools and commercial buildings have been pushing the boundaries of sustainable design for years, most skyscrapers built today still fail to embrace

Figure 1.2 Global energy-related CO_2 emissions by sector, 2015
Source: Philip Oldfield; data from UN Environment and International Energy Agency, 2017

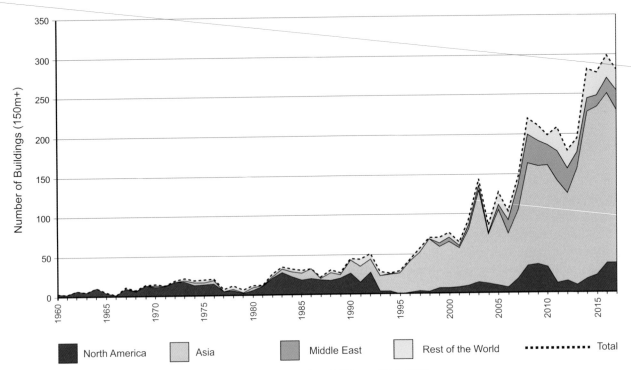

Figure 1.3 Annual tall building construction by region, for heights of 150m+, 1960–2017
Source: Philip Oldfield; data from Skyscrapercenter, 2018

environmental design beyond simply meeting local energy performance regulations; very few built skyscrapers put sustainability at the top of their design agenda. This only goes to further enhance the typology's reputation as the building equivalent of the SUV – energy hungry and embracing a bigger-is-better philosophy at any environmental cost.

With these pressures in mind, it is unsurprising that many consider the tall building an inappropriate typology for our future low-carbon cities. However, the sustainability of building tall is a complex and multi-faceted issue, and hugely dependent on climate, programme and architectural design; it is far too simplistic to merely state that tall buildings are less, or even more, sustainable than low-rise typologies. This chapter untangles the arguments for and against tall buildings in terms of sustainability. It demonstrates how height and verticality can provide sustainability challenges but also opportunities as compared to low- and medium-rise buildings, across environmental, social and economic realms. This chapter concludes that it can be difficult to consider many tall buildings

sustainable at the building scale, as often their designs fail to mitigate these challenges or seize the opportunities for improved performance. However, it also suggests that where tall building design does respond to local climate, and tackle the inherent challenges that height presents, sustainable and energy-efficient high-rise are readily achievable.

Environmental sustainability

One of the primary criticisms of high-rises is that they have been found to use much more energy (both in their day-to-day operation and their initial construction) than low- and medium-rise buildings, due to factors moderated by their height. However, fundamentally, changes in environmental factors due to height can provide both energy benefits and challenges. Exposure to wind, solar energy and air characteristics all change with height, impacting the way tall buildings use energy and how much they consume. Whether such changes are positive or negative is dependent on design, climate and programme, amongst other factors.

Air temperature, for example, decreases linearly with height, at a rate of around 1°C per 150 metres (Ellis & Torcellini, 2005). For office buildings or those that are cooling dominated (such that most of their conditioning needs throughout the year are for cooling rather than heating), this can provide energy benefits. In a study on the Freedom Tower (the initial design for One World Trade Center) in New York, Ellis and Torcellini (2005) show that the outside air temperature decreases by 1.85°C between the ground level and the uppermost floor at 284 metres above grade. Cooler outdoor air at height can be beneficial in offices since it means reduced conductive heat gain through the envelope, along with cooler air entering the building through infiltration and ventilation. The study predicts this would result in the top floor's energy requirement for heating and cooling being 2.4% lower than the ground-level floor. Air pressure and density also decrease with altitude (Leung & Weismantle, 2008). Since less energy is required to cool this thinner outdoor air, it makes sense in cooling-dominated towers to bring in outdoor air for ventilation at the highest level possible.

A study by Saroglou *et al.* (2017) explores the heating and cooling impact of these changing microclimatic conditions with altitude in a theoretical 400-metre-tall building in hot and humid Tel Aviv.

In an office scenario, they found heating requirements increased slightly with height from 0.94 kWh/m²/annum at ground to 3.44 kWh/m²/annum at a height of 343.2 metres. However, the more dominant cooling loads decrease with height to a much greater extent, from 46.6 kWh/m²/annum at ground to 30.9 kWh/m²/annum at the top, meaning increased height, in this instance, is an intrinsic energy benefit. In a residential scenario in the same climate, due to greater heating requirements, the reduced cooling loads at height are offset by increased heating loads (Figure 1.4). For residential programmes in colder climates, floor levels at higher altitudes will likely have greater energy demands, since they require more heating to offset cooler outdoor temperatures, although they may also gain access to greater levels of passive solar gain, for free heating.

Perhaps the most significant environmental factor that tall buildings face is that of wind speed, which increases with height. Typically, wind has been the nemesis of the tall building designer since greater wind loads mean more force acting laterally on the building, and therefore greater structural resistance required in terms of bracing. These effects increase exponentially such that in the world's tallest towers, resisting wind load becomes the predominant design factor in the building's form, orientation

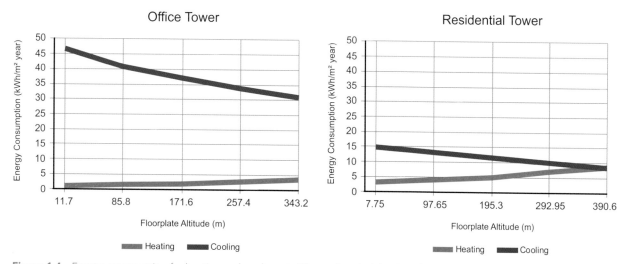

Figure 1.4   Energy consumption for heating and cooling at different floor heights in a theoretical 400-metre-tall tower in Tel Aviv
Source: Philip Oldfield; data from Saroglou *et al.*, 2017

and structure. In terms of sustainability, the result is that tall buildings require much greater quantities of structural steel and concrete, and thus consume more embodied energy/carbon,[4] than low-rise buildings. A study by Treloar *et al.* (2001) calculated the initial embodied energy in five office buildings in Melbourne, Australia – 3, 7, 15, 42 and 52 storeys tall – and found embodied energy increases significantly with height, predominantly due to increased structural requirements (Figure 1.5). However, the issue of embodied energy and high-rise is not simply a case of being better or worse than low-rise construction, and there are a variety of both advantages and disadvantages to building tall in terms of material sustainability. These issues are outlined in more detail in Chapter 7.

Increased wind at height can provide environmental benefits. The exposed nature of tall buildings can give upper floors greater access to wind for natural ventilation as compared to low-rise buildings sited in a dense urban setting, where surrounding buildings may block wind paths. Of course, the flip side of this

is that groups of towers, particularly when clustered tightly together, or lined up, can create 'urban walls' and block the wind path to other buildings or public spaces, limiting their access to ventilation. Wind speeds at height can also be relatively large, providing far more ventilation than necessary for internal spaces. In theory, opening windows for natural ventilation becomes unviable when wind speeds reach 8 m/s and above (Gonçalves & Umakoshi, 2010). Open a window on the 40th storey and, rather than a fresh breeze, you might receive a gust of wind strong enough to cause discomfort or even danger. Tall building designs geared towards incorporating natural ventilation strategies therefore need to operate over a variety of wind pressures, which can cause control difficulties that are expensive to overcome (Etheridge & Ford, 2008). The upshot is, despite the potential for greater access to wind, many tall buildings fail to take advantage of the natural ventilation opportunities height can provide. Instead, they typically rely on sealed environments, coupled with energy-intensive air-conditioning, to the planet's detriment.

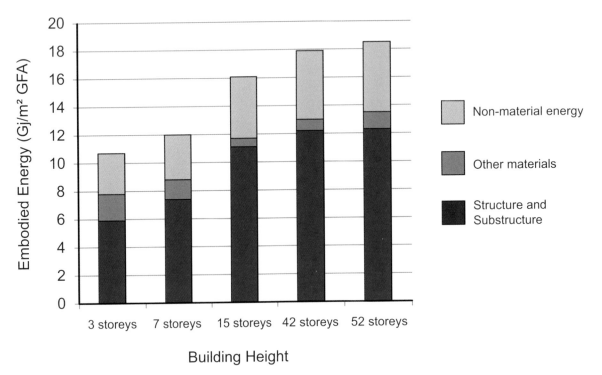

Figure 1.5 Initial embodied energy increasing with height in five buildings in Melbourne
Source: Treloar *et al.*, 2001

Increased wind speeds at height can also provide opportunities for renewable energy generation. Positioning wind turbines atop a tall building can be an optimum location in the dense urban environment, since this is where speeds are highest, and turbines can benefit from unobstructed access to the wind. In practice, however, there have been challenges with the integration of wind turbines into high-rise forms, specifically with regard to turbulence and noise, and the concept is still very much an emerging one (for more on this topic, see Chapter 4).

Tower design and location can have a significant impact on the comfort and safety of pedestrians in the surrounding public realm. By creating large exposed façade surfaces, tall buildings, and especially wide slab blocks, can redirect wind flow in undesirable ways. Of importance is the impact of wind downdraft, where a tower form redirects wind downwards towards the pedestrian realm, causing discomfort and occasionally danger.[5] Mitigation strategies typically include careful siting and orientation of towers in consideration of prevailing wind directions, as well as the use of podiums or set-backs, pedestrian canopies or aerodynamic tower forms (Figure 1.6).

The exposed nature of tall buildings will often provide greater access to solar energy and daylight, since other buildings and trees rarely cast shadows on high-rises, at least on the upper floors. In heating-dominated buildings, such as residential towers in cold climates, this can be beneficial, providing passive solar heat gain and reducing the energy needed for artificial heating. Of course, in hot climates (or cooling-dominated buildings) this would be a disadvantage, and the extra solar gain would be unwanted (and impact negatively on building energy use). Greater access to solar energy can also provide renewable energy generation opportunities from photovoltaic panels or solar-thermal installations. Although these energy solutions are generally most efficient when installed on rooftops, allowing panels to be tilted towards the sun for maximum output, low-rise roofs are often shaded in dense urban environments. High-rise façades are generally less shaded and provide an opportune location for solar energy systems.

However, some see this greater access to solar energy as selfish. By rising above its surroundings, the tall building can be seen to 'steal' sunshine, casting significant shadows across adjacent areas, leading to a loss of both solar gain and daylight for its neighbours. This result can have a negative impact on quality of life, comfort and energy demands; any energy savings made in the tower from greater access to passive solar gains could be offset by the increased heating and lighting demands of its neighbours in the shadows. Effects can be particularly significant when multiple towers are involved. The eight towers originally proposed for Bishopsgate Goodsyard in London, for example, were sited to the south of low-rise streets and estates (Figure 1.7). Studies suggested the towers' construction would result in 44% of windows in the buildings to the north having less access to sunlight over the course of a year (More Light More Power, 2016). Such impacts can cause legal disputes regarding rights of light. In Nanjing, China, the developer of one of the tallest buildings in the world, the 450-metre-tall Zifeng Tower, was found guilty of shading adjacent buildings to such an extent that their access to sunlight fell below the local legal minimum of two hours each winter's day (Lam, 2015).

It is worth noting that shadows are not an environmental problem everywhere. In hot and tropical climates, the creation of shaded areas from towers can be beneficial, shading streets and public spaces, reducing direct solar gain and creating more comfortable public

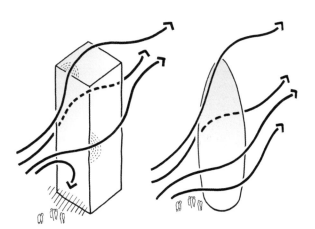

Figure 1.6 Design thinking for London's 30 St Mary Axe (the 'Gherkin'), showing the use of an aerodynamic form to reduce wind downdraft

Source: Norman Foster

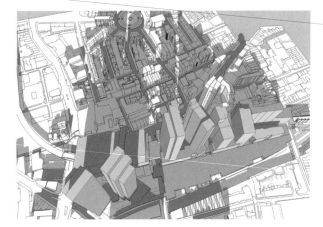

Figure 1.7   Digital model of the Bishopsgate Goodsyard
Towers, London, and the anticipated shadows they would cast
over adjacent buildings
Source: More Light More Power

Figure 1.8   The creation of an 'urban canyon' along Adams
Street, Chicago
Source: Philip Oldfield

environments. In the hot, tropical context of Singapore, one of the key community spaces for residents is the 'void deck'. This is the space at the base of high-rise housing clusters made comfortable and popular since surrounding towers provide a shaded area for community interaction.

The concentration and proximity of tall buildings to each other can have other impacts on microclimate. The creation of rows of towers along narrow streets creates 'urban canyons', which can trap heat, contributing to the Urban Heat Island (UHI) effect (Figure 1.8). This is a phenomenon where urban areas suffer higher ambient temperatures as compared to rural or suburban surroundings, caused by heat being released from vehicles and air-conditioning units in the city, but also due to solar heat being stored and re-radiated by large buildings, paving and roads (Memon *et al.*, 2008). According to Santamouris *et al.* (2017), over 400 major cities in the world suffer from increased urban temperatures. These can be in the order of 4–5°C higher than surrounding areas, and in some cases 7–8°C. Urban canyons are particularly prone to UHI effects, as they suffer from a low sky view factor – which is the amount of visible sky area. This means the lower floors in urban canyons cannot easily release the heat they have absorbed during the day as long-wave radiation to the cooler open sky at night. Thus, heat becomes trapped in the canyon, contributing to higher ambient temperatures. This is especially detrimental in warmer climates, where any additional heat is unwanted.

The form and shape of tall buildings has a significant impact on the amount of energy they use, as compared to other typologies. High-rise buildings generally have a much lower surface-area-to-volume ratio as compared to low- and medium-rise construction. That is, they have less exposed envelope area per unit building volume, meaning they are more compact than other typologies. Research has shown that in cold and temperate climates a building's energy needs for space heating is proportional to surface-area-to-volume ratio; the higher the ratio, the higher the heating requirements due to an increased quantity of envelope area facilitating heat loss by conduction and infiltration (Oldfield, 2017; Depecker *et al.*, 2001). To illustrate this point, consider a terraced house versus an apartment in a tall building; in the terraced house, heat loss may occur through the front wall, back wall, roof and ground. In a high-rise apartment, heat is typically lost through just a single façade, or perhaps two façades at a corner unit (Figure 1.9).

In the European context, space heating represents the greatest overall energy demand in buildings, making up 70% of overall usage in residential buildings (WBCSD, 2009). Given this, the compact nature of high-rise housing can be of significant environmental benefit. Urban energy modelling has found that taller buildings in Europe are more compact, and thus can have lower heating requirements than those of low-rise buildings (Figure 1.10). This means reduced GHG emissions and lower bills for residents as energy prices continue to rise. These advantages, and issues surrounding surface-area-to-volume ratio and compactness, are discussed in more detail in Chapters 3 and 4.

Of course, a compact form can provide environmental challenges, too. Reduced surface-area-to-volume

ratios mean less envelope to facilitate heat loss in buildings with high internal gains (such as offices), or buildings that need to dissipate heat to the outside in the summer months to achieve thermal comfort. For example, empirical data collected by Beizaee *et al.* (2013) demonstrates that even in the mild English summer season, rooms in apartment buildings tended to overheat more regularly than rooms in other dwelling types (Figure 1.11). Overcoming overheating can be a significant challenge in tall buildings; their inherently compact nature means it can be more difficult to ventilate spaces via opening windows, since there is less envelope available than in low-rise buildings. Deep floor plans, typical of tall office buildings, can also mean interior spaces fail to gain access to natural light and ventilation, which is compensated for by air-conditioning and artificial lighting (Figure 1.12).

A final notable challenge to tall buildings is the need to move people and resources (water, air, equipment, etc.) up and down the building, at a greater energy cost than in low-rise buildings. Elevators, in particular, are widely considered to be major contributors of skyscraper energy requirements, and they are often used as a key part of the argument to suggest tall buildings are more energy hungry than low-rise (Roaf *et al.*, 2009; Leung & Ray, 2013). However, there have been significant technological developments in vertical transportation over the past few decades. In modern elevator motors, most of the energy needed to move

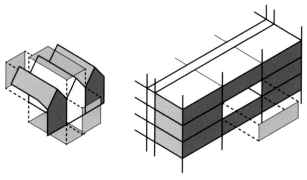

Figure 1.9   Exposed façade surface area facilitating heat loss in a typical terraced house and a high-rise apartment
Source: Philip Oldfield

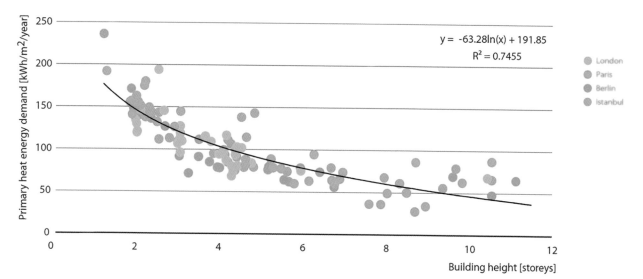

Figure 1.10   Correlation between building height and primary heat energy demand in four European cities
Source: LSE Cities & EIFER, 2014

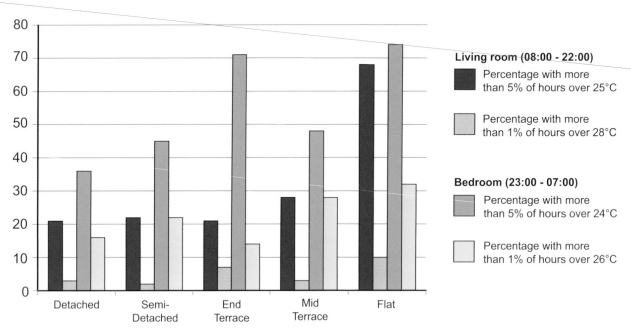

Figure 1.11   Percentage of living rooms and bedrooms exceeding overheating thresholds in a study of 192 UK households during the summer of 2007

Source: Philip Oldfield; data from Beizaee *et al.*, 2013

Figure 1.12   Shanghai Tower, Shanghai – deep office floor plans and large structural elements can limit access to natural light and ventilation in tall buildings

Source: Philip Oldfield

people up the building, against gravity, can be recaptured when an elevator cab is returned to ground in a process known as 'elevator regeneration'. This advancement means modern elevators typically consume just 2% of tall building energy needs, as compared to values around 8% about 30 years ago (de Jong, 2008). In a study comparing the energy use of office buildings in Hong Kong, Lam *et al.* (2004) found no trend between taller buildings and increased elevator energy needs.

What should become clear from this discussion is that a myriad of opportunities and challenges exist for reducing the energy use and the environmental impact of tall buildings, as compared to shorter typologies (Figure 1.13). In theory, height can be of significant environmental benefit in some circumstances and an environmental weakness in others; however, in practice a different story emerges. There are, unfortunately, only a few studies that compare the energy use of low-, medium- and high-rise buildings, but in those that do, the empirical data suggests the operation of taller buildings does require more energy, and thus contribute to the release of more GHG emissions – just as Yeang suggested at the beginning of the chapter.

Myors *et al.* (2005) studied the delivered energy[6] and subsequent carbon emissions of 3,670 dwellings across 41 residential developments in Sydney, Australia, through a combination of energy audits and collating energy bills. They found that high-rise housing had the highest carbon emissions per person – over twice that of townhouses and villas (Figure 1.14). This, the authors suggest, is due to the higher energy consumption in

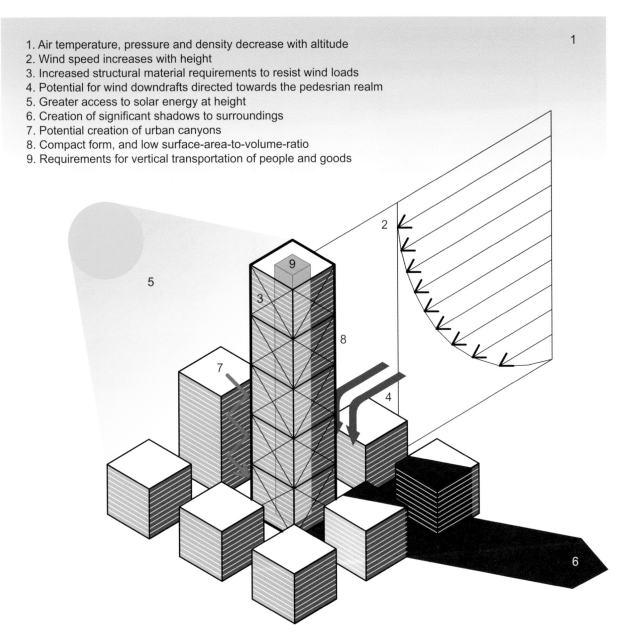

1. Air temperature, pressure and density decrease with altitude
2. Wind speed increases with height
3. Increased structural material requirements to resist wind loads
4. Potential for wind downdrafts directed towards the pedesrian realm
5. Greater access to solar energy at height
6. Creation of significant shadows to surroundings
7. Potential creation of urban canyons
8. Compact form, and low surface-area-to-volume-ratio
9. Requirements for vertical transportation of people and goods

Figure 1.13 A summary of environmental and microclimate factors influenced by height
Source: Philip Oldfield

common areas in tall buildings (e.g. for heated swimming pools) as well as the lower occupancy rates of the apartments as compared to the other dwelling types. Similar results have been found in office buildings; Leung and Ray (2013) gathered the delivered energy consumption of 706 office buildings in New York from city benchmarking data. They too found that high-rises had greater operational energy requirements than low-rise buildings, with a distinct jump at 30–39 storeys,

before levelling off at taller heights (Figure 1.14). They suggest this is due to changes in microclimate with height, such as increasing wind speeds, but also the prevalence of energy-intensive data centres and trading floors being located in tall buildings.

One of the most comprehensive studies in the field of height and operational energy was conducted at University College London between 2015 and 2017. The study looked at 700 office buildings across the

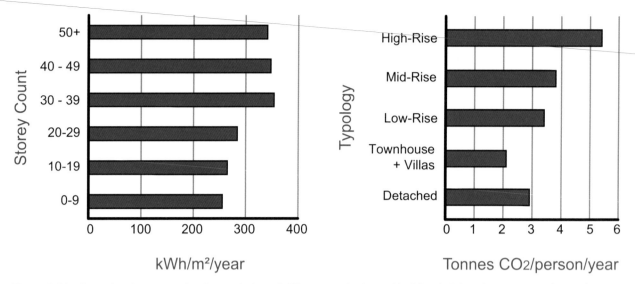

Figure 1.14 Operational energy and carbon emissions of different typologies and building heights, showing a trend towards higher operational energy requirements and emissions in tall buildings
Source: Philip Oldfield; data from Leung & Ray, 2013 (left) and Myors *et al.*, 2005 (right)

UK, and all residential buildings across 12 London boroughs, determining energy loads from electricity and gas records and statistical analysis. In office buildings, the authors found towers over 20 storeys tall have on average more than double the operational carbon emissions as compared to office buildings of six storeys and lower. In residential buildings, they found a significant increase in gas use with increased building height, but only a slight increase in the use of electricity.[7] In conclusion, the authors are damning about the typology, suggesting "that much energy could be saved by discouraging tall buildings and encouraging low-rise in their place" (Steadman *et al.*, 2017).

Armed with this data, how should we build our future cities? With the pressing challenge of climate change, should we no longer build tall buildings due to their higher energy needs? A first conclusion is that more studies are required; it is only when armed with actual building performance data that we can make the strategic decisions necessary to improve the energy efficiency of our built environment. Although the studies outlined here go some way in achieving this task, it's clear we still have an undeveloped understanding of energy performance in low- versus high-rise buildings in different climates and cities around the world.[8] A second conclusion is that we should acknowledge that currently tall buildings *do* typically use more

energy than their low-rise counterparts. But, we should also be aware that a building's environmental impact is not just limited to its energy requirements, nor to the boundaries of its site. Insert a building into any cityscape and that building will impact the way energy is used, and the amount of GHGs released at an urban scale, across a variety of different dimensions. This includes impacts on transport-related GHG emissions, impacts on surrounding buildings and their energy loads, impacts on the amount of materials needed to construct infrastructure such as roads, etc. One of the primary environmental arguments for building tall is to create higher densities, and a more compact city, reducing urban sprawl and thus GHG emissions from transportation and infrastructure. This argument is discussed in detail in Chapter 2, but the conclusion here is that at a building scale it is currently difficult to consider the skyscraper as a sustainable building type. A further conclusion is that these results show the environmental failures of past and present tall building design, but that there are significant opportunities for the typology's environmental performance to be improved. We have a choice; stop building towers or build *better* towers. As discussed, height provides inherent environmental opportunities and challenges for the tall building designer in terms of air, sun, wind, form, etc. Too often though, these opportunities are not seized, and these challenges not mitigated. Where tall building design does respond to local climate and to the challenges and opportunities presented by height, there is evidence that operational energy consumption can be significantly lower than the norm.

Commerzbank, Frankfurt

The Commerzbank is a 259-metre-tall, 56-storey office tower, built in Frankfurt. It is the tallest building in Germany, and on completion in 1997, it was the tallest in Europe (Figure 1.15). The building is the result of an international design competition, won by Fosters and Partners, the brief of which insisted any skyscraper proposal for the site would have to embrace environmental design and energy efficiency before planning permission was granted by the local government (Davies & Lambot, 1997). As such, the design was set on a trajectory that most tall buildings do not benefit from.

A key driving factor in the building's design was local German building regulations which require that offices must have visual contact with the outside world. While regulations give no specific maximum distance between a workstation and a window, in practice this means that workstations are located less than six metres from the façade, since beyond this an occupant's access to natural light and ventilation is significantly diminished (van Meel, 2000). In the Commerzbank design, this meant the traditional model of the deep-floored office tower with a central core, where occupants often sit 12–14 metres from the façade, became an impossibility. Instead, the architects hollowed out the traditional skyscraper plan, replacing the central core with an atrium, effectively reducing the plan depth and giving all occupants proximity to the façade, be it the external envelope or the internal atrium (Figures 1.16 and 1.17).

As discussed previously, to provide natural ventilation in a tall building, there is the need to overcome the erratic nature of wind speed at height. To meet this challenge the Commerzbank façade incorporates a second skin, which acts as a buffer to the external

Figure 1.15 The Commerzbank, Frankfurt
Source: Ian Lambot

Figure 1.16 Commerzbank, view up the central atrium
Source: Ian Lambot

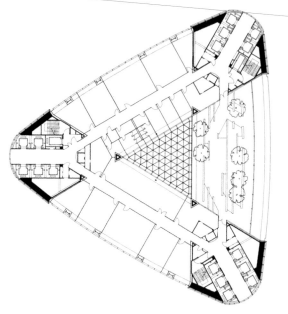

Figure 1.17 Typical plan of the Commerzbank with a central atrium and perimeter cores
Source: Foster + Partners

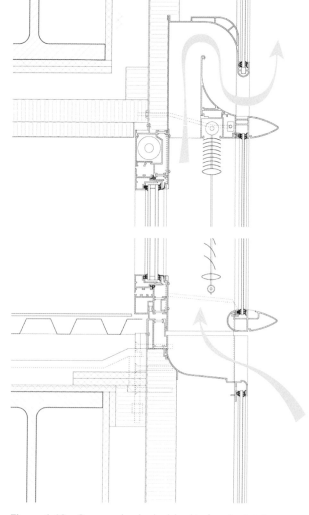

Figure 1.18 Commerzbank, double-skin façade detail showing air inlet and outlet. The internal operable window allows this airflow into the building
Source: Foster + Partners

elements. Air is drawn into a cavity between an openable inner skin and a fixed outer skin via a slot at sill level (Figure 1.18). This process slows the wind speed, mediating its path into the building, allowing windows to be opened in windy and rainy conditions – an impossibility in most towers (Davies & Lambot, 1997).

Internal offices are naturally ventilated from air drawn into the atrium via spiralling three-storey skygardens punctured into the tower's mass (Figure 1.19). To manage airflow in the atrium, the building is segmented into a series of 12-storey stacked vertical villages, each with three skygardens. The spiralling nature of the skygardens means no matter which direction the wind is blowing from, there is always a windward garden to admit air and a leeward garden to exhaust it (Davies & Lambot, 1997). The gardens also provide places of recreation and contemplation, spaces for meetings or relaxation at height in the city.

Whereas the vast majority of commercial tall buildings rely on air-conditioning all year round, at significant energy expense, the Commerzbank's mediating of wind speed at height through design and technology allows the building to be naturally ventilated for 80% of the year[9] (Gonçalves & Umakoshi, 2010). During the 20% of time when natural ventilation alone cannot

provide comfort (e.g. on the hottest summer days and coldest winter days), heating, cooling and ventilation are provided mechanically. This hybrid model, utilising natural ventilation when feasible but artificial conditioning when outside temperatures become too extreme, is known as 'mixed mode'.

In terms of energy performance, what is the impact of these strategies? According to 10 years of post-occupancy data presented by Gonçalves and Umakoshi (2010), the Commerzbank uses less energy

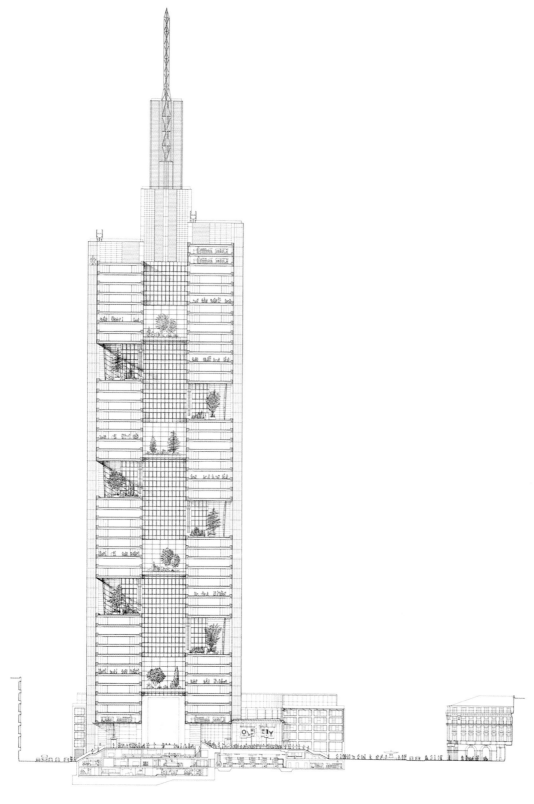

Figure 1.19 Commerzbank, section showing skygardens
Source: Foster + Partners

for heating and cooling than German energy benchmarks (ENEV, 2007), even benchmarks for naturally ventilated buildings (Figure 1.20). What's more impressive is that these benchmarks were enacted 10 years after the construction of the Commerzbank, during which time mechanical system efficiencies and building energy performances will have improved. And yet, it still betters them.

The Commerzbank is over 20 years old now, but was arguably the first tall building to truly use passive environmental design as the predominant driver of architectural form, organisation and technology (Oldfield *et al.*, 2009). In the years since, many other high-rise buildings have emerged that are designed around maximising environmental performance, far beyond that of the Commerzbank, be it generating energy on-site from renewable sources, fostering natural ventilation, or using low-energy materials such as timber

to achieve previously unimagined heights. Many of these exemplars are highlighted across the following chapters of this book. Yet, the environmentally responsive skyscraper still remains in the minority, and we must conclude that evidence suggests on the whole that tall buildings use more operational energy than low-rise buildings, and thus contribute to more GHG emissions at the building scale. But, as the Commerzbank demonstrates, when high-rise design responds to climate, and to the unique opportunities and challenges presented by height, energy-efficient tall buildings can be realised.

Social sustainability

A further case often made against the tall building is that the typology is *socially* unsustainable, and that compared to low-rise buildings, towers are less

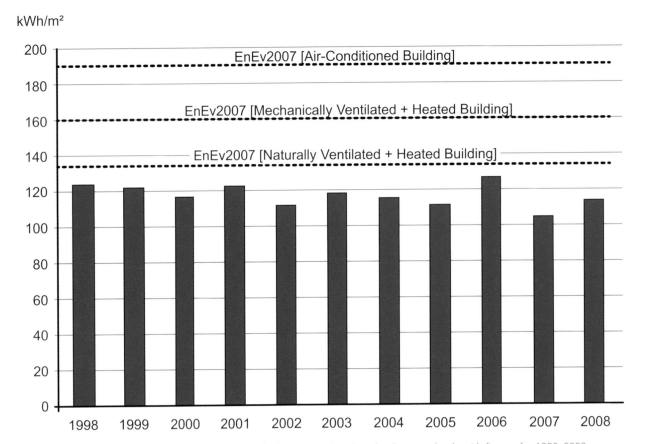

kWh/m²

Figure 1.20 Average monthly energy consumption for heating and cooling the Commerzbank, with figures for 1998–2008 compared to German benchmarks

Source: Gonçalves & Umakoshi, 2010, p. 318

conducive to forming successful and attractive residential communities. In this context we can define a socially sustainable development as one that creates "an environment favourable to the compatible cohabitation of culturally and socially diverse groups, while at the same time encouraging social integration, with improvement in the quality of life for all segments of the population" (Polese & Stren, 2000, p. 229).

High-rise housing, and in particular high-rise *social housing*, has become significantly politicised in recent years and, for some, represents an outdated and unappealing lifestyle. In the UK, for example, former Prime Minster David Cameron suggested brutal high-rise towers "are a gift to criminals and drug dealers" (BBC, 2016), and vowed to demolish the worst examples. In France, high-rise housing on city peripheries has even been blamed for contributing to riots, fuelled in part by the apparent alienation the housing type instils in its occupants (Appold, 2011; Caldwell, 2005). In reality, it is challenging to compare the social sustainability of low- and high-rise housing types given the variety of non-architectural factors that influence occupants' experience of living there, such as socio-economic status, local economy, building governance and whether residents chose to live there or if it was their only option. Even considering such factors, a review of studies has suggested that tall buildings are less satisfactory than other housing forms across three main areas (Gifford, 2007):

- Tall buildings are less suited to families with children than low-rise forms
- Social relations and helping behaviour are less in tall buildings
- Crime, and fear of crime, is greater in tall buildings

However, it's worth noting that many studies examining the social sustainability of tall buildings are quite old, often from the 1960s and 1970s. Many of the towers built during this period were of inadequate build quality and poorly maintained, which no doubt contributed to residents' dissatisfaction. Historic studies have also tended to focus on the social sustainability of people from poorer economic backgrounds who reside in tall buildings. There are few studies on middle-class occupants, who are likely to be more satisfied with their housing, as they have greater ability to choose where they live and in what building typology. Contemporary studies also offer more nuanced results. Rollwagon (2016), for example, found that residents in tall buildings do have a greater fear of neighbourhood crime, but their fear of crime in the home is lower than that experienced by residents in low-rise and detached buildings, due to the protection offered by being lifted above the ground in an apartment.

Tall buildings do offer some social sustainability advantages too, as compared to low-rise buildings. Building tall can create higher densities, and thus provide more people for the vitality of public spaces (Appold, 2011). Housing at higher densities can provide residents with easier access to local community services and facilities, which tend to be more generous in city-centre locations (Dempsey *et al.*, 2012). The general criticism of high-rise housing also tends to focus on western failures. Other studies in cities where high-rise living is more commonplace have found that residents are happy with living in towers. In Singapore, over 80% of the population live in high-rise social housing, 91% of whom were found to be satisfied with doing so[10] (Yuen *et al.*, 2006).

However, it is necessary to acknowledge that many tall building designs are not optimised for social sustainability – far from it in fact. One of the most notable failings of building tall is that the typology is generally less appealing for families with children, as compared to low-rise typologies. Central to this failure is the lack of open play space for children. Suburban low-rise living can offer the defensible front garden, the protected back garden and the tree-lined street as places to play, interact and socialise. In comparison, the tall building can often only offer the corridor and the lift lobby, both squeezed down to the absolute minimum that regulations allow, and more often than not, without access to natural light and view (Oldfield, 2013). Social spaces created at ground level can provide opportunities to overcome this lack of space, but are far below the home, and well out of eye-shot, meaning it's difficult for parents to supervise their children. The result is the traditional suburban home and garden often remain the 'ideal' typology for many families. This is not to say that families with children don't live in high-rise housing – increasingly they do, lured by the proximity and vitality of the city centre and places of employment and

Figure 1.21   The vertical monotony, and lack of space for social interaction, community and play adjacent to the home, means high-rise living can be unappealing for many people

Source: Philip Oldfield

culture – but more that the current procurement and subsequent design of high-rise housing fails to provide the spaces, facilities and services that families need and desire (Figure 1.21). The unsuitability of high-rise living for families with children provides one of the biggest future challenges to the typology – what's the point of an energy-efficient skyscraper if it only caters to a fraction of society, and a large percentage of the population doesn't want to, or simply cannot live there? Increasingly, architects and developers are rising to this challenge and incorporating social and recreational spaces at both the ground level and at height within high-rise design in order to improve their social sustainability and make them more attractive to a wider sociodemographic. These opportunities are discussed in greater detail in Chapter 5.

Economic sustainability

Tall buildings have always been intrinsically linked to economics. As far back as 1900, Cass Gilbert, a prominent skyscraper architect of the time, famously referred to the typology as "A machine that makes the land pay" (Gilbert, 1900, p. 624), such was the link between profit and building vertically. While the technological inventions of the elevator and load-bearing steel frame are often highlighted as key drivers behind the development of the first skyscrapers in the late nineteenth century, arguably it was the quest for economic efficiency that primarily influenced their form and expression (Willis, 1995).

Financial drivers still play the most important role in the formation of skyscrapers today, steering every aspect of their design articulation. This is due, in part, to skyscrapers being costlier to construct per unit floor area than low-rise buildings because of increased structural, lifting and service requirements, coupled with the complexity of their materials and construction methods (Watts, 2005). A further economic challenge the typology faces is its efficiency, given that increasing height usually results in reduced net-to-gross ratios (Figure 1.22). That is, tall buildings have less net lettable floor area per unit gross floor area[11] than low-rise buildings, due to greater structural and core requirements with increased height (e.g. larger columns, a greater number of elevators to service more floors, etc.).

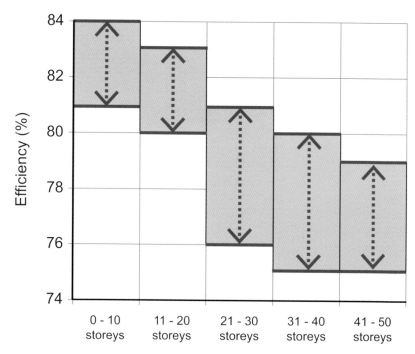

Figure 1.22 Typical office net-to-gross efficiencies compared by height
Source: Philip Oldfield; data from Barton & Watts, 2013

This in turn has environmental impacts; tall buildings effectively require *more* materials and therefore greater cost to create *less* useable floor space – a further criticism of the typology's sustainable credentials.

Improving the efficiency of a skyscraper then is inherently sustainable, not only economically, but environmentally too; a higher net-to-gross ratio means fewer materials (and therefore embodied carbon emissions) are needed for more useable space. If repeated, such a strategy would mean fewer buildings are needed across the city, saving land and cost. In addition, an efficient tower would be cheaper to construct and provide greater rents. Significant efforts go into making tall building planning as efficient as possible, and in particular, using advanced vertical transportation technologies to reduce the size of the core and improve net-to-gross efficiencies.

There are other links between tall building economic and environmental sustainability too. Although the capital costs of building tall are initially very high, compared to the salary of its occupants such costs are actually relatively low. Collins *et al.* (2008) note that over a high-rise office building's whole life-cycle, the salaries of the occupants can make up 85% of total company costs, with the building construction cost a mere 6.5%.

Sustainable strategies designed to improve the environmental performance of a building – for example, reducing energy requirements by harnessing natural light and natural ventilation – can also benefit the occupants' well-being, and in doing so, increase productivity and staff satisfaction and reduce absenteeism, a potentially significant economic benefit to the organisation (Singh *et al.*, 2010). In the Commerzbank example, the developer recognised that the additional capital cost of the full-height building atrium, skygardens and double-skin façade could be offset by even a 1% or 2% increase in staff productivity (Davies & Lambot, 1997).

This joined-up thinking in terms of sustainability is especially important for the realisation of sustainable tall buildings. In particular, identifying the future benefits and impacts of design strategies and technologies across the full spectrum of economic, environmental and social sustainability will give developers, architects and engineers the information to be able to decide whether their integration into a tall building is appropriate or not. Collins *et al.* (2008) support this notion, suggesting that a lack of awareness of the future financial benefits of sustainable strategies often leads to these being value engineered out of final designs.

Conclusion

In conclusion, it is challenging to say whether tall buildings are more or less sustainable than other building types. In reality there are a number of factors both for and against tall buildings, across the full spectrum of environmental, social and economic dimensions. What we must acknowledge though is that our current tall building stock and the way we design skyscrapers at present is far from optimised for holistic sustainability. We rarely design skyscrapers to take advantage of the environmental benefits of height or to mitigate the environmental challenges. The result is tall buildings use more energy and resources than low-rises do. Socially, they remain unappealing or inaccessible for much of society.

It's clear we need to change the way high-rises are designed to move sustainability to the forefront of the typology's agenda. Failure to evolve will mean tall buildings' contribution to the challenge of climate change in the twenty-first century will be negligible, or even detrimental. The case of the Commerzbank demonstrates how innovative design thinking can create high-rises that are energy-efficient, with places for social interaction while being economically viable. The Commerzbank is by no means alone in this sense, and other towers have pushed sustainable design thinking, but for the majority of high-rise, environmental and social concerns come second to financial factors. Too often, the tall building is designed as an economic product, rather than an economic, environmental and social one (Collins *et al.*, 2008).

These conclusions, and this chapter in general, have considered the skyscraper in isolation, as an object within the city. The next chapter challenges this notion by exploring the sustainability of the tall building at the urban level. In doing so, it argues that we only begin to see the greatest environmental benefits of building vertically if a tall building is successfully integrated into the urban realm, and in particular, to public transportation networks.

Notes

1   Ken Yeang is widely perceived to be one of the earliest pioneers of sustainable tall building design through both his built work with T.R. Hamzah & Yeang and his published theories on bioclimatic skyscrapers (Hamzah & Yeang, 2000). Despite this achievement, Yeang argues that the skyscraper is inherently un-ecological, but inevitable due to growing city populations. As such, attempts should be made to mitigate its environmental impacts as much as possible (Richards, 2007).

2   As of 2018, 195 countries have signed the agreement. However, the United States of America, the world's second highest emitter of carbon dioxide behind China, has issued official notice to the United Nations that it will withdraw from the Paris Climate Agreement by 2020.

3   According to data from Skyscrapercenter (2018), the hundred years spanning between 1900 and 1999 saw the construction of 1,032 tall buildings of 150 metres or greater in height, at an average rate of around 10 per year. In comparison, the 17 years from 2000 to 2017 saw 3,203 constructed, at an average rate of 188 per year.

4   The embodied energy/carbon of a building comprises the energy used (or carbon emitted) from extracting, transporting and refining the raw materials (e.g. mining iron ore), manufacturing the building components (e.g. creating steel beams) and constructing, renovating and maintaining the building (Fay *et al.*, 2000). For more details on this definition, and its impact on tall building sustainability, see Chapter 7.

5   In hot and humid climates, wind downdrafts caused by tall buildings can actually be desirable, to provide free cooling and thermal comfort in urban spaces (see also Chapter 4).

6   The energy used within a building is known as 'delivered energy' or sometimes 'site energy'. When this is measured, it excludes the energy used in mining the raw fuels (such as coal, crude oil, natural gas, etc.), converting them into a useable format in a power station (which may only be around 40% efficient) and transmitting the energy to the building. This broader boundary is known as 'primary energy' or 'source energy'. For example, for every unit of delivered electricity used in Australia, on average, approximately 3.4 units of primary energy are required (Fay *et al.*, 2000).

7   The authors speculate the reasons for this increase with height are two-fold: firstly, the taller buildings

tended to have more glazing than the low-rise buildings, contributing to greater unwanted heat losses and gains, and thus increased energy use. Secondly, they suggest the changing microclimate conditions with height, as noted previously in this chapter, play a role, such as increased wind loads causing infiltration, a lack of over-shadowing and reduced air temperature with height (Steadman *et al.*, 2017).

8   Unfortunately, real-life energy data is rarely released by building owners/managers. This limits our ability to substantiate and assess environmental design claims and to compare the impact of different design strategies and technologies, including low-rise versus high-rise (Goncalves & Bode, 2011; Oldfield, 2011). It is often through large-scale regulation that such data is made available. For example, Leung and Ray's study was only possible due to New York City Local Law 84, which requires all large buildings in the city to publicly release energy consumption data.

9   According to Goncalves and Umakoshi (2010), the windows in the Commerzbank still have to be closed when outside wind speeds reach 15 m/s, but only on the prevailing wind side. Natural ventilation in the atrium is available all year round, regardless of external conditions, as the space is protected from the elements. Overall, they suggest the figure of 80% can vary by ± 5% depending on the specific climatic conditions of the year.

10 The success of Singapore's high-rise housing is due to a variety of factors, including innovative architectural design, active social mixing of residents, progressive planning policies, good maintenance of social spaces and a lack of space in the city, meaning building up is the only real option available. These issues are discussed in more detail in Chapter 5.

11 A building's net-to-gross ratio is a measurement of efficiency defined as total gross floor area divided by net floor area. The latter is considered the lettable, or saleable, floor area – e.g. excluding the core, toilets, lobbies, machine rooms, etc. A net-to-gross of 75% means essentially three-quarters of the total floor area is 'lettable' and useable for typical activities (e.g. office space or housing). Care should be taken when comparing and contrasting net-to-gross ratios as the definition has different inclusions and exclusions in different markets and countries.

References

Adams, W. M. (2006). *The Future of Sustainability: Re-Thinking Environment and Development in the Twenty First Century*. Report of the IUCN Renowned Thinkers Meeting, 29–31 January.

Appold, S. J. (2011). Community Development in Tall Residential Buildings. In: Yuen, B. & Yeh, A. G. O. (eds.) *High-Rise Living in Asian Cities*. Springer-Verlag, London and New York, pp. 149–178.

Barton, J. & Watts, S. (2013). Office vs. Residential: The Economics of Building Tall. *CTBUH Journal*, No. II, pp. 38–43.

BBC. (2016). Housing Estate "Turnaround" Pledged by David Cameron. *BBC News*. www.bbc.com/news/uk-politics-35274783

Beizaee, A., Lomas, K. J. & Firth, S. K. (2013). National Survey of Summertime Temperatures and Overheating Risk in English Homes. *Building and Environment*, Vol. 65, pp. 1–17.

Bristol City Council. (2005). *Supplementary Planning Document 1: Tall Buildings* www.bristol.gov.uk/documents/20182/34520/SPD1%20-%20tallbuildings.pdf/2a44c0d4-fb3b-4da3-ae6e-c1bf96999481

Caldwell, C. (2005). Revolting High-Rises. *New York Times*, 27 November. www.nytimes.com/2005/11/27/magazine/revolting-high-rises.html?_r=0

Caron, C. & Stevens, M. (2018). Mudslides Close Part of Highway 101 in California. *New York Times*, 14 January. www.nytimes.com/2018/01/14/us/mudslides-california-highway-101.html?smid=tw-nytimes&smtyp=cur&referer=https://t.co/hL9kMaAtAT%3famp=1

Collins, A., Watts, S. & McAlister, M. (2008). *The Economics of Sustainable Tall Buildings*. Proceedings of the CTBUH 8th World Congress, "Tall & Green: Typology for a Sustainable Urban Future", Dubai, 3–5 March, pp. 175–185.

CTBUH. (2018). *CTBUH Height Criteria*. www.ctbuh.org/TallBuildings/HeightStatistics/Criteria/tabid/446/language/en-US/Default.aspx

Davies, C. & Lambot, I. (1997). *Commerzbank Frankfurt: Prototype for an Ecological High-Rise*. Birkhäuser, Basel.

De Jong, J. (2008). *Advances in Elevator Technology: Sustainable and Energy Implications*. Proceedings of the CTBUH 8th World Congress, "Tall & Green: Typology for a Sustainable Urban Future", Dubai, 3–5 March, pp. 212–217.

Dempsey, N., Brown, C. & Bramley, G. (2012). The Key to Sustainable Urban Development in UK Cities? The Influence of Density on Social Sustainability. *Progress in Planning*, Vol. 77, pp. 89–141.

Depecker, P., Menezo, C., Virgone, J. & Lepers, S. (2001). Design of Buildings Shape and Energetic Consumption. *Building and Environment*, No. 36, pp. 627–635.

Ellis, P. G. & Torcellini, P. A. (2005). *Simulating Tall Buildings Using EnergyPlus*. Ninth International Building Performance Simulation Association (IBPSA) Conference and Exhibition (Building Simulation 2005), Montreal, Quebec, 15–18 August.

Etheridge, D. & Ford, B. (2008). *Natural Ventilation of Tall Buildings: Options and Limitations*. Proceedings of the CTBUH 8th World Congress, "Tall & Green: Typology for a Sustainable Urban Future", Dubai, 3–5 March, pp. 226–232.

Fay, R., Treloar, G. & Iyer-Raniga, U. (2000). Life-Cycle Energy Analysis of Buildings: A Case Study. *Building Research and Information*, Vol. 28, No. 1, pp. 31–41.

Gifford, R. (2007). The Consequences of Living in Tall Buildings. *Architectural Science Review*, Vol. 50, No. 1, pp. 2–17.

Gilbert, C. (1900). The Financial Importance of Rapid Building. *Engineering Record*, 30 June, Vol. 41, p. 624.

Gonçalves, J. C. S. & Bode, K. (2011). The Importance of Real Life Data to Support the Environmental Claims for Tall Buildings. *CTBUH Journal*, No. II, pp. 24–29.

Gonçalves, J. C. S. & Umakoshi, E. M. (2010). *The Environmental Performance of Tall Buildings*. Earthscan, Washington.

Hamzah, T. R. & Yeang, K. (2000). *Bioclimatic Skyscrapers Revised Edition*. Ellipsis London Pr Ltd, London.

IPCC. (2014). *Climate Change 2014: Synthesis Report*. Contribution of Working Groups I, II and III to the Fifth Assessment Report of the Intergovernmental Panel on Climate Change. IPCC, Geneva, Switzerland.

Lam, E. (2015). Nanjing Skyscraper Developers Found Guilty of Stealing Nearby Residents' Sunshine. *Shanghaiist*, 26 November. http://shanghaiist.com/2015/11/26/if_you_steal_their_sunshine.php

Lam, J. C., Chan, R. Y. C., Tsang, C. L. & Li, D. H. W. (2004). Electricity Use Characteristics of Purpose-Built Office Buildings in Subtropical Climates. *Energy Conservation and Management*, Vol. 45, pp. 829–844.

Leung, L. & Ray, S. D. (2013). Low Energy Tall Buildings? Room for Improvement as Demonstrated by New York City Energy Benchmarking Data. *International Journal of High-Rise Buildings*, December, Vol. 2, No. 4, pp. 285–291.

Leung, L. & Weismantle, P. (2008). *How Supertall Buildings Can Benefit from Height*. Proceedings of the CTBUH 8th World Congress "Tall & Green: Typology for a Sustainable Urban Future", Dubai, 3–5 March, pp. 328–335.

LSE Cities & Eifer. (2014). *Cities and Energy: Urban Morphology and Heat Energy Demand*. LSE Cities, London and Karlsruhe.

Lucon, O., Ürge-Vorsatz, D., Zain Ahmed, A., Akbari, H., Bertoldi, P., Cabeza, L. F., Eyre, N., Gadgil, A., Harvey, L. D. D., Jiang, Y., Liphoto, E., Mirasgedis, S., Murakami, S., Parikh, J., Pyke, C. & Vilariño, M. V. (2014). Buildings. In: *Climate Change 2014: Mitigation of Climate Change: Contribution of Working Group III to the Fifth Assessment Report of the Intergovernmental Panel on Climate Change*, Cambridge University Press, Cambridge and New York.

Memon, R. A., Leung, D. Y. C. & Chunho, L. (2008). A Review on the Generation, Determination and Mitigation of Urban Heat Island. *Journal of Environmental Sciences*, Vol. 20, pp. 120–128.

More Light More Power. (2016). *Loss of Light*. www.morelightmorepower.co.uk/light-issue//

Myors, P., O'Leary, R. & Helstroom, R. (2005). Multi-Unit Residential Building Energy and Peak Demand Study. *Energy News*, Vol. 23, No. 4, pp. 113–116.

Oldfield, P. (2011). Real Life Data to Support Environmental Claims for Tall Buildings. *CTBUH Journal*, No. III, p. 61.

Oldfield, P. (2013). Successful High-Rise Means Building Gardens and Streets in the Sky, Too. *The Guardian*, Housing Network. www.theguardian.com/housing-network/2013/sep/30/successful-high-rise-gardens-streets

Oldfield, P. (2017). A "Fabric-First" Approach to Sustainable Tall Building Design. *International Journal of High-Rise Buildings*, Vol. 6, No. 2, pp. 177–185.

Oldfield, P., Trabucco, D. & Wood, A. (2009). Five Energy Generations of Tall Buildings: An Historical Analysis of Energy Consumption in High-Rise Buildings. *Journal of Architecture*, Vol. 14, No. 5, pp. 591–614.

Polèse, M. & Stren, R. (eds.) (2000). *The Social Sustainability of Cities*. University of Toronto Press, Toronto.

Richards, I. (ed.) (2007). *Ken Yeang: Eco-Skyscrapers*. Images Publishing, Mulgrave, Australia.

Roaf, S., Crichton, D. & Nichol, F. (2009). *Adapting Buildings and Cities for Climate Change: A 21st Century Survival Guide*, Second Edition. Princeton Architectural Press, Oxford.

Rogelj, J., Den Elzen, M., Höhne, N., Fransen, T., Fekete, H., Winkler, H., Schaeffer, R., Sha, F., Riahi, K. & Meinshausen, M. (2016). Paris Agreement Climate Proposals Need a Boost to Keep Warming Well Below 2°C. *Nature*, Vol. 534, pp. 631–639.

Rollwagon, H. (2016). The Relationship Between Dwelling Type and Fear of Crime. *Environment and Behaviour*, Vol. 48, No. 2, pp. 365–387.

Santamouris, M., Ding, L., Fiorito, F., Oldfield, P., Osmond, P., Paolini, R., Prasad, D. & Synnefa, A. (2017). Passive and Active Cooling for the Outdoor Built Environment – Analysis and Assessment of the Cooling Potential of Mitigation Technologies Using Performance Data from 220 Large Scale Projects. *Solar Energy*, Vol. 154, pp. 14–33.

Saroglou, T., Meir, I. A., Theodosiou, T. & Givoni, B. (2017). Towards Energy Efficient Skyscrapers. *Energy and Buildings*, Vol. 149, pp. 437–449.

Singh, A., Syal, M., Grady, S. C. & Korkmaz, S. (2010). Effects of Green Buildings on Employee Health and Productivity. *American Journal of Public Health*, September, Vol. 100, No. 9, pp. 1665–1668.

Skyscrapercenter. (2018). *The Skyscraper Center – The Global Tall Building Database of the CTBUH*. www.skyscrapercenter.com

Steadman, P., Hamilton, I., Godoy-Shimizu, D., Shayesteh, H., Evans, S., Moreno, G. & Donn, M. (2017).

UCL-Energy "High-Rise Buildings: Energy and Density" Research Project Results, 13 June. www.ucl.ac.uk/bartlett/energy/news/2017/jun/ucl-energy-high-rise-buildings-energy-and-density-research-project-results

Treloar, G. J., Fay, R., Llozor, B. & Love, P. E. D. (2001). An Analysis of the Embodied Energy of Office Buildings by Height. *Facilities*, Vol. 19, No. 5–6, pp. 204–214.

UN Environment & International Energy Agency. (2017). *Towards a Zero-Emission, Efficient, and Resilient Buildings and Construction Sector*. Global Status Report 2017.

United Nations General Assembly. (1987). *Report of the World Commission on Environment and Development: Our Common Future*. Transmitted to the General Assembly as an Annex to document A/42/427.

Van Meel, J. (2000). *The European Office: Office Design and National Context*. 010 Publishers, Rotterdam.

Watts, S. (2005). Cost. In: Strelitz, Z. (ed.) *Tall Buildings: A Strategic Design Guide*. RIBA Publishing, London, pp. 106–123.

WBCSD. (2009). *Energy Efficiency in Buildings: Transforming the Market*. World Business Council for Sustainable Development.

Willis, C. (1995). *Form Follows Finance*. Princeton Architectural Press, New York.

Woetzel, J., Mendonca, L., Devan, J., Negri, S., Hu, Y., Jordan, L., Li, X., Maasry, A., Tsen, G. & Yu, F. (2009). *Preparing for China's Urban Billion*. McKinsley Global Institute, March. www.mckinsey.com/insights/urbanization/preparing_for_urban_billion_in_china

World Meterological Organization. (2015). *WMO: 2015 Likely to Be Warmest on Record, 2011–2015 Warmest Five Year Period*. https://public.wmo.int/en/media/press-release/wmo-2015-likely-be-warmest-record-2011-2015-warmest-five-year-period

Yuen, B., Yeh, A., Appold, S. J., Earl, G., Ting, J. & Kwee, L. K. (2006). High-Rise Living in Singapore Public Housing. *Urban Studies*, Vol. 43, No. 3, pp. 583–600.

CHAPTER TWO

Density, the city and the tower

Introduction: the compact city

At some point in 2008, a unique event occurred. For the first time in history, half the world's population – some 3.3 billion people – lived in urban as opposed to rural areas (Figure 2.1). According to the United Nations, 193,107 new city dwellers are added to this figure every day, meaning urban populations will nearly double by 2050 (United Nations, 2014; Unhabitat, 2008). This growth is equivalent to around 1.4 million people each week, or the population of London every six and a half weeks. To accommodate these new urban dwellers will require the largest construction boom of all time. According to Ürge-Vorsatz *et al.* (2015), total global residential floor area was 141 billion square metres in 2010, but with population growth and larger houses being built, this is anticipated to almost double to 274 billion square metres by 2050. To put this into perspective, this is an increase equivalent to building over half a million new Empire State Buildings, or 1.6 billion new terraced houses. And this is just for residential space, not including the new buildings needed for work, culture, civic, education and industrial programmes.

If these statistics sound shocking, or dramatic, it is because they are. Alongside mitigating climate change, accommodating our dramatically increasing global (and mostly urban) population in a sustainable and harmonious manner is surely one of the greatest challenges of the twenty-first century. For the architect, developer, urban designer and city planner, the question that arises is what is the best urban form for our future populations, to benefit both the planet and the people who reside upon it? In what kind of city should people live?

The generally agreed answer to this question has changed several times over the last couple of hundred years, from the countryside, to the suburb, to the city. In the late nineteenth century, the city was the place of industry, and as such suffered from extremes of overcrowding, poverty and ill health with open sewers and overflowing tenements (Rogers & Gumuchdjian, 1997). This led to movements against the city and propositions to house populations in low-density semi-rural towns known as Garden Cities. The first of these – Letchworth – was designed by Raymond Unwin and Barry Parker in 1902, 80 miles north of London on the railway. Unwin's motto was "twelve houses to the acre", a density equivalent to 30 units/hectare[1] (Kostof, 1991). This rejection of the congested and 'unhealthy' city continued throughout the twentieth century with the rise of suburbia. Fuelled by the automobile, urban areas spread dramatically and populations dispersed. Cities became polarised, with downtown commercial areas, and vast swaths of surrounding residential suburbs, often up to 50 kilometres from the city centre, with densities typically in the region of 15–25 units/hectare. While populations grew steadily, the geographic spread of cities grew rapidly, meaning the density of our built-up areas dropped across the latter half of the twentieth century (Figure 2.2).

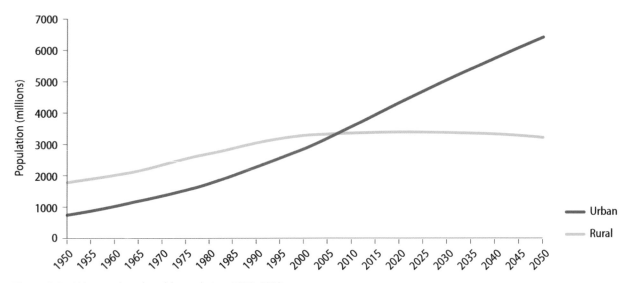

Figure 2.1   Urban and rural world population, 1950–2050
Source: World Urbanisation Prospects: *The 2014 Revision, Highlights*, by the United Nations Department of Economic and Social Affairs, ©2014 United Nations. Reprinted with the permission of the United Nations

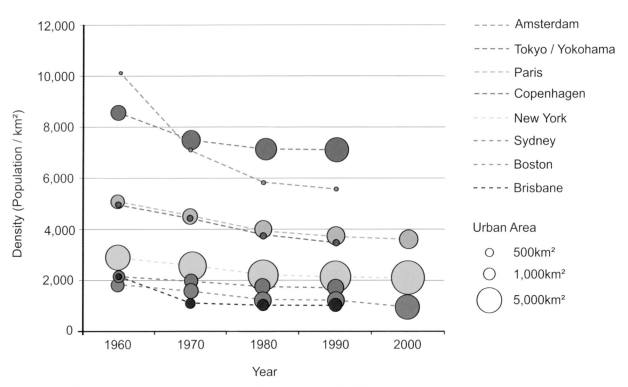

Figure 2.2   Changes in density and size of developed urban areas, 1960–2000
Source: Philip Oldfield; data from Demographia, 2001

Today, however, there is a general recognition that this model of suburban spread has been to the environmental, economic and social detriment of our cities and those who live in them. Such low-density urban patterns limit the ability of residents to walk or cycle for their daily transit and make access to mass rapid public transportation cost prohibitive. The result is a reliance on the automobile for transportation, which in turn increases pollution and CO_2 emissions while limiting physical activity (Stevenson *et al.*, 2016).

American-style suburbia, aka sprawl, was an emergent, self-organising system made possible only by lavish and exorbitant supplies of cheap fossil fuels, and once those conditions no longer obtain, not only will there be no further elaboration of this development pattern, but all the existing stuff built according to that pattern . . . will drastically lose its usefulness and its relative "market" value. . . . Suburbia will be coming off the menu. We will no longer be able to resort to the stupid argument that it is okay because we chose it.

[James Howard Kunstler, 2006, p. 176]

In response, a movement against urban and suburban sprawl has developed, instead promoting the idea of the *compact city*. This can be defined as an urban area with a high residential density, a diverse mixture of different land uses, an ease of access to public transport and the promotion of walkability.[2] The environmental benefits of the compact city are widely publicised. Perhaps most notable is the work of Newman and Kenworthy (1999), who berate low-density suburban development for the resulting automobile dependency it creates. Road transit is responsible for 18.4% of total global greenhouse gas emissions and is expected to increase significantly in future decades due to rising incomes in developing countries fuelling greater access to car ownership (Sims *et al.*, 2014). Low-density suburban sprawl, typified by North American cities, is highly car dependent, resulting in significant transit-related CO_2 emissions. However, as the density of urban areas increases, the energy needed for private transportation can often be seen to reduce exponentially[3] (Figure 2.3). This is

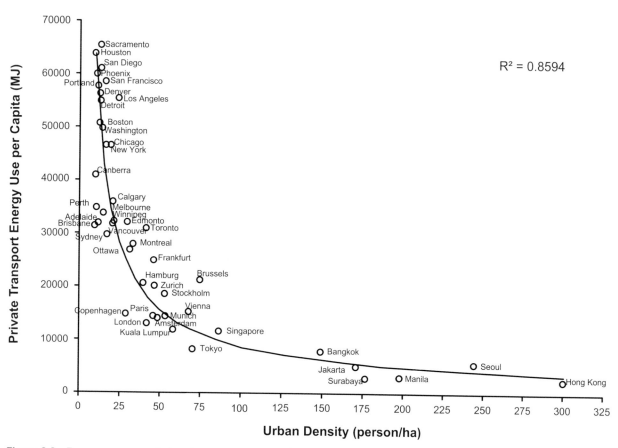

Figure 2.3 Energy use per capita in private passenger travel versus urban density in global cities, 1990

Source: From *Sustainability and Cities* by Peter Newman and Jeffrey Kenworthy. Copyright © 1999 by the authors. Reproduced by permission of Island Press, Washington, DC.

supported by Norman *et al.* (2006), who compared the carbon footprint of residents living in a 15-storey inner-city apartment block (density 150 units/hectare) with those living in suburban detached housing (density 19 units/hectare) in Toronto, Canada. Their analysis considered the carbon emitted from the materials needed to build the housing (embodied carbon), the emissions from using the building (operating carbon), and the emissions from occupants' daily transportation. In this scenario suburban living is 2.5 times more carbon intensive per person, and 1.5 times more carbon intensive per square metre than high-density living, mainly due to increased transportation emissions (Figure 2.4).

It is not only the emissions from road transit that can be reduced with increased density, but also the carbon emissions required to create the infrastructure that supports the city. Suburbs require vast highway and road networks to link them to the city centre and to other urban nodes. This requires millions of tonnes of concrete, at a significant economic and environmental cost. Increasing urban density, and compacting the city, can reduce the length and service run of infrastructure, such as pipelines and roads. Research by Müller *et al.* (2013) suggests that the length of water, waste water and road networks per capita and their associated material requirements decline with increasing urban density. What's more, since higher densities often provide incentives for a modal switch from cars to walking, cycling and public transit, they were found to also reduce car ownership (Figure 2.5).

However, other studies have generated more nuanced findings. Du and Wood (2017) compared high-rise living in the centre of Chicago (n = 249) with low-rise suburban living in Oak Park (n = 273) on the city's periphery. They found high-rise residents used less water, had far less infrastructure network requirements, had access to greater areas of open space, and travelled greater distances by bicycle and walking. However, suburban residents benefitted from lower operational and embodied energy requirements, had a greater sense of community and, interestingly, had on average lower car ownership and travelled fewer miles by car – a finding that goes against common assumptions. The authors put the greater car usage in the high-rise buildings down to the specific demographics of those who lived there, with many high-rise residents being older, retired and with a greater household income than the suburban dwellers.

Cities can be seen to contribute to other environmental issues beyond carbon emissions. As cities disperse and consume more land, they can be

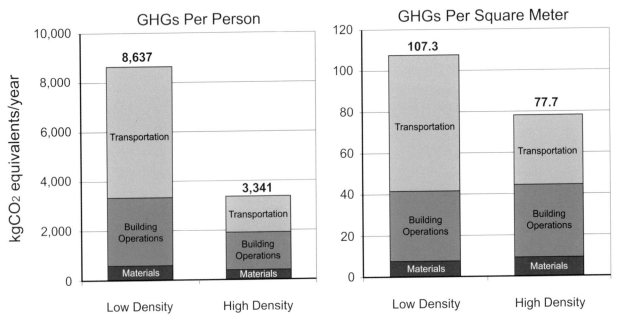

Figure 2.4 Annual greenhouse gas emissions associated with low- and high-density development in Toronto
Source: Norman *et al.*, 2006, with permission from ASCE

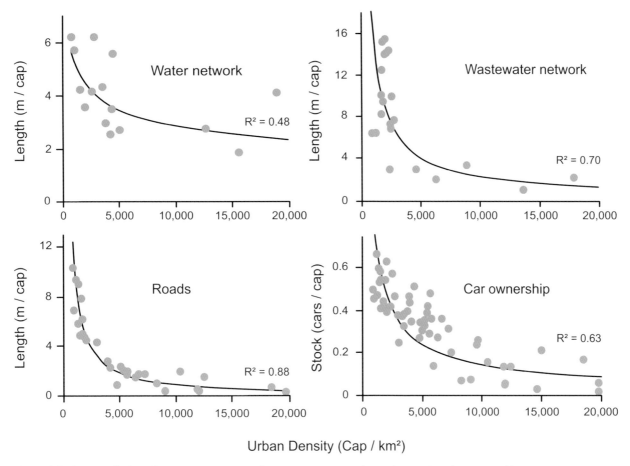

Figure 2.5 Impact of urban density on water network, waste water network, road network and car ownership

Source: Adapted with permission from Müller, D. B., Løvik, A. N., Modaresi, R. & Brattebø, H. (2013). Carbon Emissions of Infrastructure Development. *Journal of Environmental Science and Technology*, Vol. 47, No. 20, pp. 11739–11746. Copyright 2013 American Chemical Society

responsible for the loss of biodiversity and regional vegetation. In Australia, the horizontal growth of major cities, along with clearing for agriculture, has contributed to significant loss of native vegetation and forest land (DSEWPaC, 2011). In general, urban development produces some of the greatest local extinction rates and frequently eliminates a large majority of native species (McKinney, 2002). Limiting the spread of built-up areas as our population grows can maintain natural environments and biodiversity outside the city boundary.

The benefits of compact urban development are not only environmental but can also support health and well-being. The eminent urbanist and activist Jane Jacobs was one of the first to acknowledge the value of high densities for city vitality, safety and community.

In *The Death and Life of Great American Cities* (1961), Jacobs suggests that city life starts flourishing at a density of around 250 units per hectare, 10 times that of the suburbs.[4] Jacobs also dispels the myth that high-density development results in overcrowding. She notes that overcrowding is a result of too many people *per dwelling*, which is not synonymous with density as measured in *units per hectare*. A development may have a very high density in units per hectare, but its residents may live in comfortable conditions that are not overcrowded. It is this confusion, perhaps more than any other, which means that 'high density' can still strike fear into an existing neighbourhood, concerned that new development will result in overcrowding.

More recent research highlights the health and fitness benefits of compactness and intensity in city planning. Stevenson *et al.* (2016) modelled existing cities and adjusted these to cater for increased residential density, mixed land use and greater access to public transportation and walkability – all key characteristics of the compact city. Their research found compact cities had health benefits in terms of diabetes, cardiovascular disease and respiratory disease, with overall gains of 420–826 disability-adjusted life-years per 100,000 people.

However, while these benefits are widely acknowledged, and the compact city is broadly recognised as the urban model to tackle the twin challenges of urbanisation and climate change in planning policy, our urban areas are not getting denser, despite a perception as such. Detailed spatial analysis of 200 cities shows urban densities have been dropping 1.5% annually over the past 25 years in developed countries and 2.1% annually in less developed countries. These trends are likely to continue throughout the first half of the twenty-first century (Angel *et al.*, 2016). Thus, while we recognise that density is sustainable, and we may have a perception that our cities are getting denser, we continue to construct our built environments in a sprawling manner. There is a pressing need for change:

> [U]rban growth is mostly taking place in an unplanned and disorderly manner, informality is becoming more common over time, cities are expanding their territories faster than their populations, residential densities are decreasing dramatically, public spaces and the lands allocated to streets and arterial roads are also in decline. All these are real, empirical facts, proving that the contemporary model of urbanization is becoming highly unsustainable.
>
> [Joan Clos, Under-Secretary-General, United Nations, Executive Director, UN-Habitat. From Angel *et al.*, 2016, p. vi]

Density and tall buildings: not as simple as it seems

Although it is accepted that compact cities are more sustainable than dispersed cities of suburban spread, a pertinent question remains: do we actually need to build tall to create high densities and sustainable urban forms? This is a topic of significant debate, and arguably confusion, in the field. It is perhaps the most common argument used to campaign *against* the use of tall buildings – that they often result in densities that are no higher, and sometimes even lower, than more traditional mid- and low-rise forms – and thus provide little benefit to the compact city. Among the first to demonstrate that 'dense' doesn't automatically mean 'tall' was the work of Lionel March. His research, combining architecture and mathematics, demonstrated that on a large, open site, a mid-rise perimeter courtyard block with a large open centre can create the same density as a very tall tower surrounded by low- and mid-rise buildings (Figure 2.6).

We also know that cities with many tall buildings aren't necessarily dense, or demonstrate the environmental or social benefits of the compact city. The twentieth-century American model of a high-rise commercial core supported by vast swathes of parking and surrounded by a hinterland of low-density suburbs is highly reliant on the automobile as residents on the city periphery commute into the centre daily (Figure 2.7). The flip side to this is that cities that have traditionally spurned the skyscraper can achieve very high densities and demonstrate many, if not all, of the sustainable benefits of the compact city. Paris and Barcelona are widely hailed as the ideal models of the compact city, maintaining mid-rise urban forms of six to eight storeys while achieving densities in the region of 200–250 units per hectare. Yet, we must remember, while Paris is often framed as a city that has 'rejected' the skyscraper, the idea that it relies on *just* mid-rise development is a myth, a fallacy. Instead, most of its modern tall buildings are clustered in a region outside of the city's political boundary, but urbanistically linked to its historic core, known as *La Défense*. This district is Paris's economic engine, with 180,000 daily workers, allowing it to compete with financial centres such as London and Frankfurt. If we include La Défense in the city's skyscraper statistics, we can see Paris is home to more towers overall than London (Figure 2.8). Paris is an excellent case study for the high densities and walkable districts achievable with mid-rise buildings, but we must remember that the skyscraper has played a role in this success, diverting new construction away from its historic centre, maintaining its famous boulevards, vistas and urban forms (Figure 2.9).

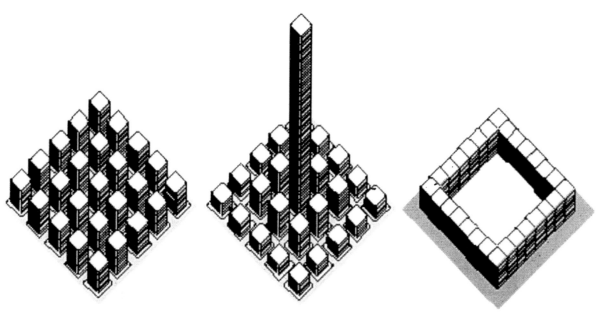

Figure 2.6   A theoretical 5 by 5 block, showing the same floor area distributed in three different forms
Source: March, 2002

Figure 2.7   Aerial view of Denver, Colorado, June 1976. The use of tall buildings does not guarantee density or a compact city form, especially if combined with large areas of surface parking
Source: Nick DeWolf

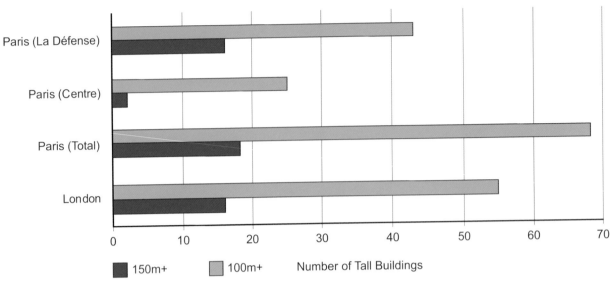

Figure 2.8 The number of tall buildings in London and Paris as of the end of 2017

Source: Philip Oldfield; data from Skyscrapercenter, 2018

Figure 2.9 Paris, looking towards La Défense. These towers sit outside of Paris's political boundary but are urbanistically and economically tied to the city

Source: Sumit Gupta/Sumit4all Photography

A common criticism of high-rise residential developments of the past is that they have often failed to achieve 'high' densities. Despite rising up to 31 storeys in height, the Red Road flats in Glasgow, constructed between 1962 and 1969, created 1,350 flats across 8.7 hectares (Gold, 2007), providing a density of 155 units/hectare (Figure 2.10). Many post-war high-rise housing estates in the UK achieved densities of around 100 units/hectare due to being planned around large open spaces with surface parking (Derbyshire *et al.*, 2015). Such densities could easily be matched or bettered by mid-rise construction. The open spaces around towers also provided little benefit to the residents, since they often provided few mixed-use activities. In Red Road, there was no play equipment for children, only one shop, and the nearest bus stop was half a mile away (Boys Smith & Morton, 2013).

It's abundantly clear that to achieve high densities, we do not need to build tall. And, even when we do build tall, the resultant urban forms are not always high density. There is little doubt that compact sustainable cities can be achieved with mid-rise built forms, without the skyscraper. So where does this leave the typology? Knowing that towers typically require more energy to operate and build than other types (as shown in Chapter 1), should we abandon the skyscraper as unnecessary in our quest for compact urban forms? The answer is no, and the tall building *does* have a significant role to play in terms of creating high densities. Two primary opportunities are highlighted here:

1 Tall buildings can create *hyperdensities*, far higher than other typologies, that have less well-documented, but still pertinent, sustainability advantages

Figure 2.10   Red Road Flats, view from Broomfield Road, 2012
Source: Daniel Naczk, CC BY 3.0 https://creativecommons.org/licenses/by/3.0/

2 Tall buildings can create high densities while providing more open public space, which if carefully planned, can provide a unique benefit to the city

These issues are discussed in more detail in the following sections.

The sustainability of 'hyperdensity'

Although high densities can be comfortably delivered by mid- and even low-rise buildings, tall building developments can achieve much greater densities still, above 350 units/hectare, which can be termed *hyperdensities*.[5] For example, Wood Wharf in London will create 3,200 new homes in a mixed-use skyscraper cluster in the city's east end with a density of 435 units/hectare (Derbyshire *et al.*, 2015). Many high-rise developments in Hong Kong have higher densities still, above even 800 units/hectare (Table 2.1). Such figures would be impossible to achieve with traditional mid-rise forms.[6]

However, debate rages about whether such hyperdensities are sustainable or desirable for our cities. Derbyshire *et al.* (2015) suggest the maximum density for new developments in London should be 350 units/hectare. Above this level, they question the long-term sustainability of hyperdense development, stating that within such projects it is "very difficult to create the conditions that allow mixed communities to thrive" (p. 10). The concept of 'good density' remains contentious, as architects and city-makers promote the

mid-rise, high-density models of Paris and Barcelona and yet deride the emerging high-rise cities of Asia as congested, characterless and rapidly expanding at any cost. Yet many Asian megacities are outperforming European capitals economically, in terms of cultural production, mass transit, environmentalism, racial integration and more (Chakrabarti, 2013).

Much of the concern for very high densities relates to perceptions of crowding. Famously, the work of Calhoun (1962) showed that rats subjected to crowding displayed pathological behaviour, such as violence, conflict and the neglect of young by their mothers. This fuelled the idea that humans living at high densities may too experience such social breakdown, and there is little doubt that crowdedness can cause social problems. McCarthy and Saegert (1978), for example, compared the experiences of residents living in three-storey walk-ups and 14-storey buildings. They found that those who lived in the high-rise came into contact with far more people, and thus felt social overload due to perceived crowding in the building.

However, others have demonstrated that it is not high densities *per se* that lead to feelings of crowdedness, but this is instead more closely related to the physical environment and social factors. The experience of crowding is dependent on socio-economic background, culture, age, education and previous living environments. For example, Anderson (1972) discusses how Asian and Chinese people have far greater tolerances to crowding due to historically large households, and unwritten social codes that inform lifestyle, making what many would

Development	Location	Height (storeys)	Density (units/hectare)
Typical Suburbia	General	1–2	12–25
Terraced Housing	General	2–3	75–150
Red Road Flats	Glasgow	31	155
Edwardian Mansion Block	London	6–8	200
Eixample District	Barcelona	6–7	230
Arundle Square, Islington	London	6	292
Wood Wharf	London	up to 57	435
Clinton Hill Co-op	New York	7–14	482
Pinnacle@Duxton	Singapore	50	740
Aldrich Garden	Hong Kong	9–34	815

Table 2.1 Densities of different buildings and typologies

Source: Philip Oldfield. Data from Derbyshire *et al.*, 2015; Density Atlas, 2011; and determined by author

perceive as crowded living environments acceptable or even pleasant. The layout of a building, the amount of open, shared and private spaces provided, and the community facilities available will also influence this experience (Yuen & Yeh, 2011). In this sense, high-rises can actually alleviate crowding by creating greater amounts of private space or open community space on a given site as compared to other typologies.

Lawson (2010) perhaps best sums up the challenges of hyperdensity, noting that it is much more a matter of design than statistics that influences the social and psychological success of a development or city. However, he goes on to note that while density itself is not the key issue, "the higher the density the harder we have to work to design our cities in such a way that makes them pleasant and fulfilling places to live" (p. 292). Rather than abandoning this challenge (as many have suggested), this should be a call to arms for the designer to create tall buildings that respond to users' needs for privacy, community and appropriate space for social interactions (for more on this topic, see Chapter 5).

These challenges to hyperdensity are widely recognised, but the benefits are perhaps less well known. Creating tall buildings with hyperdensities beyond the capabilities of mid-rise development can provide environmental, economic and urban gains to the city and to its residents. Hong Kong is an excellent example. Perhaps more than anywhere, Hong Kong has truly embraced the tall building, being home to more towers than any city in the world.[7] This, in part, has been fuelled by Hong Kong's unique geography, with a limited land area and challenging topography of hills, meaning there is no opportunity to build out, with the only way being to build up (Figure 2.11). The result is some of the highest densities in the world, with areas such as Mong Kok achieving a density of 130,000 people/km^2, several times higher than typical urban densities in Paris.

Hong Kong's hyperdensity has created an extremely compact urban form, providing the basis for one of the most successful public transit networks in the world. The result is that 90% of journeys made in the city are on public transportation, with half of the population living within a 500-metre radius of a mass rapid transit station (Shelton *et al.*, 2015). With public transit so popular, car ownership is extremely low as compared

to other wealthy nations at just 48 cars/1,000 population. In the USA the figures are 485, the UK 377 and Japan 325 (Cullinane, 2003). In the year 2000, car use in Hong Kong averaged 493 km per capita, eight times less than London at 3,892 km/capita, 12 times less than Sydney at 5,885 km/capita and, perhaps unsurprisingly, 24 times less than Los Angeles at 11,587 km/capita (Newman & Kenworthy, 2000). This all means that Hong Kong has one of the lowest energy needs for personal transit of any developed city in the world, of huge environmental benefit. Other factors such as strict parking controls and the high costs of motoring have contributed to this achievement, but there is little doubt that Hong Kong's hyperdense urban morphology has played a major role in making widespread public transit economically viable, thus restricting its reliance on the automobile.

Yet, it is not just in Asia where hyperdensities are having a positive effect. In Europe, where the traditional model of mid-rise high-density prevails, tall buildings and hyperdensites are providing environmental and economic advantages to the city. London is embarking on a massive building project of skyscrapers, with 436 new towers over 20 storeys either under construction or proposed (NLA, 2016). To many, this is a frightening transformation which will destroy the city's historic urban fabric, leading some to suggest London will turn into a "bad version of Dubai or Shanghai" (de Botton, 2015). Yet, while there are valid concerns that too many of these towers house only luxury apartments, with too little in the way of affordable homes, an urban comparison with Shanghai is misleading; Shanghai already had 6,461 towers over 20 storeys in 2014, with thousands more in the pipeline (Shanghai Bureau of Statistics, 2015). A few hundred new towers will not see London turn into a vertical city.

Tall building development in London is restricted by the existence of protected viewing corridors; these are strategic historic views and panoramas of important landmarks in the city, such as St Paul's Cathedral, within which high-rise development is limited. The result is tall buildings in London tend to be grouped together in clusters, outside of these strategic viewing corridors, and sited close to mass rapid transit. One such cluster is the 'City Eastern Cluster', home to some of the most recognisable skyscrapers in London

Figure 2.11   Hong Kong: Informed by a challenging mountainous topography, Hong Kong is one of the densest cities in the world
Source: Philip Oldfield

(Figure 2.12). This cluster accommodates six office sky-scrapers over 100 metres in height, with a further six either under construction or proposed as of 2017, all situated within an unbelievably tight area of approximately one-third of a square kilometre. The intense proximity of so many office towers has created one of the highest employment densities in the world, with a peak of 141,600 jobs/km^2 in the City of London in 2012, greater even than Central Hong Kong, which peaks at 120,200 jobs/km^2 (Urban Age, LSE Cities, 2012). This figure will be higher still, upon completion of future towers.

There can be little denying that the skyscraper has been a huge contributor to this hyperdensity of employment. The 12 office towers in the Eastern City Cluster will, when finished, create 1,070,098 m^2 of gross floor area, of which 746,051 m^2 (around 70%) is above the 10th floor (Table 2.2, Figure 2.13). If we had limited construction in the City to 10 storeys, comparable to say Paris or Barcelona, this would mean that the same buildings would only be able to supply around 30% of this floor space. In fact, to achieve the extra 746,051 m^2 that would have been lost if we 'capped' these buildings at 10 storeys, we would need to build an additional 42 ten-storey office blocks.[8] What this means is the same office space created in just 12 skyscrapers would require some 54 ten-storey buildings to achieve. In terms of occupants, we can estimate the number of employees working in this hyperdense space above the 10th floor. Occupational density in London offices is on average one person per 11.3 m^2 of net internal area (BCO, 2013). Assuming

Figure 2.12   Render of the London City Eastern Cluster, showing completed and future buildings
Source: Vertex Modelling www.vertexmodelling.co.uk

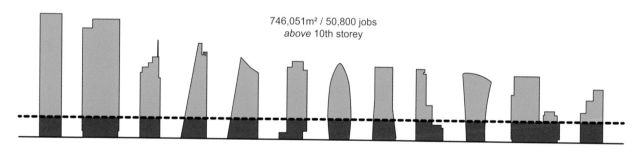

746,051m² / 50,800 jobs
above 10th storey

324,027m² / 22,000 jobs
below 10th storey

Figure 2.13   Tall office buildings in the London Eastern City Cluster, with floor areas and jobs above and below the 10th storey
Source: Philip Oldfield

net internal area is 77% of the gross floor area in these London towers, we can estimate there will be around 50,800 people working above the 10th storey, in these 12 towers alone. These occupants would otherwise have to be distributed across a far wider area, had London restricted the City Cluster to mid-rise development.

The use of the skyscraper, and hyperdensity, within the City of London has limited new development to strategic sites. If we were to build an additional 42

buildings to achieve the same floor area, this would force the City to spread, losing the intensity and proximity of employment created by the skyscraper. What's more, 42 additional buildings would put existing heritage and the character of London's streetscape at risk through masses of new construction. In this sense, by providing pockets of hyperdensity, we can effectively preserve low- and mid-rise areas. Rather than the tall building damaging the character of the city, it can be argued that hyperdensity is actually contributing to the preservation of its historic realm – much like with La Défense in Paris.

There are other benefits, too. Economically, the spikes of high employment created by the skyscraper provide concentrations of financial, creative and business industries, where information can be quickly exchanged and face-to-face interaction can occur (Figure 2.14). It provides an intensity of competition, efficiency and quality, which has established the City of London as one of the world's economic powerhouses (Urban Age, LSE Cities, 2012; Wynne Rees, 2008).

Environmentally, the greatest value of the hyperdensity created in the City of London is its contribution to the use of public transportation. The 12 towers that make up the Eastern City Cluster are serviced by just 149 car parking spaces, equivalent to one space per 7,182 m² (Table 2.2). In fact, most of the newer towers have around only five car parking spaces for disability access, meaning public transit, bicycling and walking effectively make up 100% of transit to and from work. Compare this to Apple

Park, the new low-rise, ring-shaped headquarters of Apple, built in suburban San Francisco. This office will be the largest naturally ventilated building on the planet and one which Tim Cook, the CEO of Apple, has described as the "greenest building in the world" (Graber, 2017). Yet it will also include some 11,000 car parking spaces for 14,200 employees, a factor of one space per 1.3 employees. Across the 12 towers in the London City Cluster, the figure is one space per 490 employees.[9] Instead, the Eastern City Cluster provides 8,000 cycle spaces, with no tower more than a 6-minute walk from a tube station, providing opportunities for sustainable and healthy transit to work. The low-density suburban location of Apple Park just cannot economically justify the kind of mass rapid transit that the hyperdensity of central London thrives on. The upshot is that while Apple Park may benefit from high-performance technology reducing its operating emissions, the transport-related carbon emissions of its mostly car-travelling occupants will be much higher than that of a comparable office worker

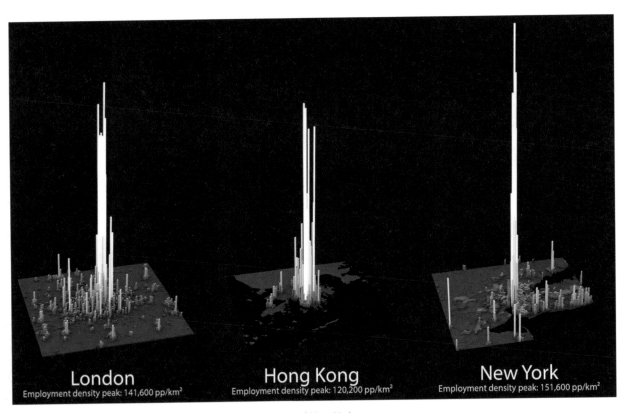

Figure 2.14   Employment densities in London, Hong Kong and New York
Source: Urban Age, LSE Cities, 2012

Building	Status as of 2017	Height (m)	Storeys	GFA (m²)	GFA above the 10th floor (m²)	Car parking spaces	Cycle parking spaces	Walking distance to the tube (minutes)
No.1 Undershaft	Proposed	290	73	132,790	112,920	6	1,600	6
22 Bishopsgate	Under construction	278	62	194,492	160,492	4	1,500	6
Heron Tower	Completed 2011	230	46	66,260	43,740	5	526	3
The Leadenhall Building	Completed 2014	224	52	84,424	57,403	22	397	6
52–54 Lime Street	Under construction	192	39	53,424	31,911	1	363	5
Tower 42	Completed 1980	183	43	50,000	38,900	60	84	5
30 St Mary Axe	Completed 2004	180	40	64,470	43,102	5	118	5
100 Bishopsgate	Under construction	172	40	82,037	52,812	5	900	5
6–8 Bishopsgate / 150 Leadenhall	Proposed	168	41	71,501	40,877	3	961	4
20 Fenchurch Street	Completed 2014	160	37	104,513	78,000	6	422	4
40 Leadenhall	Proposed	155	37	125,699	65,614	2	1,068	4
Willis Building	Completed 2007	125	28	40,488	20,280	30	200	3
			TOTAL	**1,070,098**	**746,051**	**149**	**8139**	

Table 2.2 Office buildings, their floor areas and parking facilities in the City of London Eastern Cluster

Source: Philip Oldfield. Floor area data calculated from Skyscrapercenter, 2018; City of London, 2016. Parking data from various sources. Walking distance information from Google Maps

in a central London skyscraper. This is because modes of mass public transportation benefit from reduced carbon emissions as compared to car travel; for example, travel on the Docklands Light Railway in London emits around 42% of the CO_2 per kilometre travelled as compared to a typical petrol car, and around 24% compared to a large petrol car (Figure 2.15). Across London there is a positive link between high-density regions and public transportation access. Car use in Central London is below 18%, although this rises to over 50% along the lower-density outer boundary of the city (Burdett *et al.*, 2004).

Tall buildings and open space

A further advantage of building high-rises is they can provide greater expanses of open space at ground as compared to other typologies. The diagrams in Figure 2.16 show a theoretical site of 50 by 100 metres and four different ways of achieving a density of 160 units/hectare. For simplicity, no private garden areas are considered. In the terraced approach, approximately 66% of the site would be given over to the building footprints, while 33% would remain open as streets. A three-storey courtyard block would leave 53% of the site open, and a five-storey block would leave 73% open. However, a 20-storey point tower would only take up 10% of the site, leaving 90% open. This is not just a theoretical advantage but one reflected in built forms today. The Pinnacle@Duxton in Singapore accommodates 1,848 units across seven towers at a density of 740 units/hectare. Despite this, it still manages to maintain 70% of the site area as open green spaces accommodating a series of mini-parks, a basketball court, shops, a food court, a kindergarten and more. Skybridges linking the towers at level 26 and level 50 mean the overall green

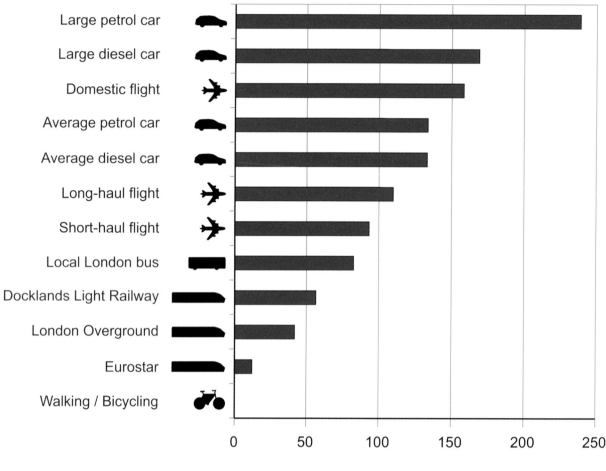

Figure 2.15   Carbon emissions for different modes of passenger transit
Source: Philip Oldfield, data from DEFRA, 2013

space provided is approximately 100% of the total site area, a figure which would be implausible with low- or mid-rise types (Figure 2.17).

Of course, it's important to recognise that more open space at ground does not necessarily equate to *better* open space. The 'tower in the park' typology was first envisioned by Le Corbusier and captured in the *Radiant City* (1932), a theoretical plan to house 1.5 million people in Cartesian towers rising out of green parkland. By using high-rises, Corbusier managed to maintain 88% of the site as open green space, with only 12% of the ground occupied by buildings. The aim was to provide residents with sun, light, space and serenity, in a high-rise version of Unwin and Parker's Garden Cities. However, the abolishment of the

street as the central place of interaction and community, and its replacement with open, boundless parkland has seen significant criticism, most notably from Jacobs (1961), who sees the well-defined and mixed-use streetscape as essential to the vitality of the city. Although it was never built, Corbusier's Radiant City was highly influential, inspiring many urban renewal projects throughout the mid-twentieth century, such as Park Hill in Sheffield and Pruitt-Igoe in Detroit (see also Chapter 5). Although Corbusier's vision of the parkland between towers included a variety of facilities and functions – libraries, sports, shops and recreation – in built examples, these rarely materialised, and the open green space often became neglected, windswept and unpopulated.

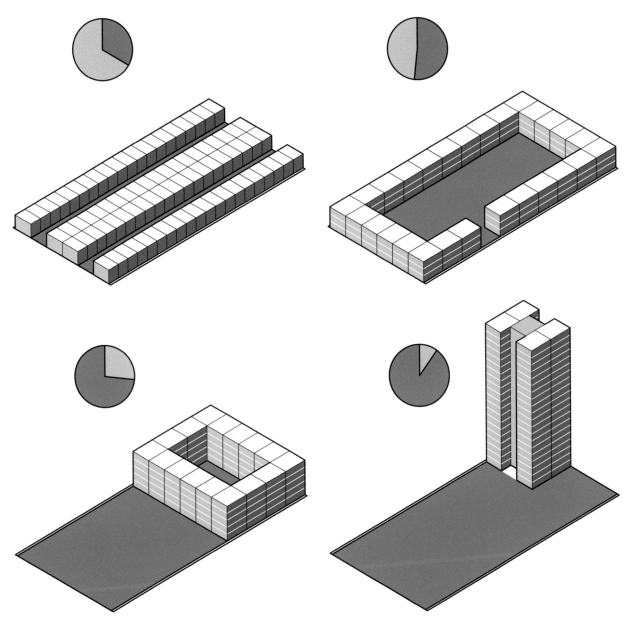

Figure 2.16 Four alternative typologies for achieving a density of 160 units/hectare on a 5,000 m² site, with different quantities of open space remaining
Source: Philip Oldfield

The significant urban limitations of the 'tower in the park' paradigm need acknowledging, but the point remains: building vertically can release greater floor space at ground level. Such space need not be a wind-swept park. It could provide area for cultural facilities, a museum or a public pool. It could still accommodate traditional low- and mid-rise streets and additional housing, creating higher densities in a *hybrid* urban model.

Hybrid models: one size does not fit all

No one way is a good way to house a city neighbourhood; no mere two or three ways are good. The more variations there can be, the better. As soon as the range and number of variations in buildings decline, the diversity of population and enterprises

Figure 2.17   The Pinnacle@Duxton, Singapore. A high-rise form with skybridges allows for a hyperdensity of 740 units/hectare, but still maintains 70% of the site area as open space

is too apt to stay static or decline, instead of increasing.

[Jacobs, 1961, p. 214]

One of the problems with the current density debate is there seems to be little middle ground. Much of the discussion seems to be pitched as a battle between mid-rise and high-rise development, as if only one is a solution to our growing urban populations. We are constantly told that cities can follow either the "Barcelona route or the Shanghai route" (Saulwick & Gair, 2016) in terms of urban development, with the Barcelona model generally preferable. However, for most cities there is no single answer to providing the increased density and housing stock we need in the future – we need multiple options and multiple typologies of development. In reality, the Barcelona and Shanghai models mark the extremes: one celebrates the boulevard and the mid-rise, whereas the other

celebrates the point tower. For most cities, embracing just a single building type or a single density seems wrong. The most vibrant cities often have a mix of different densities and building types, influenced by local history, context, culture and the connectedness of a place. For most cities, accommodating the dramatic growth of our future urban populations will require a *hybrid approach*, including an intensification of the suburbs, a large proportion of mid-rise development and tall buildings strategically located within close proximity to mass rapid transit.

In London this hybrid approach is exactly what's happening. The 2016 tall building audit by New London Architecture suggests there are 436 new tall buildings in the pipeline, of which 320 will be residential (NLA, 2016). If we assume 200 apartments per tower, these will provide an estimated 64,000 new units. Yet London requires a far greater number of homes, with the CBRE suggesting 52,000 are needed each year to satisfy current and future demand (CBRE, 2014). If we assume these new 320 towers are completed in five years, they will contribute around 25% of the 260,000 houses needed in the city during this time; the remainder will come from the more traditional low- and mid-rise development (Figure 2.18).

A hybrid approach to density and typology can also be created at the site scale. By combining mid-rise blocks that maintain the traditional scale of the streetscape with towers set back, a mix of both densities and typologies can be achieved, while also opening up public spaces at ground (Figures 2.19 and 2.20). In

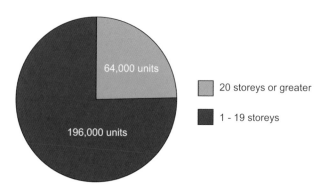

Figure 2.18   Projected housing in London 2017–2021, assuming all planned tall buildings are completed and CBRE future housing demand estimates are met

Source: Philip Oldfield

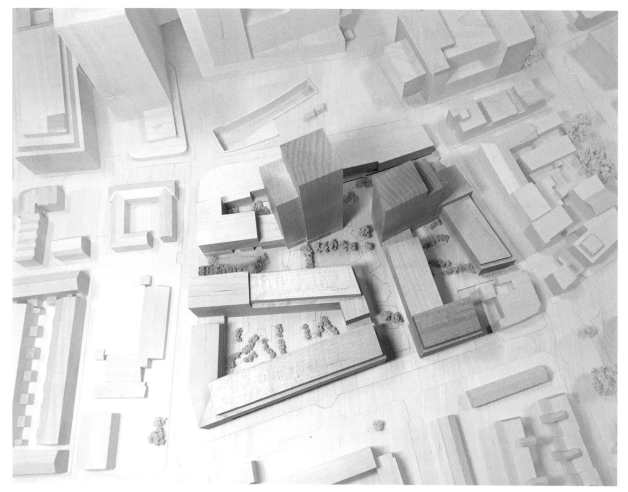

Figure 2.19   Whitechapel Central, London, by Stockwool. Mid-rise blocks along the site edge maintains the street scale, while a high-rise tower, set back from the street, provides additional density

Source: Stockwool

the theoretical example of a 100 metre by 50 metre site discussed previously, a hybrid approach of terraces, mid-rise and a high-rise tower could achieve a density of 342 units/hectare, while still maintaining 50% of the site area for green space (Figure 2.21). Such a hybrid approach provides a mix of typologies, suitable for different tastes, desires and needs.

Nowhere has this model been embraced more than in the city of Vancouver. Here, the standard downtown development is a hybrid mix of mid-rise perimeter blocks, with slender high-rise residential towers above, a model so celebrated that it has its own name: *Vancouverism*. Brent Toderian, the former head of Planning for the City of Vancouver, sings the praises of this approach by noting it blends "the best of both scales"

(Toderian, 2014), at a density that would otherwise be unachievable with just mid-rise construction. Toderian goes on to discuss the block he lives in which includes two mid-rise buildings and two towers, with shared amenities and a link to mass rapid transit. Retail at ground level activates the street, while a raised courtyard provides a green community space for the residents.

Conclusion

Urbanisation, along with the mitigation of climate change, is likely to be one of the greatest challenges of the twenty-first century. Three billion new urban dwellers will need to live, work and play in our future

Figure 2.20   Whitechapel Central, London
Source: Stockwool

cities within just a few decades, requiring vast and unprecedented levels of construction. It is widely accepted that to accommodate our growing city populations in a sustainable and efficient manner, we need to focus on creating compact cities, with better access to public transportation, and ease of proximity to work, home and leisure. However, debate still rages about what form such compact cities should take. For many, the mid-rise models of Paris and Barcelona are heralded as the solution for cities around the world, creating high densities, yet maintaining a familiarity of scale with six- to eight-storey blocks. Towers are frequently derided as unnecessary, often creating densities no higher than these mid-rise forms, and at a greater environmental and economic cost.

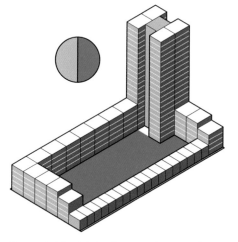

Figure 2.21   A hybrid approach to typology, achieving a density of 342 units/hectare
Source: Philip Oldfield

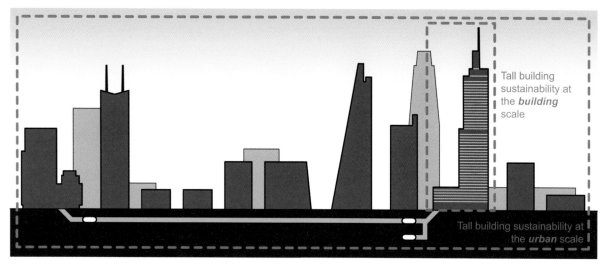

Figure 2.22 Tall building sustainability at the *building scale* often suffers from high material requirements and operating energy needs. Tall building sustainability at the *urban scale* includes the advantages of density and proximity to public transit networks

Source: Philip Oldfield

However, density is not a simple concept, and the narrative linking tall buildings and high densities is complex and multi-faceted. Although mid-rise typologies can create high densities, building tall can create hyperdensities, with additional and less well-documented benefits. These include limiting development to strategic sites and preserving historic areas; promoting high use of public transit, cycling and walkability; creating intensities of competition, efficiency and creativity; and maximising open space at ground. Of course, such hyperdensities do not make sense everywhere. Such is the challenge of urbanisation, that there is no 'one solution' and no magic bullet. For most cities, to accommodate their growing populations in a compact and sustainable manner will require multiple approaches, including the intensification of the suburbs, urban infill with more traditional mid-rise blocks, and strategically located towers and areas of hyperdensity. It's just as foolish to say that only the Parisian model of mid-rise development will solve all of our urban and environmental problems as it is to say that only towers will do so.

Environmentally, the optimum height and density of our cities is dependent on a multitude of factors. However, there is evidence that taller cities are more optimal from a purely energy perspective. A parametric study of theoretical cities of different densities, heights and populations by Resch *et al.* (2016) suggests that the optimal building height for urban energy use is in the region of 7–26 storeys when considering initial embodied energy, heating energy, transportation energy and the embodied energy needed to create road infrastructure. The authors state that this range is informed mostly by building lifecycle and population. For the combination of a low population of 10,000 and a low building lifecycle of 40 years, the optimal number of storeys is seven. At the other end of the scale, a city with a population of 10 million and a 150-year building lifecycle, the optimal number of storeys is 26. At both ends though, such building heights are far above the norm in many cities. Of course, few cities desire a consistent plateau of building heights, and the 'optimum' height for any building will change across different sites and districts within our cities. But there is evidence that building taller buildings, particularly in megacities, can have an environmental benefit at the urban scale.

The conclusion we must draw is that the sustainable performance of tall buildings is intrinsically linked to their location and integration with the urban realm, specifically transit networks. Chapter 1 showed us that at the *building scale*, tall buildings often use more energy and emit more CO_2 in both their operation and in the materials needed for their realisation. It's predominantly at the *urban scale* that a convincing sustainability argument for building tall can be made, creating higher densities that can foster intensity of use of public transit and contribute to a lower carbon lifestyle. As an 'object' the skyscraper is often unsustainable; integrate it into the low-carbon infrastructure of the compact city, however, and its sustainable credentials become more apparent (Figure 2.22).

So, it is not just *what* we build that is important in skyscraper design. Arguably more vital is *where* we build it. The key sustainability factor in tall building design is *location, location, location*. Tall buildings should be integrated in close proximity to public transit networks for their full sustainability potential to be met. When cities fail in this sense, and where we see the construction of 'icons before infrastructure', transportation becomes automobile dependent, causing congestion, pollution and greater carbon emissions (Pramati & Oldfield, 2015). This means we should be siting our tall buildings and clusters of hyperdensity ideally no further than a walkable 800 metres from a public transit node, or closer still, to foster greater access and use.

Notes

1   Although density may seem a simple concept, it is actually complex and multi-faceted. Density can be defined as a measurement of the concentration of individuals or physical structures within a given geographical unit (Cheng, 2010). In this sense a variety of different metrics exist. Density can measure the amount of people, homes (often referred to as 'units') or habitable rooms per geographical area. Densities can be measured at the building, site, region, city or even urban agglomeration scale. As such, it is often difficult to compare densities, since measurements are not always consistent. For example, two widely different density figures are given for Hong Kong, one including its lush green mountainous regions and the other excluding them. In this chapter two primary metrics are used. The first is the measurement of density at the site level, which is presented in units/hectare – a measurement of the amount of homes per hectare of land (10,000 m²). Such a measurement makes no consideration for if the homes are large

or small, but is the standard metric for comparing different typologies and case studies at a site level (Derbyshire *et al.*, 2015). Density at a city or urban agglomeration level is presented as people/km², a measurement of the people living within a square kilometre. Other metrics are also touched on as required.

2   It's worth noting that the definition of the compact city presented here is kept purposely general. In the literature a variety of definitions exist (Jenks *et al.*, 1996). However, common to most are the characteristics of a high residential density, limited sprawl, mixed-use planning and the promotion of public transportation and walkability.

3   It is worth noting that Newman and Kenworthy's graph as shown in Figure 2.3 has provoked debate regarding whether it proves that higher urban densities contribute to reduced fuel use. Brindle (1994) suggests their data instead demonstrates total fuel consumption is more significantly related to city area, not density in itself. Thus, the aim should be to create compact cities, not only to increase density (even though these two parameters of density and city size clearly interact).

4   Jacobs is keen to stress though that not all areas of high density are vibrant and successful, merely that high densities are one factor that can contribute towards flourishing city diversity. In particular, she notes that high densities can suppress vitality if they become too standardised, noting that such areas must have variation in building character, age and programmes for success.

5   There is no common definition in the literature as to what constitutes hyperdensity. Chakrabarti (2013, p. 126) defines it as density "sufficient to support subways", but this leaves the term open to interpretation. In this sense, the author here refers to the definition in Derbyshire *et al.* (2015), who define it as development above 350 units/hectare.

6   Perhaps the highest residential density ever recorded was that of Kowloon Walled City in Hong Kong, with an estimated figure of 2,743 units/hectare (Density Atlas, 2011). Set over a site of around 25,000 m², Kowloon Walled City consisted of multiple blocks, between five and 14 storeys, clustered together, built without planning permission, administration or basic services and infrastructure. At its

peak it housed 35,000 residents, with an average of around 3 m² per person – barely enough room to lie down (Girard & Lambot, 2014). The extremity of such conditions, unsurprisingly, led to a whole host of social problems, with the development often described as a slum, leading to its demolition in 1993.

7   As of the end of 2017, Hong Kong had 317 towers of 150 metres in height or taller. This is more than New York (257), Dubai (177), Tokyo (145) and Shanghai (141), the next ranked cities (Skyscrapercenter, 2018).

8   This figure assumes that all of the additional midrise office buildings required to achieve the same floor area as the skyscrapers have a floor plan of 40 by 40 metres, across 11 storeys – a basement and 10 above-ground floors. This gives a total gross floor area of 17,600 m². Just over 42 of such buildings would be needed to achieve a floor area of 746,051 m², the area which is created above the 10th floor in the 12 skyscrapers within the City Eastern cluster.

9   This figure is based on an occupation density of one person per 11.3 m² of net internal area (BCO, 2013) and an assumed net internal area of 77% of gross floor space. It gives a total occupancy across the 12 towers in the City Cluster as 73,000 office workers.

References

Anderson, E. N. (1972). Chinese Methods of Dealing with Crowding. *Urban Anthropology*, Vol. 1, No. 2, pp. 141–150.

Angel, S., Blei, A. M., Parent, J., Lamson-Hall, P., Sánchez, N. G., Civco, D. L., Lei, R. Q. & Thom, K. (2016). *Atlas of Urban Expansion – 2016 Edition, Volume 1: Areas and Densities*. New York University, New York, UN-Habitat, Nairobi and Lincoln Institute of Land Policy, Cambridge, MA.

BCO. (2013). *Occupier Density Study 2013*, September. British Council for Offices, London.

Boys Smith, N. & Morton, A. (2013). *Create Streets: Not Just Multi-Storey Estates*. Policy Exchange, London.

Brindle, R. E. (1994). *Lies, Damned Lies and "Automobile Dependence" – Some Hyperbolic Reflections*. Proceedings of the 1994 Australian Transport Research Forum, Melbourne, pp. 117–131.

Burdett, R., Travers, T., Czischke, D., Rode, P. & Moser, B. (2004). *Density in Urban Neighbourhood in London: Summary Report*. LSE Cities, London.

Calhoun, J. B. (1962). Population Density and Social Pathology. *Scientific American*, Vol. 206, pp. 139–146.

CBRE. (2014). *Supplying London's Housing Needs: Building to Match Demand*. www.cbreresidential.com/uk/en-GB/content/supplying-londons-housing-needs

Chakrabarti, V. (2013). *A Country of Cities: A Manifesto for Urban America*. Metropolis Books, New York.

Cheng, V. (2010). Understanding Density and High Density. In: Ng, E. (ed.) *Designing High-Density Cities: For Social and Environmental Sustainability*, Taylor & Francis, New York.

City of London. (2016). *Planning Applications*. www.cityoflondon.gov.uk/services/environment-and-planning/planning/planning-applications/Pages/default.aspx

Cullinane, S. (2003). Hong Kong's Low Car Dependence: Lessons and Prospects. *Journal of Transport Geography*, Vol. 11, pp. 25–35.

De Botton, A. (2015). London Is Becoming a Bad Version of Dubai. *The Guardian*, 14 July. www.theguardian.com/artanddesign/video/2015/jul/14/alain-de-botton-london-becoming-bad-version-of-dubai?CMP=embed_video

DEFRA. (2013). *2013 Government GHG Conversion Factors for Company Reporting: Methodology Paper for Emission Factors*, July, London.

Demographia. (2001). *International Urbanized Area Data: Population, Area & Density*. http://demographia.com/db-intlua-data.htm

Density Atlas. (2011). *Density Atlas: Case Studies*. http://densityatlas.org/casestudies/index.php?sort=du_area_ac&s=desc

Derbyshire, B., Goulcher, M., Beharrell, A. & Von Bradsky, A. (2015). *Superdensity: The Sequel*. www.superdensity.co.uk

DSEWPaC. (2011). *Australia State of the Environment 2011*. Independent report to the Australian Government Minister for Sustainability, Environment, Water, Population and Communities, Canberra.

Du, P. & Wood, A. (2017). *Downtown High-Rise vs. Suburban Low-Rise Living: A Pilot Study on Urban Sustainability*. CTBUH, Chicago.

Girard, G. & Lambot, I. (2014). *City of Darkness: Revisited*. Watermark Publications, UK.

Gold, J. R. (2007). *The Practice of Modernism: Modern Architects and Urban Transformation, 1954–1972.* Routledge, London and New York.

Graber, H. (2017). Apple Says Its New Headquarters Could Be the Greenest Building in the World. Not with 11,000 Parking Spaces! *Slate*, 12 April. www.slate.com/blogs/moneybox/2017/04/12/apple_says_its_new_headquarters_is_the_greenest_building_in_the_world_not.html

Jacobs, J. (1961). *The Death and Life of Great American Cities.* Random House, New York.

Jenks, M., Burton, E. & Williams, K. (eds.) (1996). *The Compact City: A Sustainable Urban Form?* E & FN Spon, Oxford.

Kostof, S. (1991). *The City Shaped: Urban Patterns and Meanings Through History.* Thames & Hudson, London.

Kunstler, J. H. (2006). Sprawl: A Compact History – A Review. *Salmagundi: The Quarterly Journal of Humanities and Social Sciences of Skidmore College*, Fall, No. 152.

Lawson, B. (2010). The Social and Psychological Issues of High-Density City Space. In: Ng, E. (ed.) *Designing High-Density Cities: For Social and Environmental Sustainability.* Taylor & Francis, New York.

March, L. (2002). Architecture and Mathematics since 1960. In: Williams, K. & Rodrigues, J. F. (eds.) *Nexus: Architecture and Mathematics.* Kim Williams Books, Florence.

McCarthy, D. & Saegert, S. (1978). Residential Density, Social Overload, and Social Withdrawal. *Human Ecology*, Vol. 6, No. 3, pp. 253–272.

McKinney, M. L. (2002). Urbanization, Biodiversity and Conservation. *Bioscience*, Vol. 52, No. 10, pp. 883–890.

Müller, D. B., Løvik, A. N., Modaresi, R. & Brattebø, H. (2013). Carbon Emissions of Infrastructure Development. *Journal of Environmental Science and Technology*, Vol. 47, No. 20, pp. 11739–11746.

Newman, P. & Kenworthy, J. (1999). *Sustainability and Cities: Overcoming Automobile Dependence.* Island Press, Washington.

Newman, P. & Kenworthy, J. (2000). Sustainable Urban Form: The Big Picture. In: Williams, K., Burton, E. & Jenks, M. (eds.) *Achieving Sustainable Urban Form*, E & FN Spon, London.

NLA. (2016). *London Tall Buildings Survey*, March, New London Architecture, London.

Norman, J., Maclean, H. & Kennedy, C. A. (2006). Comparing High and Low Residential Density: Life-Cycle Analysis of Energy Use and Greenhouse Gas Emissions. *Journal of Urban Planning and Development*, Vol. 132, No. 1, pp. 10–21.

Pramati, L. & Oldfield, P. (2015). *Tall Building Planning Strategy and Governance: What Can Jakarta Learn from Other Cities?* 3rd International Conference on Architecture and Civil Engineering (ACE 2015), 13–14 April, Singapore, pp. 469–478.

Resch, E., Bohne, R. A., Kvamsdal, T. & Lohne, J. (2016). Impact of Urban Density and Building Height on Energy Use in Cities. *Energy Procedia*, Vol. 96, pp. 800–814.

Rogers, R. & Gumuchdjian, P. (1997). *Cities for a Small Planet.* Faber & Faber, London.

Saulwick, J. & Gair, K. (2016). Sydney Population Booms and the Only Way Is Up and In. *The Sydney Morning Herald*, 12 September. www.smh.com.au/nsw/sydney-population-booms-and-the-only-way-is-up-and-in-20160911-grdv4b.html

Shanghai Bureau of Statistics. (2015). *Buildings Over Eight Storeys in Main Years.* www.stats-sh.gov.cn

Shelton, B., Karakiewicz, J. & Kvan, T. (2015). *The Making of Hong Kong: From Vertical to Volumetric.* Routledge, Oxford.

Sims, R., Schaeffer, R., Creutzig, F., Cruz-Núñez, X., D'Agosto, M., Dimitriu, D., Figueroa Meza, M. J., Fulton, L., Kobayashi, S., Lah, O., McKinnon, A., Newman, P., Ouyang, M., Schauer, J. J., Sperlind, D. & Tiwari, G. (2014). Transport. In: *Climate Change 2014: Mitigation of Climate Change: Contribution of Working Group III to the Fifth Assessment Report of the Intergovernmental Panel on Climate Change.* Cambridge University Press, Cambridge and New York.

Skyscrapercenter. (2018). *The Skyscraper Center – The Global Tall Building Database of the CTBUH.* www.skyscrapercenter.com/

Stevenson, M., Thompson, J., Hérick De Sá, T., Ewing, R., Mohan, D., McClure, R., Roberts, I., Tiwari, G., Giles-Corti, B., Sun, X., Wallace, M. & Woodcock, J. (2016). Land Use, Transport, and Population Health: Estimating the Health Benefits of Compact Cities. *The Lancet*, Vol. 388, No. 10062, pp. 2925–2935.

Toderian, B. (2014). Tall Tower Debate Could Use Less Dogma, Better Design. *Planetizen*, 1 June. www.planetizen.com/node/69073

Unhabitat. (2008). *State of the World's Cities 2008/09: Harmonious Cities*. Earthscan, London.

United Nations. (2014). *World Urbanization Prospects: The 2014 Revision, Highlights*. Department of Economic and Social Affairs, United Nations, New York.

Urban Age, LSE Cities. (2012). *Electric City*, December. https://urbanage.lsecities.net/newspapers/electriccity-1

Ürge-Vorsatz, D., Cabeza, L. F., Serrano, S., Barreneche, C. & Petrichenko, K. (2015). Heating and Cooling Energy Trends in Buildings. *Renewable and Sustainable Energy Reviews*, Vol. 41, pp. 85–98.

Wynne Rees, P. (2008). *It's Not What You Build, But the Place That You Build It: Urban Sustainability in London*. Proceedings of the CTBUH 8th World Congress – "Tall and Green: Typology for a Sustainable Urban Future", CTBUH, Chicago, pp. 1–7.

Yuen, B. & Yeh, A. G. O. (eds.) (2011). *High-Rise Living in Asian Cities*. Springer-Verlag, London and New York.

CHAPTER THREE

Five energy generations of tall buildings

Philip Oldfield, Dario Trabucco and Antony Wood[1]

Introduction

Over the past 130 years, the high-rise typology has undergone a variety of paradigm shifts, influenced by regulatory changes, developments in technology and materials, changes in architectural style, economics and commercial drivers. Developments such as the New York Zoning Law of 1916, the post-war innovations in curtain wall façades and the energy crises of the 1970s have all impacted on the way tall buildings of the time were designed and operated. These events also had a significant impact on the quantity of, and way in which, energy was consumed in tall buildings of the time.

Although there have been numerous categorisations of high-rise buildings according to their function, architectural style, height or structural strategy, historically little work has been undertaken to classify them based on factors affecting their energy performance – their shape and form, façade, attitude to natural lighting, ventilation strategies, etc. With this in mind, this chapter examines the history of energy use in tall buildings, from their origins in North America in the late nineteenth century to the present day. In doing so, it categorises tall buildings into five chronological 'generations', based on their energy consumption characteristics.

The first energy generation: from the birth of tall buildings in 1885 to the 1916 Zoning Law

Born out of a desire to maximise the financial return of a given plot of land, combined with developments in structural steel framing and the invention of the elevator in the mid-nineteenth century, tall buildings quickly spread across North America, becoming the symbol of economic growth and prosperity. The Home Insurance Building, completed in Chicago in 1885, is generally regarded as the first of these high-rises, although debate continues regarding its credentials for this title. We can state that this first generation of tall buildings originally required relatively little operating energy as technologies such as air-conditioning and fluorescent lighting were not yet developed. Primary energy was predominantly consumed in the heating of occupied spaces and providing vertical transportation between floors. Ventilation was achieved naturally via opening windows, and artificial lighting levels were very low – typically between 22 and 43 lux[2] in office buildings in 1913 (Osterhaus, 1993) due to the inefficiencies of lighting technologies of the time (Figure 3.1). The quality and rentability of office space thus depended on large windows and high ceilings that allowed daylight to penetrate as deeply as possible into the interior

Figure 3.1   Artificial lighting in an early twentieth-century skyscraper, Chicago
Source: Philip Oldfield

Figure 3.2   The Equitable Building, New York, 1915
Source: Dario Trabucco

(Willis, 1995). Windows occupied some 20–40% of the façade in these first-generation buildings, which while high for the time, is still significantly lower than modern high-rise buildings with their glazed curtain walls allowing values of 50–75% façade transparency.[3]

These buildings utilised the latest structural innovations, but their envelope construction remained heavily influenced by traditional, load-bearing technology; external walls, although freed from any structural role, were thick, of masonry construction, with an internal finish of dense plasterwork. Although this construction suffers from a lack of thermal insulation (i.e. due to the use of single glazing) and poor air-tightness, it does provide a high degree of exposed thermal mass. This would assist in creating comfortable internal environments in North America by maintaining warmth in the winter and absorbing excess heat gains in the summer.

The form and shape of these early high-rise buildings also impacted their primary energy usage; typically, those constructed prior to the 1916 Zoning Law were bulky, compact forms, the result of repetitive stacking of large floor plates to maximise rentable floor area. These buildings were large volumes, but had relatively small envelope surface areas, allowing them to retain a high degree of heat in the winter. However, these bulky forms often disguised relatively shallow lease spans with a maximum of 6.1–8.5 metres almost universally observed (Willis, 1995), maintaining natural light penetration into office spaces.

These characteristics of dense, solid façade and compact, bulky shape are best reflected in the Equitable Building of New York, completed in 1915 (Figure 3.2). This building – the vertical extrapolation of an H-shaped floor plan over 40 storeys – is an immense volume, while its façade consists of limestone cladding, backed by thick masonry, with punctured windows.

In more recent times, buildings of this era have experienced significant refurbishments to improve lighting, enhance façade and glazing performance, and introduce mechanical space conditioning. However, their energy performance still benefits to a certain extent from their shape (compact and bulky) and their envelope construction (solidity and thermal mass).

The second energy generation: from the 1916 Zoning Law to the development of the glazed curtain wall, 1951

The construction of the Equitable Building in New York marked a significant watershed in high-rise design. This massive building, covering an entire city block, would, according to its detractors, "steal" light and views from surrounding buildings (Weiss, 1992). In fact, similar concerns about skyscrapers of the time had been growing for years; the lack of planning legislation for this new typology had allowed the number and size of tall buildings in Manhattan to increase steadily, blocking sunlight from streets and other buildings, culminating in the construction of the Equitable Building, which cast a seven-acre shadow across its surroundings. In response, the New York City authorities developed the landmark Zoning Law of 1916, restricting the bulk of tall buildings, requiring them to preserve the penetration of light and air onto the streets below. The subsequent 'set-backs' prescribed by the law created the familiar 'wedding cake' skyscraper style that would dominate future skylines (Figure 3.3).

In order to determine the impact that the 1916 Zoning Law had upon the energy consumption of tall buildings, 10 New York skyscrapers – five pre-dating the law and five in its aftermath – have been studied. For each building a calculation of its envelope surface-area-to-volume ratio (*AVr*) was made using the formula outlined below:

$$AVr = \frac{SA}{V} \; (\mathrm{m}^2 / \mathrm{m}^3)$$

In this instance, *SA* is the envelope surface area of the building and *V* is its volume. The results of this analysis are outlined in Figure 3.4.

As could be expected, tall buildings constructed after the Zoning Law have an increased amount of envelope surface area per unit volume compared to those that predate the law, which are typically bulkier. So what does this mean in terms of energy use? Studies

by Depecker *et al.* (2001) show that in a climate with cold, severe winters – such as New York – a building's energy requirement for space heating is proportional to its surface-area-to-volume ratio (*AVr*); the higher the ratio, the higher the heating requirements due to an increased quantity of envelope area facilitating heat

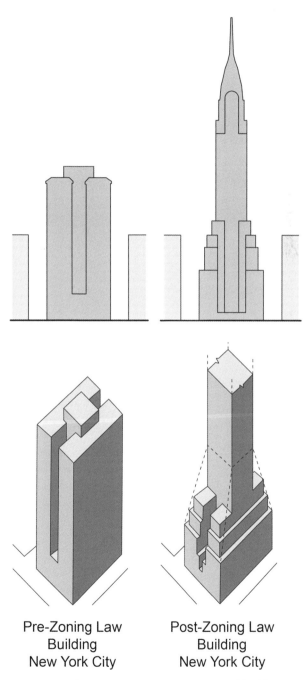

Pre-Zoning Law
Building
New York City

Post-Zoning Law
Building
New York City

Figure 3.3 The 1916 Zoning Law – impact on tall building form and mass
Source: Oldfield *et al.*, 2009; adapted from Barnett, 1982

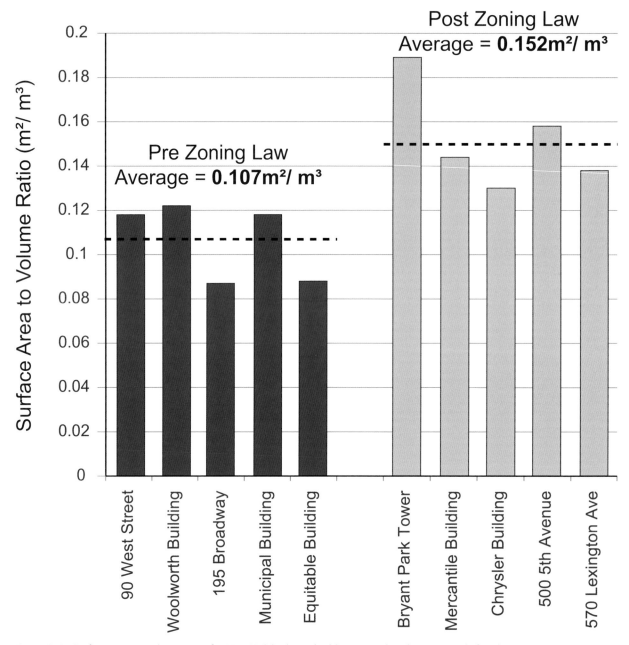

Figure 3.4   Surface-area-to-volume ratios for New York high-rise buildings completed prior to and after the 1916 Zoning Law
Source: Oldfield *et al.*, 2009

loss. However, at the same time, the slender Zoning Law buildings have smaller floor plans compared to 'first generation' buildings, at least at the higher levels. As the proportion of glazing within the façade stayed similar across both generations, this would result in greater natural light penetration, potentially reducing artificial lighting loads at the higher floor levels (Figure 3.5). However, despite this greater potential,

artificial lighting standards actually increased in this second generation time period; whereas in 1916 the recommendation by the New York City Department of Health for adequate lighting levels in offices was 86–97 lux, it rose to 108–129 lux in the 1920s and, spurred on by the aggressive sales tactics of large power companies, some experts urged up to 269 lux by the 1930s (Willis, 1995).

Figure 3.5 The slender upper floors of the Chrysler Building, New York, 1930

Source: Philip Oldfield

So, it can be seen that the 1916 Zoning Law directly influenced the primary energy consumption of tall buildings. Prior to the law's inception, high-rise buildings were large rectilinear blocks, designed with a high degree of compactness. Those that followed the law were increasingly slender, resulting in greater requirements for space heating (due to increased heat loss through higher quantities of envelope), but with increased natural light penetration at the higher floor levels.

It is worth noting that while these attributes are consistent with the majority of tall buildings in New York, there are obviously a few exceptions to the rule. For example, the Flatiron Building, constructed prior to the Zoning Law in 1902, has a surface-area-to-volume ratio of 0.17 m²/m³, a figure characteristic of the more slender post–Zoning Law buildings. The Empire State Building (1931), arguably the most famous of the 'wedding cake' skyscrapers, has a ratio of 0.09 m²/m³,

which shows a high degree of compactness similar to buildings that predate the law. However, both of these examples can be seen as unusual; the Flatiron's slender form is obviously influenced by its unique site, and the Empire State was a massive building on an unprecedented scale – the tallest in the world for over 40 years.

For reasons of depth, quality and number of buildings affected, this study focused solely on the Zoning Law of New York. However, it is reasonable to assume similar characteristics in other North American cities with cold winters. By the late 1920s, many cities had developed their own zoning laws based on the New York system of set-backs and volumetric controls. Although these regulations were not identical to those in New York, the architectural results were the same – an increased slenderness of tall buildings – whether they were in Chicago (Palmolive Building, 1929; Chicago Board of Trade, 1930), Detroit (Penobscot Building, 1928) or Cincinnati (Carew Tower, 1931).

It is also within this generation that air-conditioning started to become more commonplace in tall buildings, although it wasn't until the 1950s and 1960s that it became a standard feature. The earliest high-rise office building that was completely air-conditioned was the Milam Building in San Antonio, Texas, which was built in 1928 (Pauken, 1999). Shortly afterwards, some existing skyscrapers were retrofitted to include air-conditioning. For example, the Chicago Tribune Tower, completed in 1925, was originally designed to be naturally ventilated through opening windows. However, following record-high summer temperatures in June 1933, the *Tribune* publisher directed the tower's management to immediately instal air-conditioning to provide more comfortable internal conditions and to boost demand for vacant space in the tower.

The Tribune believes, and has said, that the next great advance in human comfort will be achieved by air conditioning. . . . The Tribune Tower will be air-conditioned as a contribution to the comfort and health of its occupants, as a contribution to the progress of air conditioning for all, as a contribution to the economic revival of the nation.

[*The Chicago Tribune* announces its intent to install air-conditioning in the Tribune Tower. From Chicago Tribune, 1934, p. 14.]

Second-generation buildings suffered increased primary energy needs through a change in shape, higher artificial lighting requirements and a part-shift to mechanical ventilation, but they still benefited from the continued use of traditional façade materials, such as stone, brick and dense plaster, providing a high degree of thermal mass to assist in occupant comfort. For example, the envelope construction of the Empire State Building consisted of vertical bands of brick back-up masonry faced with limestone, alternating with vertical bands of steel-framed windows with cast aluminium spandrel panels and an internal finish of dense plasterwork (Nacheman, 2006).

The third energy generation: from the development of the glazed curtain wall, 1951,[4] to the 1973 energy crisis

By the middle of the twentieth century, visions of fully glazed skyscrapers had been around for decades but had yet to be realised due to technical limitations at the time. However, after World War II, technological innovations gave rise to the realisation of such proposals: a development that dramatically changed the high-rise typology (see also Chapter 8).

Whereas tall buildings completed prior to the war had between 20% and 40% glazing within their façades (Fine Arts Building, Chicago, 1885 – 40%; Equitable Building, New York, 1915 – 25%; Chrysler Building, New York, 1930 – 32%), 'third-generation' buildings had a significantly higher ratio, typically between 50% and 75% (Lake Shore Drive Apartments, Chicago, 1951 – 72%; Lever House, New York, 1952 – 53%). These rectilinear glass boxes quickly spread around the world, regardless of site, climate or orientation, becoming symbols of reconstruction and economic wealth.

> Towering, glazed office blocks became fashionable as company headquarters. . . . Glass curtain walls became the status symbol of confident companies and the silhouette of glass towers the sign of a prosperous city.
>
> [Schittich *et al.*, 2007, p. 30]

Lever House in New York was one of the first high-rise buildings to utilise this technology. Its façade build-up consisted of a tinted, single-glazed curtain wall with low-level spandrel panels backed by a concrete upstand for fire legislation purposes (Figure 3.6). This lightweight façade construction, made possible only through the use of fixed single glazing, has a significantly inferior thermal/insulation performance compared to the heavyweight façades of first- and second-generation buildings. For example, the façade of Lever House has a U-value of 3.3 W/m²K, compared to 2.6 W/m²K for the Empire State Building, which was completed 20 years previously (Table 3.1). Other buildings of this period, with greater proportions of single glazing, suffered a further reduction in façade performance; the Lake Shore Drive Apartments had a U-value of approximately 4.2 W/m²K, compared to values of 1.1 W/m²K and below, common in modern high-rise buildings.[5]

The problems that buildings with large quantities of single glazing suffer are well-documented; internal

Figure 3.6   Lever House, New York, 1952
Source: Dario Trabucco

Second energy generation: Empire State Building, 1931, New York	Thickness (m)	Thermal conductivity (W/mK)	Thermal resistance (m²K/W)
1. Wall (52.4%)			
External Surface	-	-	0.06
Limestone Cladding	0.102	1.3	0.078
Brickwork	0.203	0.62	0.327
Dense Plaster	0.024	0.5	0.048
Internal Surface	-	-	0.12
Total Resistance	-	-	**0.633**

U-value of Wall Element = (1/0.633) = 1.58 W/m²K

	Thickness (m)	Thermal conductivity (W/mK)	Thermal resistance (m²K/W)
2. Spandrel Panel (24.7%)			
External Surface	-	-	0.06
Aluminium Spandrel Panel	0.04	237	0.00017
Brickwork	0.203	0.62	0.327
Dense Plaster	0.024	0.5	0.048
Internal Surface	-	-	0.12
Total Resistance	-	-	**0.555**

U-value of Spandrel Panel Element = (1/0.555) = 1.802 W/m²K

3. Glazing (22.9%)

6mm Clear Single Glazing with no Coatings

U-value of Glazing Element = 5.7 W/m²K

(Figure courtesy of Pilkington Glass)

Average Envelope U-value = (0.524 × 1.58) + (0.247 × 1.802) + (0.229 × 5.7) = **2.578 W/m²K**

Third energy generation: Lever House, 1952, New York	Thickness (m)	Thermal conductivity (W/mK)	Thermal resistance (m²K/W)
1. Wall/Upstand (47%)			
External Surface	-	-	0.06
Glazed Spandrel Panel	0.06	1	0.06
Air Gap	-	-	0.18
Concrete Upstand	0.125	1.4	0.089
Insulation	0.05	0.035	1.429
Internal Surface	-	-	0.12
Total Resistance			**1.938**

U-value of Wall/Upstand Element = (1/1.938) = 0.516 W/m²K

2. Glazing (53%)

6mm Blue/Green-tinted Single Glazing

U-value of Glazing Element = 5.7 W/m²K

(Figure courtesy of Pilkington Glass)

Average Envelope U-value = (0.47 × 0.516) + (0.53 × 5.7) = **3.264 W/m²K**

Table 3.1 Envelope U-value calculations for the Empire State Building and Lever House

Source: Oldfield *et al.*, 2009; Façade make-up taken from Nacheman, 2006; Schittich *et al.*, 2007

spaces experience vast heat losses in the winter but also overheat from excess solar gain in the summer. If compensated for by air-conditioning alone, this leads to excessively high primary energy consumption. In fact, due to its façade performance, Lever House was one of the first office buildings where air-conditioning was so fundamental to the building design that it could not operate without it (Arnold, 1999).

A further interesting characteristic of this period is the high number of black skyscrapers constructed. Influenced by the International Style represented in Mies van der Rohe's designs such as the Lake Shore Drive Apartments (1951), the Seagram Building (1958), Toronto Dominion Bank Tower (1967) and IBM Building (1973), these black monoliths spread not just across North America but to many cities and climates around the world, such as Paris (Tour Fiat, 1974) and Tokyo (Shinjuku Mitsui Building, 1974) (Figure 3.7). Due to the high solar absorption characteristics of black or dark-coloured cladding, these buildings would have suffered higher quantities of unwanted heat gain in the summer, compared to other buildings with brick or lighter-coloured façades (Table 3.2). The result is that the black skyscraper would further rely on energy-intensive air-conditioning to create a comfortable internal environment.

Figure 3.7   IBM Building, Chicago, 1973
Source: Philip Oldfield

Material	Solar absorptance
Flat black paint	0.95
Dark grey paint	0.91
Red bricks	0.7
Uncoloured concrete	0.65
Light buff bricks	0.6
White semi-gloss paint	0.3

Table 3.2 Solar absorptance values for different coloured materials

Source: Oldfield *et al.*, 2009; data from Yeang, 2006

Glazing colour (float glass, 6mm thick single glazing with no coatings)	Light transmission (%)
Clear	88
Green	75
Bronze	50
Grey	44

Table 3.3 Light transmission values for coloured and clear glazing

Source: Oldfield *et al.*, 2009; data courtesy of Pilkington Glass

In addition to black cladding, many of these buildings also incorporated bronze or dark-tinted glazing. In his seminal Seagram Building, van der Rohe utilised iron oxide and selenium in the glass melt to give the glazing a bronze hue to match the bronze sections of the curtain walling. This strategy was copied in virtually all black skyscrapers of the period, many utilising grey or bronze-tinted glass to create the required aesthetic. The impact this strategy would have on the building's primary energy consumption would likely be detrimental; despite the high quantities of glazing in the façade, low amounts of natural light would actually penetrate into the office spaces beyond due to the poor light transmittance properties of the dark-coloured glass (Table 3.3). This in turn would increase reliance upon artificial lighting.

In terms of shape and form, tall buildings of this period were predominantly large rectilinear boxes, with deep office floor plans – a response to the economics of real estate in city centre areas. No longer slender like the Zoning Law–inspired buildings, these new towers typically displayed shape characteristics similar to first-generation buildings with a high degree of bulk and compactness. Generally, their surface-area-to-volume ratio was between 0.085 m^2/m^3 and 0.13 m^2/m^3, comparable to those built prior to the Zoning Law (see Table 3.4 at the end of this chapter). The 1961 New York Zoning Law replaced the 1916 'wedding cake' set-back requirements with restrictions based on floor area ratios, in recognition of the corporate need for deep floor plans (as many firms found floor areas in the slender towers of the 1920s too shallow for their needs). In addition, the new zoning law allowed a 20% density bonus for buildings that created a public plaza on a portion of their plot (Weiss, 1992). Although the

bulky form of these buildings would be beneficial in colder climates, reducing heat loss in winter through the low-performance curtain walling, the deep floor plans would also restrict the passage of natural light into office spaces. Recommended office lighting levels also rose dramatically in this generation; whereas in the 1930s the recommended levels were around 269 lux, the *1960 Recommended Practice for Office Lighting* guidelines advised illuminance levels several times higher, between 1076 and 1615 lux (Osterhaus, 1993).

In the 1950s, advances in technology and changes in architectural ideology liberated the tall office building from its dependence on nature and site. Fluorescent lighting and air conditioning were as important to the transformation of post-World War II skyscrapers as were elevator and steel-cage construction to the first tall office buildings of the late nineteenth century.

[Willis, 1995, p. 132]

The paradigm shift from a traditional, solid façade construction with punctured windows to the new, lightweight glazed curtain wall had a significant impact on the primary energy consumption of tall buildings of this period. High-rises became hermetically sealed glass boxes, completely reliant on air-conditioning and fluorescent lighting to compensate for overheating, excessive heat loss and poor natural light penetration. These characteristics were only exaggerated by the high number of black skyscrapers constructed at the time. In fact, tall building primary energy consumption grew dramatically in this period, as demonstrated by a study on 86 office buildings constructed in Manhattan

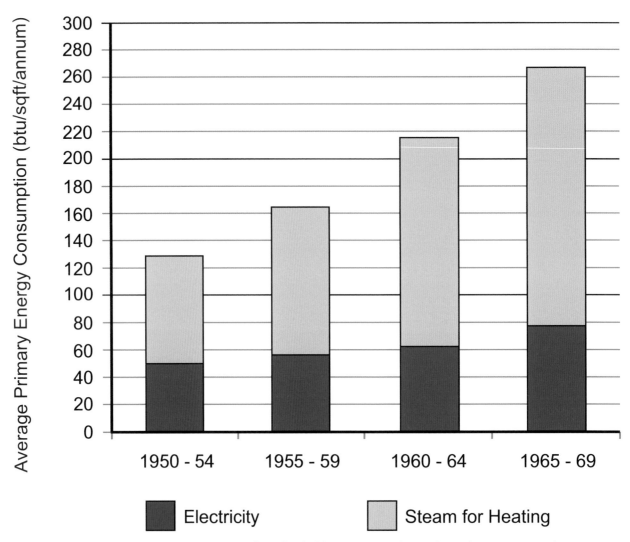

Figure 3.8 Average primary energy consumption of 86 office buildings constructed in Manhattan between 1950 and 1970
Source: Oldfield *et al.*, 2009; data from Stein, 1977

between 1950 and 1970 (Stein, 1977). The results of the study show that, on average, buildings completed in the late 1960s have primary energy requirements more than double those of buildings constructed in the early 1950s, less than 20 years previous (Figure 3.8).

The fourth energy generation: from the energy crisis of 1973 to the present day

The popularity of the single-glazed curtain wall façade, so prevalent in the previous generation, was abruptly interrupted by two major events in the 1970s: the energy crises of 1973 and 1979. Whereas prior to these crises it was still considered sophisticated to isolate the tall building from its surroundings, generating a comfortable internal environment with gas-guzzling air-conditioning and artificial lighting alone, the amount of primary energy these buildings required suddenly became a major issue. Responding to this new attitude towards energy, many developed nations now brought in building energy performance codes,[6] forcing a widespread switch to double-glazing (Johnson, 1991). In fact, the strong criticism the single-glazed curtain wall faced resulted in many changes to the design of high-rise façades.

Following the two oil crises of the 1970s, the fully glazed curtain façade was criticised for its poor energy performance and reliance on mechanical systems to provide a comfortable climate in hermetically sealed buildings. This brief setback to the use of glass in tall buildings forced architects and engineers to act – research led to the development of better insulating and solar control glass. Furthermore the demand for coloured and mirror glazing dropped significantly, in favour of clearer glass with better daylight transmittance.

[Schittich *et al.*, 2007, p. 36]

These developments led to a significant improvement in tall building façade performance; where third-generation buildings had façade U-values in the range of 3.0–4.2 W/m²K, the use of double-glazing, low-e coatings and argon-filled cavities reduced these figures to between 1.0 and 1.5 W/m²K in fourth-generation buildings (Figure 3.9). At the same time, the move away from dark-tinted glazing would reduce artificial light loads, which were further diminished by a reduction in overall recommended lighting levels for offices of the period. The 1982 revision of the *American National*

Standard Practice for Office Lighting proposed roughly a 25–50% decrease in office illuminance levels, due to the rising energy costs and environmental concerns brought about by the energy crises (Osterhaus, 1993).

This new energy-conscious era also claimed a high-rise casualty in the form of the original design for the Tour Elf in Paris. Initially proposed as a twin tower for the adjacent Tour Fiat completed in 1974, it was later redesigned with energy efficiency in mind and completed in 1985. Comparing these two designs indicates some of the major differences between third- and fourth-generation tall buildings (Figure 3.10). The Tour Fiat is a monolithic box clad in black granite, where deep office floors only benefit from minimal natural lighting through dark-tinted windows. Alternatively, the redesigned Tour Elf required good levels of natural lighting for all office workers. This was achieved by specifying a glass that allows for a higher standard of light transmission, yet is still well insulated, a reflection of the strides forward made by the glazing industry after the energy crises. This, in conjunction with a computerised building management system, resulted in a building of the same height and gross floor area as its predecessor, but one that is half as expensive to heat, light and maintain (Ayers, 2004).

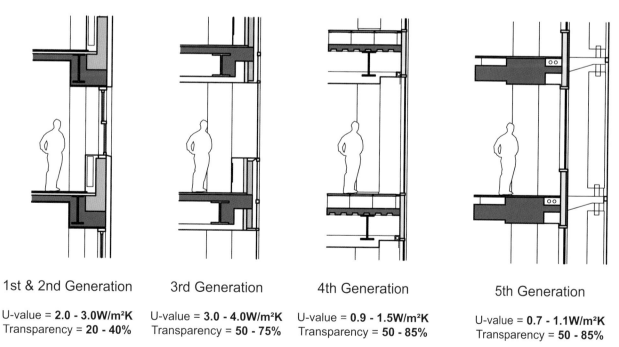

1st & 2nd Generation

U-value = **2.0 - 3.0W/m²K**
Transparency = **20 - 40%**

3rd Generation

U-value = **3.0 - 4.0W/m²K**
Transparency = **50 - 75%**

4th Generation

U-value = **0.9 - 1.5W/m²K**
Transparency = **50 - 85%**

5th Generation

U-value = **0.7 - 1.1W/m²K**
Transparency = **50 - 85%**

Figure 3.9 Evolution of office tall building façades
Source: Philip Oldfield

Figure 3.10 Tour Fiat (left) and Tour Elf (right), La Défense, Paris. The original design of the Tour Elf called for a twin tower to the Tour Fiat
Source: Steven Henry

It is not only the original Tour Elf proposal that was shunned in this era, but black skyscrapers in general became increasingly unpopular due to their inherent energy-efficiency flaws. At their peak in 1971, 17 black skyscrapers were completed in major American cities (Figure 3.11). However, following the first energy crisis, this figure had fallen to only three in 1976 and zero the following year.

Although tall buildings of this generation benefited greatly from improvements in façade performance and a reduction in the number of black skyscrapers, technological developments in office equipment would have a negative impact on building primary energy consumption. For example, the dramatic rise in the use of computers in this era not only required additional electricity for their power, but their use also increases internal heat gains. Figures suggest electronic equipment in office spaces provide on average 17.5 W/m^2 of additional heat gains[7] – a value that is compensated for by increasing levels of mechanical cooling in summer.

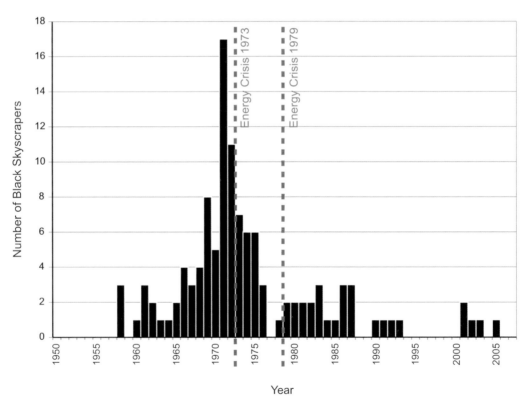

Figure 3.11 Number of black skyscrapers constructed in North America, 1950–2007. Buildings over 100m in height and located in Atlanta, Chicago, Houston, Los Angeles, Miami, New York and San Francisco considered
Source: Oldfield *et al.*, 2009

The fifth energy generation: from the rise of an environmental consciousness (1997) to the present day

The majority of tall buildings constructed today continue to demonstrate 'fourth-generation' characteristics – meeting regulatory energy performance criteria, but not bettering these by any significant amount – but a growing number of high-rise designs and completed buildings aim to go above and beyond the norm in terms of reducing primary energy consumption.

Arguably the first significant tall building reflecting these new environmentally conscious principles was the Commerzbank in Frankfurt (by Foster & Partners, 1997), although one could look to the bioclimatic skyscrapers of Ken Yeang, SOM's National Commercial Bank in Jeddah (1984), or even Frank Lloyd Wright's Price Tower in Oklahoma (1956) as earlier examples of sustainable high-rise buildings (Wood, 2008). The Commerzbank incorporates a high degree of energy-reducing design strategies and technologies that include:

- A full-building-height central atrium, providing natural lighting and ventilation to internal office spaces that are usually artificially lit and ventilated in fourth-generation buildings
- The use of large, open skygardens to further increase daylight penetration to office areas and to provide a place of social interaction and leisure at height
- A double-skin façade that allows for natural ventilation for 80% of the year via operable windows
- A water-based cooling system of chilled ceilings

(For more details on the Commerzbank, see Chapter 1.)

In fact, many qualities of the Commerzbank are typical of fifth-generation skyscrapers. In terms of form and shape, tall buildings of this generation have high surface-area-to-volume ratios – typically between 0.10 m^2/m^3 and 0.22 m^2/m^3 – compared to around 0.09 m^2/m^3 for the bulkier fourth-generation buildings (see Table 3.4 at the end of this chapter). This is achieved by utilising shallow floor plans (e.g. GSW Headquarters, Berlin, 1999) or by using large atria to effectively reduce the depth of deeper floor plates (e.g. Deutsche Post Tower, Bonn, 2002; 'Swiss Re' Tower,

London, 2004; 1 Bligh Street, Sydney, 2011), allowing air and natural light to penetrate deep into office spaces (Figures 3.12 and 3.13). A further characteristic common to many of these tall buildings is a move away from the total reliance upon air-conditioning to strategies that utilise natural and mixed-mode[8] ventilation where climatic conditions allow. For example, the GSW Headquarters in Berlin (designed by Sauerbruch Hutton Architects) utilises a west-facing, double-skin façade that acts as a thermal flue; air in the façade cavity rises due to buoyancy, and when windows are opened, used air is drawn out from the office spaces into the flue and is replaced with fresh air from the east façade. This strategy allows the building to be naturally ventilated for around 70% of the year, significantly reducing air-conditioning energy needs (Clemmetsen *et al.*, 2000) (Figures 3.14 and 3.15).

In more recent years, a new trend in fifth-generation skyscrapers has been the exploitation of on-site energy generation from low- and zero-carbon sources. Although the integration of many of these technologies into tall buildings is still at the experimental stage, increasing numbers of designs and some completed projects utilise technologies such as building-augmented wind turbines, photovoltaic panels, cogeneration and trigeneration systems, fuel cells and ground-source heat pumps to reduce primary energy consumption (for more on this, see Chapter 4).

Conclusion

Table 3.4 summarises the overall findings of this research. Basically, we can note a number of trends affecting tall building energy performance throughout history. Primary energy in first-generation buildings (1885–1916) was predominantly consumed in the heating of occupied spaces and providing vertical transportation, as other technologies were not yet developed. These towers benefited from their compact and bulky shape (large volume vs. small surface area), reducing winter heat loss through the building envelope, which also contained a high degree of thermal mass.

Second-generation buildings (1916–1951) were increasingly slender (small volume vs. large surface area) – a direct result of the New York Zoning Law of 1916. This change in shape would increase winter

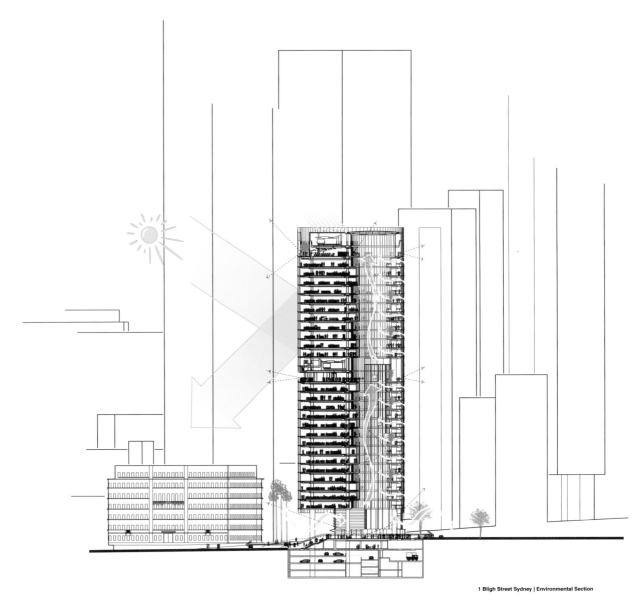

1 Bligh Street Sydney | Environmental Section

Figure 3.12 1 Blight Street, Sydney. Section showing the 120-metre-tall atrium. This allows natural light to penetrate to some of the deepest spaces in the office floors and, using the stack effect, drives natural ventilation for thermal comfort in the ground floor public spaces. The offices are mechanically ventilated for commercial reasons, although a double-skin façade allows perimeter spaces to be naturally ventilated if desired by tenants

Source: Architectus + Ingenhoven Architects

heat loss, but at the same time allow for a greater level of daylight penetration at the upper floors. Like first-generation buildings, these towers also benefited from thermal mass within the envelope construction.

Third-generation buildings (1951–1973) were heavily influenced by the development of glazed curtain walls; 50–75% of tall building façade area in this generation consisted of glazing, compared to 20–40% in the previous two generations. Subsequently, façade U-values increased due to the high proportions of single glazing used. Tall buildings of this generation were hermetically sealed boxes, totally reliant on mechanical conditioning and artificial lighting; despite high levels of façade transparency, tinted glazing and deep floor plans significantly restricted daylight penetration. At the same time, office illuminance recommendations were significantly higher in this era than at any other time.

Figure 3.13   1 Blight Street, view up the central atrium from the ground floor lobby
Source: Philip Oldfield

Fourth-generation buildings (1973 to the present day) benefited from a widespread switch to double-glazing and increased technological developments in curtain wall façades. Although envelope glazing percentages remained high, façade U-values decreased from around 3.0–4.2 W/m²K in third-generation buildings to levels of 1.0–1.5 W/m²K. The majority of tall buildings constructed today continue to demonstrate the characteristics of fourth-generation buildings: compact shape (surface-area-to-volume ratios of around 0.07 m²/m³ – 0.12 m²/m³), high levels of façade glazing (40–85%) and a reliance on air-conditioning for comfort.

Fifth-generation buildings (1997 to the present day) are still relatively rare, at least in completed form.

Generally these towers have a high surface-area-to-volume ratio (often achieved by the use of atria) and high quantities of envelope transparency, allowing for daylight penetration, but at the cost of higher winter heating loads. The use of natural and mixed-mode ventilation strategies is also common in these towers. Lastly, buildings of this category have begun exploring the potential to harness on-site energy generation from low- and zero-carbon sources.

Postscript: Philip Oldfield, January 2018

It is almost a decade since the research in this chapter was first conducted. Yet despite the passage of time,

Figure 3.14   GSW HQ, Berlin, view of the west-facing double-skin façade
Source: © Annette Kisling/Sauerbruch Hutton

fifth-generation tall buildings, where the design aims to maximise energy efficiency and improve environmental performance, are still in the minority. Instead, fourth-generation tall buildings remain the standard design model of our times. This is worrying given the rapid increase in high-rise construction around the world and the urgent need for more sustainable designs to tackle climate change.

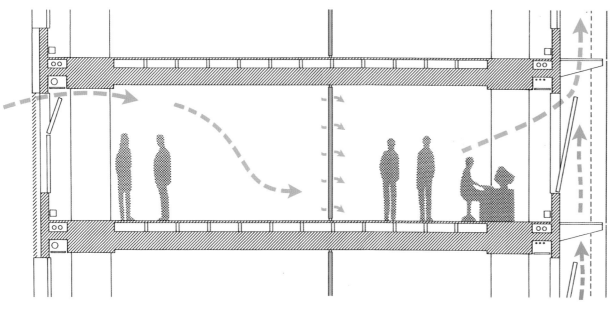

querlüftung - kombi/ost   *cross ventilation - combi/east*

Figure 3.15   GSW HQ. A shallow floor plan of 11.5 metres wide, along with a west-facing double-skin façade, allows for natural ventilation for around 70% of the year

Source: © Sauerbruch Hutton

This slow shift from fourth- to fifth-generation tall building design is being influenced by commercial, cultural and regulatory drivers. On the plus side, sustainable design is increasingly recognised as a significant factor in generating status and revenue. For example, the *World Green Building Trends 2016 Report* surveyed over 1,000 people in the construction industry and found that client demand was the biggest trigger for green building construction, with 40% of clients now expecting a green building – up from 34% in 2008 (Dodge Data and Analytics, 2016). It goes without saying though that 40% is still far lower than where we need to be.

Regulatory demands and incentives are also driving this shift towards fifth energy generation towers, but again at a pace not fast enough to meet necessary GHG reduction targets. At a national level, building regulations have been incrementally tightening across the last four decades, moving towards the goal of establishing widespread Net Zero Energy Buildings (NZEB) that generate as much energy on-site from renewable sources as they need for their day-to-day operations (Papadopoulos, 2016). Yet, while NZEB performance

is both technologically and economical feasible in high-rises, there are few incentives for developers to strive to achieve such levels of environmental performance[11] (Harrington, 2016). Some cities and regions are progressing more rigorous regulations and incentives; for example, the European Commission has set in place legislation for all members to ensure new buildings are nearly Zero Energy Buildings (nZEB) by 2020 (European Commission, 2016). In San Francisco, priority permits that put projects at the front of queues for planning decisions are made available for designs achieving LEED Platinum status or other high levels of green building certification (City and County of San Francisco, 2014). These developments are promising, but often building regulations do not go far enough, nor is their spread wide enough to cover the emerging locations of high-rise cities. For example, the International Energy Agency reports that over the next 20 years, two-thirds of all new buildings will be constructed in countries that do not currently have mandatory building energy codes (UN Environment and International Energy Agency, 2017). What's more, it is not enough to implement widespread fifth-generation

	1st energy generation From the birth of tall buildings in 1885, to the 1916 Zoning Law	2nd energy generation From the 1916 Zoning Law to the development of the glazed curtain wall, 1951	3rd energy generation From the development of the glazed curtain wall, 1951, to the 1973 energy crisis	4th energy generation From the energy crisis of 1973, ongoing to the present day	5th energy generation From the rise of an environmental consciousness in 1997, ongoing to the present day
Typical Energy Performance Characteristics	- Compact shape (large volume vs. small façade area) - High levels of thermal mass in façade - Low percentage of façade transparency compared to modern tall buildings - Reliance on natural light penetration - Heating and elevators main consumers of primary energy	- Slender shape (small volume vs. large façade area) - High levels of thermal mass in façade - Low percentage of façade transparency compared to modern tall buildings - Greater levels of artificial lighting - The use of air-conditioning becoming more common	- Compact shape (large volume vs. small façade area) - Low-performance, single-glazed curtain wall façade systems - High quantities of façade transparency with tinted glazing - Total reliance on mechanical conditioning and fluorescent lighting - Large quantity of 'black skyscrapers'	- Compact shape (large volume vs. small façade area) - Good performance, double-glazed curtain wall façade systems - High quantities of façade transparency with good solar transmittance - Total reliance on mechanical conditioning	- Slender shape (small volume vs. large façade area) - High performance double-skin and triple-glazed curtain wall façade systems - High quantities of façade transparency with good solar transmittance - Natural and mixed-mode ventilation possibilities exploited - On-site energy generation promoted
Surface-Area-to-Volume Ratios (m²/m³)	- 90 West Street, *New York*: **0.118** - Woolworth Building, *New York*: **0.122** - 195 Broadway, *New York*: **0.087** - Municipal Building, *New York*: **0.118** - Equitable Building, *New York*: **0.088** ***Average: 0.107***	- Bryant Park Tower, *New York*: **0.189** - Mercantile Building, *New York*: **0.144** - Chrysler Building, *New York*: **0.130** - 500 5th Avenue, *New York*: **0.158** - 570 Lexington Ave, *New York*: **0.138** ***Average: 0.152***	- Lever House, *New York*: **0.164** - Seagram Building, *New York*: **0.123** - City National Tower, *LA*: **0.089** - One IBM Plaza, *Chicago*: **0.088** - Tour Fiat, *Paris*: **0.089** ***Average: 0.111***	- First Canadian Place, *Toronto*: **0.077** - Wells Fargo Plaza, *Houston*: **0.087** - One Canada Square, *London*: **0.079** - UOB Plaza, *Singapore*: **0.112** - Cheung Kong Center, *Hong Kong*: **0.084** ***Average: 0.088***	- Commerzbank, *Frankfurt*: **0.161** - GSW Headquarters, *Berlin*: **0.221** - Deutsche Post Building, *Bonn*: **0.152** - Hearst Tower, *New York*: **0.100** - Bank of America Tower, *New York*: **0.096** ***Average: 0.146***
Typical Office Lighting Levels (lux)	86–97	108–269	1076–1615	377–1076	377–484
Typical Façade U-values (W/m²K)	Information unavailable. Figures likely to be in 2.0–3.0 range.	- Empire State Building, *New York*: **2.6**	- Lake Shore Drive Apartments, *Chicago*: **4.2** - Lever House, *New York*: **3.3**	- Wells Fargo Plaza, *Houston*: **1.5** - Cheung Kong Center, *Hong Kong*: **0.9**	- Deutsche Post Building, *Bonn*: **1.1** - Bank of America Tower, *New York*: **0.9**
Transparency within Façade	- Fine Arts Building, *Chicago*: **40%** - Woolworth Building, *New York*: **21%** - Equitable Building, *New York*: **25%**	- Chrysler Building, *New York*: **32%** - Empire State Building, *New York*: **23%** - 500 5th Ave, *New York*: **32%**	- Lake Shore Drive Apartments, *Chicago*: **72%** - Lever House, *New York*: **53%** - City National Tower, *LA*: **53%**	- Wells Fargo Plaza, *Houston*: **82%** - One Canada Square, *London*: **43%** - Cheung Kong Center, *Hong Kong*: **52%**	- Commerzbank, *Frankfurt*: **54%** - Hearst Tower, New York: **63%** - Bank of America Tower, *New York*: **71%**
Ventilation Strategies	Naturally ventilated via opening lights. Later renovated to be fully air-conditioned.	Naturally ventilated via opening lights. Later renovated to be fully air-conditioned.	Hermetically sealed and totally reliant on mechanical conditioning.	Hermetically sealed and totally reliant on mechanical conditioning.	Opportunities for natural and mixed-mode ventilation exploited. Double-skin façades often utilised where climatic conditions allow.

Table 3.4 Summary of data and findings

All values calculated by Philip Oldfield, Dario Trabucco and Antony Wood from a variety of sources, unless otherwise stated.[9,10]

characteristics in just new tall building design. There's an urgent need to improve the current stock of first-, second-, third- and fourth-generation skyscrapers – many of which have become heritage landmarks and international icons – through high-performance energy and environmental retrofits. Nor is it enough to only focus on operating energy, reducing artificial lighting and conditioning loads through passive design. There is increasing acknowledgement in the building industry that the materials we use to build our cities, and the manufacturing, transport, construction and demolition processes undertaken contribute significantly to CO_2 emissions in the built environment. This means our next generation of tall buildings have to go far beyond fifth-generation characteristics outlined previously and seek to radically reduce embodied carbon emissions as well. Fortunately, advanced structural modelling techniques are resulting in the optimisation of tower forms and structural systems, allowing for dematerialisation – reducing the quantity of steel and concrete in construction to the minimum necessary for safety and security. Alternative materials are also being used. A growing trend is the use of wood, such as cross-laminated timber (CLT), which has a far lower embodied carbon than steel and concrete structures. The importance of embodied carbon and strategies to reduce its impact in high-rise design is discussed in more detail in Chapter 7.

Overall, we can say that time is seriously running out for a wholescale shift from the fourth to fifth generation of skyscrapers and beyond, if the typology is going to contribute to the carbon emission reductions necessary to limit global warming to 2°C or lower, as set out in the Paris Climate Agreement. The skyscrapers built today will potentially last over a hundred years, well into the next century. They will carry with them their environmental performance for many decades, unless subject to costly and challenging energy refurbishments – by which time, much of the damage will already be done. The urgent adoption of stringent energy codes, incentives and state-of-the-art knowledge sharing to foster the fifth generation of tall buildings and beyond will avoid locking in carbon-intensive designs, which we will have to live with for several decades into the future (Lucon *et al.*, 2014).

Notes

1   This chapter was originally published as: Oldfield, P., Trabucco, D. & Wood, A. (2009). Five Energy Generations of Tall Buildings: An Historical Analysis of Energy Consumption in High-Rise Buildings. *Journal of Architecture*, Vol. 14, No. 5. pp. 591–614. Taylor & Francis Ltd, www.tandfonline.com. It is reprinted by permission of the publisher.

2   All measurements of illuminance within this chapter are converted to lux from foot-candles (a non-SI unit of illuminance which was used historically).

3   Façade transparencies refer to the percentage of transparent glazing within a typical section of building façade. This is also often known as Window-to-Wall-Ratio (WWR). All data calculated by the authors from a variety of photos and drawings (see Table 3.4).

4   Whereas mid-rise buildings with glazed curtain wall façades had been completed in the early twentieth century (such as the Hallidie Building in San Francisco, 1918), such systems did not make it into high-rise buildings until later. The first tall buildings constructed with glazed curtain wall façades were the 1951 Lake Shore Drive Apartments in Chicago, designed by Mies van der Rohe.

5   Unless stated otherwise, all U-value data is calculated by the authors from published technical details and descriptions of the building façade construction. Figures refer to the average U-value of the façade, including both glazed and solid wall elements.

6   Few building energy efficiency regulations existed prior to the 1973 energy crisis. However, building envelope thermal performance regulations existed as far back as the 1950s and '60s in Germany and Scandinavia. The Swedish building code of BABS, for example, stipulated double-glazing for comfort and economics as far back as 1960 (Papadopoulos, 2016).

7   In comparison, prior to the use of computers in the workplace, non-climatic internal heat gains in office buildings would mostly arise from people (8.5 W/m², assuming an average of 15 m² of floor space per person) and lighting (13 W/m²). All data from Knight & Dunn, 2003.

8   This is a hybrid ventilation strategy where natural ventilation is used when feasible, often in

temperate months, but mechanical conditioning is used when outside temperatures become too extreme in peak summer and winter periods.

9 Surface-area-to-volume ratios only include the tower element of projects and not adjacent low-level buildings that form part of the complex. Figures also do not include large atria/skygarden spaces, double-skin façade cavities and the ground floor footprint area as part of the calculations. The value for the Hearst Tower only includes the tower from the first office floor above; it does not include the surface area/volume of the renovated ground floor lobby.

10 Typical office lighting levels are taken from Osterhaus (1993), Willis (1995) and a personal communication with Wilson Dau, Head of the IESNA Office Lighting Committee (2008). All measurements converted to lux from foot-candles.

11 This is not to say that NZEB performance should necessarily be the ultimate target for future tall buildings. Most NZEB definitions exclude embodied carbon, and such a goal doesn't consider the environmental impact the building has on its surrounding context. These issues are discussed in more depth in Chapter 4.

References

Arnold, D. (1999). Air Conditioning in Office Buildings After World War II. *ASHRAE Journal*, July, pp. 33–41.

Ayers, A. (2004). *The Architecture of Paris*. Edition Axel Menges, Stuttgart/London.

Barnett, J. (1982). *An Introduction to Urban Design*. Harper Collins, New York.

Chicago Tribune. (1934). Air Conditioning for the Tribune Tower. *Chicago Daily Tribune*, 10 June, p. 14.

City and County of San Francisco. (2014). *Establishing Policy and Guidelines for Department of Public Works (DPW) Permit Priority Processing*. DPW Order No: 182974. www.sfpublicworks.org/sites/default/files/K2%20DPW%20Order(182974)_0.pdf

Clemmetsen, N., Muller, W. & Trott, C. (2000). GSW Headquarters, Berlin. *The Arup Journal*, February, pp. 8–12.

Depecker, P., Menezo, C., Virgone, J. & Lepers, S. (2001). Design of Buildings Shape and Energetic Consumption. *Building and Environment*, Vol. 36, pp. 627–635.

Dodge Data and Analytics. (2016). *World Green Building Trends 2016: Developing Markets Accelerate Global Green Growth*. Dodge Data and Analytics, New York.

European Commission. (2016). *Commission Recommendation (EU) 2016/1318 of 29 July 2016 on Guidelines for the Promotion of Nearly Zero-Energy Buildings and Best Practices to Ensure That, by 2020, All New Buildings Are Nearly Zero-Energy Buildings*. http://eur-lex.europa.eu/legal-content/EN/TXT/?uri=CELEX:32016H1318

Harrington, P. (2016). *Accelerating Net-Zero High-Rise Residential Buildings in Australia*. Pitt & Sherry, Sydney.

Johnson, T. E. (1991). *Low E-Glazing Design Guide*. Butterworth Architecture, Stoneham, MA.

Knight, I. & Dunn, G. (2003). *Evaluation of Heat Gains in UK Office Environments*. Proceedings of CIBSE/ASHRAE Conference, Edinburgh, 24–26 September.

Lucon, O., Ürge-Vorsatz, D., Zain Ahmed, A., Akbari, H., Bertoldi, P., Cabeza, L. F., Eyre, N., Gadgil, A., Harvey, L. D. D., Jiang, Y., Liphoto, E., Mirasgedis, S., Murakami, S., Parikh, J., Pyke, C. & Vilariño, M. V. (2014). Buildings. In: *Climate Change 2014: Mitigation of Climate Change. Contribution of Working Group III to the Fifth Assessment Report of the Intergovernmental Panel on Climate Change* Cambridge University Press, Cambridge and New York.

Nachemann, R. J. (2006). The Empire State Building: Façade Evaluation and Repair of an Engineering Landmark. *Structure Magazine*, January, pp. 39–43.

Oldfield, P., Trabucco, D. & Wood, A. (2009). Five Energy Generations of Tall Buildings: An Historical Analysis of Energy Consumption in High-Rise Buildings. *Journal of Architecture*, Vol. 14, No. 5, pp. 591–614.

Osterhaus, W. K. E. (1993). *Office Lighting: A Review of 80 Years of Standards and Recommendations*. Proceedings of the IEEE Industry Applications Society Annual Meeting, Toronto, 2–8 October.

Papadopoulos, A. M. (2016). Forty Years of Regulations on the Thermal Performance of the Building Envelope in Europe: Achievements, Perspectives and Challenges. *Energy and Buildings*, Vol. 127, pp. 942–952.

Pauken, M. (1999). Sleeping Soundly on Summer Nights: The First Century of Air Conditioning. *ASHRAE Journal*, May, pp. 40–47.

Schittich, C., Staib, G., Balkow, D., Schuler, M. & Sobek, W. (2007). *Glass Construction Manual: Second Edition*. Birkhäuer Verlag AG, Basel.

Stein, R. G. (1977). Observations on Energy Use in Buildings. *Journal of Architectural Education*, Vol. 30, pp. 36–41.

UN Environment & International Energy Agency. (2017). *Towards A Zero-Emission, Efficient, And Resilient Buildings and Construction Sector*. Global Status Report.

Weiss, M. A. (1992). Skyscraper Zoning: New York's Pioneering Role. *Journal of the American Planning Association*, Vol. 58, pp. 201–212.

Willis, C. (1995). *Form follows Finance: Skyscrapers and Skylines in New York and Chicago*. Princeton Architectural Press, New York.

Wood, A. (2008). *Green or Grey: The Aesthetics of Tall Building Sustainability*. Proceedings of the CTBUH 8th World Congress, "Tall and Green: Typology for a Sustainable Urban Future", Dubai, 3–5 March, pp. 194–202.

Yeang, K. (2006). *Ecodesign: A Manual for Ecological Design*. Wiley Academy, London.

PART II

Design drivers

CHAPTER FOUR

Climate and the environment

The 'international' skyscraper

Climate has always played a pivotal role in the formation of the built environment. For thousands of years, designers have used ingenuity and innovation to harness the natural forces of the sun, wind and temperature to provide thermal comfort and visual delight for occupants. In cold climates, windows or openings would be orientated towards the sun to capture passive solar gain for free heating. In tropical regions, typologies such as the Kampong House in South-East Asia are lifted on stilts, allowing the living spaces to capture breezes for cooling, while large projecting eaves offer shade and protection from heavy rains. In hot-arid climates, thick adobe or ceramic walls would provide thermal mass to dampen the extremes of temperature, while windcatcher towers capture elevated breezes to provide free cooling (Figure 4.1). The result is a diversity of architectural form, from region to region, with buildings shaped by the unique qualities and challenges climate provides. Of course, these strategies were also a necessity since the technologies we have come to rely on for thermal comfort today – electricity, air-conditioning and mechanical heating – were non-existent.

Much of this regional diversity changed in the early twentieth century. Fuelled by the industrial revolution, artificial heating, cooling and conditioning became more reliable, economic and subsequently commonplace. As far back as 1904, the journal *Ice and Refrigeration* stated that "the day is at hand, or soon will be, when the modern office building, factory, church, theatre and even residence will be incomplete without a mechanical air cooling plant" (Nagengast, 1999, p. 55). Although this prediction perhaps took until the end of the twentieth century to truly come to fruition, it is apparent today, and nowhere more than in our dense urban centres. There is little doubt that such technological advances have improved thermal comfort, especially in extreme climates, where passive techniques alone may not be sufficient to facilitate comfortable conditions in all building types, at all times of the year. But, their reliance on fossil fuels for power has had a vast and negative impact on the environment. Our use of such technologies will increase dramatically in the future. Isaac and Vuuran (2009) expect energy demand for air-conditioning to increase over 30-fold in the twenty-first century, from 300 TWh in 2000 to 10,000 TWh in 2100, driven mostly by greater levels of income in developing countries. If powered by fossil fuels alone, such growth could lead to vast carbon dioxide emissions, further exacerbating climate change. Mitigating the potential effects of this requires societal and policy changes – such as a widespread switch to renewable sources for energy generation – but at the building scale the need for building design to better adapt to local climate and environment is vital, reducing heat loss in colder conditions and protecting against unwanted ambient heat gain in hotter climates (Santamouris, 2016).

Figure 4.1 Windcatcher tower, Dubai
Source: Philip Oldfield

So, what of the tall building in this situation? As discussed in Chapter 3, early skyscrapers embraced some passive design strategies to provide thermal comfort, primarily due to the limitation of artificial conditioning technologies of the era. However, after World War II, economic growth and technological development saw towers shift towards a total and complete reliance on mechanical conditioning (Oldfield *et al.*, 2009). The rise of Modernism in the mid-twentieth century saw architectural design increasingly detached from its surroundings, often (although not always) prioritising functionality and aesthetics over local climate, culture or context. The problem is, despite an urgent need for low-energy, climate-responsive design to reduce the high-energy requirements of towers, little seems to have changed, and many contemporary tall building designs fail to respond to, or draw inspiration from, local climate. Antony Wood, Executive Director of the CTBUH, is one of the most vocal critics of this issue,

noting that "the rectilinear, air-conditioned, glass-skinned box is still the main template for the majority of tall buildings developing around the world" (Wood, 2015, p. 93). His critique is not only environmental – lamenting the impact highly transparent towers have, in say, hot desert climates – but aesthetic too, noting how this is contributing towards a homogenisation of skylines and the loss of the identity of place. It seems while the *International Style* of Modernism is no longer in vogue, the *International Skyscraper* remains the standard architectural approach – no matter what the city, no matter what the climate.

Our climates are hugely diverse and varied. The Köppen Climate Classification categorises global climates into five main groups: tropical, arid, temperate, cold and polar (Peel *et al.*, 2007) (Figure 4.2). With the exception of polar, all of these climates are now home to thousands of tall buildings. This provides us with significant scope for climate to act as a primary driver for tall building design and for a greater diversity of high-rise architecture to emerge.

In recent years the skyscraper has become a truly international typology, one that dominates the imaginations of planners and officials charged with ensuring their cities stand out in the competition for global attention (Kong, 2007). But tall buildings need to do more than just stand out; they also need to *fit in* to local climate, culture and context. This fitting in does not mean they need to conform to their surroundings, attempting to merge into the local context. Nor does it mean rejecting global advances in technology or design thinking. Tall buildings are always going to be global and regional icons, and they will always benefit from international best practice in structure, safety, systems and more. But this does not restrict them from taking better advantage of the unique qualities and challenges that local climate provides to improve their environmental performance. As Chris Abel notes, towers require a delicate balancing between the global and the local (Abel, 2006). It's just that from an environmental perspective, this balance is out of whack, too skewed towards creating air-conditioned global icons and not enough towards responding to local climate to improve thermal comfort and reduce energy consumption.

This chapter explores how climate can be a more substantive design driver for the tall building architect.

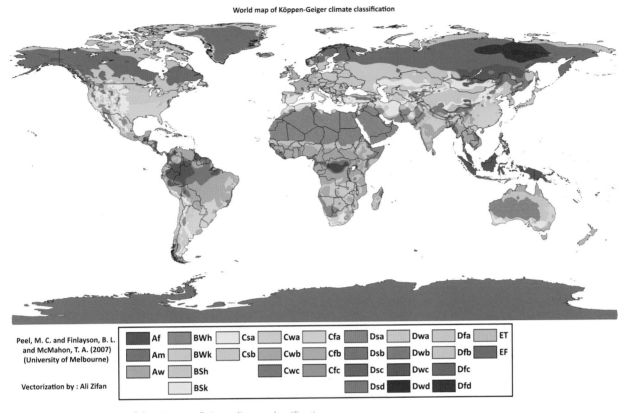

World map of Köppen-Geiger climate classification

Peel, M. C. and Finlayson, B. L.
and McMahon, T. A. (2007)
(University of Melbourne)

Vectorization by : Ali Zifan

Af	BWh	Csa	Cwa	Cfa	Dsa	Dwa	Dfa	ET
Am	BWk	Csb	Cwb	Cfb	Dsb	Dwb	Dfb	EF
Aw	BSh		Cwc	Cfc	Dsc	Dwc	Dfc	
	BSk				Dsd	Dwd	Dfd	

Figure 4.2 World map of the Köppen-Geiger climate classification

Legend: A – Tropical, B – Arid, C – Temperate, D – Cold, E – Polar

Source: Peel, M. C., Finlayson, B. L., and McMahon, T. A., (2007) CC BY-SA 4.0 https://creativecommons.org/licenses/by-sa/4.0/deed.en

It focusses on high-rise design in three climatic conditions: 'cold and temperate', 'tropical' and 'hot desert'. In each condition, potential design strategies, technologies and exemplar precedents are presented. The chapter concludes by exploring how the tall building architect can harness natural energy sources from the sun, wind and ground to achieve 'net zero energy', or 'net zero carbon' performance.

There is much more to our current place in architectural history than symbol and iconography. Rather than symbol, the specifics of each environmental condition, culture, lifestyle and the tools and methods we use to build should be the basis for a new kind of high-rise building that would inherently "add value" but also transform cities.

[Jeanne Gang, 2008, p. 497]

The 'cold and temperate' skyscraper

Cold climates (Köppen Climate Classification D) are typified by very cold winters with an average temperature in the coldest month below 0°C, and summer months ranging from cool to hot (Peel *et al.*, 2007). These include cities such as Chicago, Beijing and Seoul. Temperate climates (Köppen Climate Classification C) are similar in many respects, although milder, with cold-to-cool winters, warm-to-hot summers and mild intermediate seasons. They include cities such as Sydney, New York and Rome. Although both of these climates are varied, they are grouped together here since passive design in these regions often requires a careful balance between minimising heat loss in the winter months and controlling heat gain in summer periods. As such, high-rise buildings in both climates require adaptability to respond to changing external conditions throughout the year to achieve indoor thermal comfort without significant energy demands. Fundamental to this is an understanding of, and response to, local sunpath since this is a key contributor to building heat gains. An obvious strategy is integrating solar shading on the façades that face the sun, designed such that they limit direct solar radiation in the summer, but allow low-angle sun to penetrate interior spaces in winter months for heating. However, manipulation of solar gain can go far beyond shading alone. Studio Gang's Solstice on the Park, in Chicago, for example, uses an innovative building form to adapt to changing seasons. Chicago's climate is extremely varied, with very cold winters and warm humid summers (Figure 4.3). In this sense, for much of the year passive solar gain is beneficial to offset the cold outside temperatures – but not in the summer months. Solstice on the Park consists of a rectilinear slab building, with the long edge facing south, orientated for views of nearby Jackson Park. Its form is carved in a sawtooth-fashion on the south façade, with inclined glazing set at an angle of 72°, corresponding to the angle of the sun in Chicago at 12 noon in mid-summer. In this sense, the form of the building self-shades the internal spaces in the summer, blocking out solar gain. But as the sun angle drops in mid-season and winter months,

the inclined façade still allows solar radiation to penetrate apartments, providing free heating. Here then is a high-rise that is both dramatic in form, but tied to the unique characteristics of its location, and specifically sunpath (Figures 4.4 and 4.5).

Residential programmes benefit from passive solar gain in cold and temperate climates, but other functions such as office space may desire less solar radiation, since high internal heat gains from occupants, computers and artificial lighting can increase interior temperatures. The Heron Tower, designed by Kohn Pedersen Fox and completed in London in 2011, responds to this by organising the building footprint around a south-facing core. This is designed to act as a solar screen, shading the north-facing office floor plates from direct solar gain since cooling is the primary energy requirement. The façade build-up and spatial organisation changes in each direction. The south-facing core is clad with an array of photovoltaics, while the east and west façades use a double-skin system, with blinds located in the cavity to control direct solar radiation and mitigate glare from low sun angles. The double-skin also allows external fresh air into the cavity; in mild conditions, this can be used as natural ventilation for perimeter office spaces, reducing the energy needs for air-conditioning (Gonçalves &

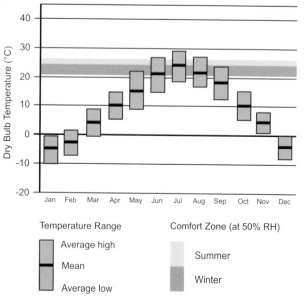

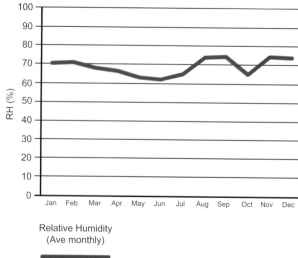

Figure 4.3 Chicago temperature, comfort and humidity data
Source: Philip Oldfield, data from Climate Consultant, 2018

Figure 4.4   Solstice on the Park, Chicago, view from the south
Source: Studio Gang

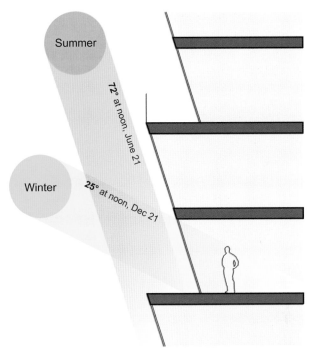

Figure 4.5   Solstice on the Park; sawtooth profile of the south
façade as a response to local sunpath
Source: Philip Oldfield

Umakoshi, 2010). The north façade is highly glazed, with no shading, since it receives little direct sunlight. Three-storey atria on the northern side of the building allow diffuse light deep into the floor plan, but also create a series of 'vertical villages' providing visual and physical connectivity between floors (Figures 4.6 and 4.7). Thus, we can see, the architectural organisation of the Heron Tower is designed to relate to the different climatic conditions each façade faces (Figure 4.8).

In cold and temperate climates, there is a need to carefully balance internal heat gains, radiant heat from the sun and heat losses through the building fabric. A strategy to achieve this is *Passivhaus* construction.[1] Here, thermal comfort is achieved to a maximum extent through a high-performance building façade, including the use of super-insulation to minimise heat loss and strategically located windows to harness solar heating. To gain Passivhaus certification, buildings need to demonstrate heating and cooling energy of less than 15 kWh/m²/annum. This is around 75% below conventional new-build construction (Passipedia,

Figure 4.6   Heron Tower, London, stacked three-storey, north-facing atria
Source: Philip Oldfield

2017). Typically, Passivhaus buildings can be characterised by six factors (Oldfield, 2017):

1   Thick insulation and triple-glazing to create a thermally high-performance building envelope. Typical

Figure 4.7   Heron Tower. North-facing atria allow diffused light deep into floor spaces, but also provide spectacular views out and visual connectivity to floors above and below

Source: Philip Oldfield

U-values are less than 0.15 W/m²K for walls and 0.85 W/m²K for windows (McLeod *et al.*, 2011).

2   The careful orientation of windows and glazing to allow for free solar heating from the sun when required, but also to minimise heat loss. In residential projects in cold northern hemisphere climates, this often results in larger expanses of south-facing glazing to harness solar gain, but smaller north-facing windows to limit heat loss.

3   Recovering waste heat from stale indoor air to pre-heat fresh air brought into the building. This is achieved using a Mechanical Ventilation and Heat Recover system (MVHR).

4   Minimising heat loss through infiltration by creating a building fabric with a high level of air-tightness, typically below 0.6 air changes per hour at 50 Pascals pressure (McLeod *et al.*, 2011).

5   Minimisation of thermal bridges in the building fabric, to reduce conductive heat losses.

6   The use of compact and bulky forms to reduce the quantities of exposed façade facilitating heat loss.

Passivhaus tall buildings can benefit from significantly reduced energy requirements. Using simulations, FxFowle (2017) found that a 26-storey Passivhaus skyscraper in Queens, New York, would have a 47% lower primary energy demand[2] and an 85% lower heating demand than a conventional tower of the same height, form and window-to-wall-ratio (WWR)[3] in the city. Although the additional systems

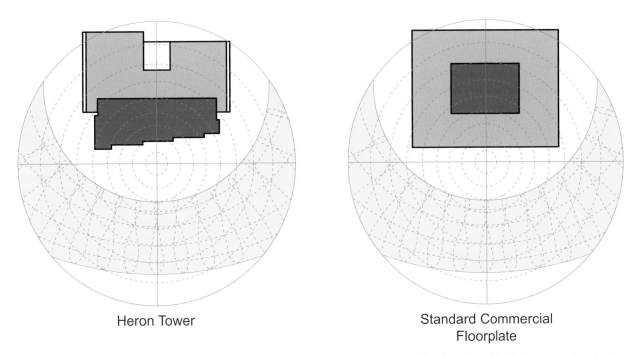

Heron Tower

Standard Commercial
Floorplate

Figure 4.8   Comparison between the Heron Tower (left) and a standard central-core office floorplate (right), demonstrating design response to the London sunpath

Source: Philip Oldfield

and high-performance façade would increase capital costs by 2.4%, this would be paid back by reduced energy costs in 24 years.

Tall buildings have intrinsic benefits in terms of Passivhaus performance as compared to other building types. Their compact form, with low surface-area-to-volume ratios, means less envelope facilitating heat loss in the winter months. Given this, tall buildings can achieve Passivhaus performance with less insulation than other building types and double-glazing rather than triple-glazing. This provides cost and constructability benefits, and potential embodied carbon savings as compared to more common low-rise and detached Passivhaus projects (Oldfield, 2017).

One of the tallest completed Passivhaus buildings in the world, at the time of this writing,[4] is Handel Architects' The House at Cornell Tech – a 26-storey residential tower for students in New York (Figure 4.9). The local climate is temperate, with cold winters, warm summers and heating the greatest energy requirement in residential accommodation (Figure 4.10). In response, the façade is designed as

Figure 4.9   The House at Cornell Tech, under construction in 2017, New York

Source: Handel Architects

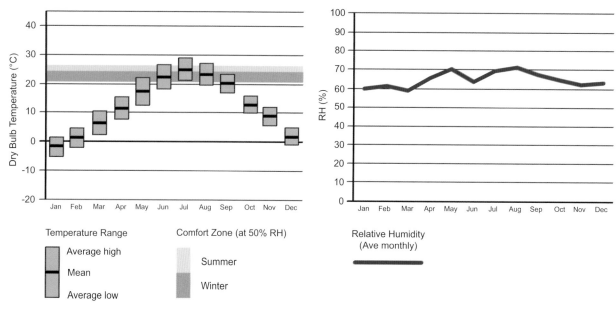

Figure 4.10   New York temperature, comfort and humidity data
Source: Philip Oldfield, data from Climate Consultant, 2018

a thermally insulated blanket wrapping the building. This consists of super-insulated panels with U-values between 0.025 and 0.053 W/m²K, triple-glazed windows and a WWR of around 30% – far below typical residential towers in the city, to keep heat losses to a minimum. The façade is prefabricated off-site, with panels shipped along the Hudson River on barges before being craned up and installed. This minimises joints on-site, therefore improving the building's air-tightness and reducing heat loss via infiltration (Figures 4.11 and 4.12). Overall, compared to a conventional building, it is expected that these Passivhaus strategies will contribute to a carbon saving of 882 tonnes of CO_2 per year (Handel Architects, 2016).

One of the challenges of achieving Passivhaus performance in any building type is minimising thermal bridges. A thermal bridge is a localised area of heat transfer due to an uninsulated part of the envelope assembly. This creates a pathway for conductive heat to escape through the building fabric, increasing heating loads and subsequent carbon emissions. In towers, this is especially prevalent in projecting concrete balconies, where the slab penetrates through the envelope insulation and creates a path for heat loss in winter months (Figure 4.13). This can be resolved by removing balconies from the design, although one would also lose a

connection to the outside for residents, with access to air, light and view. Instead, an alternative is introducing a structural thermal break into the slab; this consists of an insulating material to limit the thermal bridge, with steel reinforcement bars to provide a structural connection between interior slab and exterior balcony (Figure 4.14). Such a subtle construction change can have a significant impact on energy performance. Ge *et al.* (2013) found that in a 26-storey residential building in Toronto, the inclusion of a thermal break between the floor slabs and balconies reduced annual heating energy requirements by between 5% and 11%.

In summary, some potential design strategies for environmentally responsive tall buildings in cold and temperate climates include:

- Optimise different building programmes for solar orientation. For example, organise the building plan and form to eliminate apartments facing north (in the northern hemisphere) where possible. Office floor plates in temperate northern hemisphere climates will benefit from reduced cooling loads when facing north, as they are subject to less solar gain. However, in colder climates, solar radiation may significantly reduce office winter heating demands, so alternative orientations may be desirable.

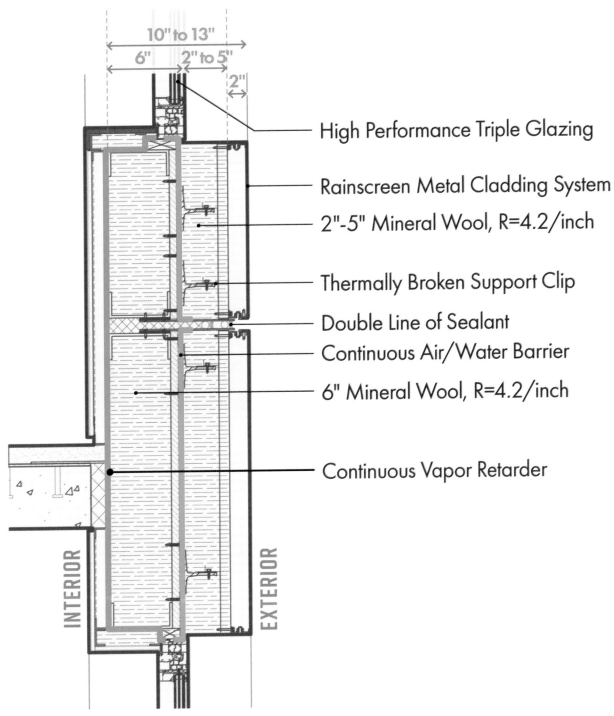

10" to 13"
6"   2" to 5"
2"

High Performance Triple Glazing

Rainscreen Metal Cladding System

2"-5" Mineral Wool, R=4.2/inch

Thermally Broken Support Clip

Double Line of Sealant

Continuous Air/Water Barrier

6" Mineral Wool, R=4.2/inch

Continuous Vapor Retarder

INTERIOR   EXTERIOR

Figure 4.11 The House at Cornell Tech, sectional façade detail showing super-insulation
Source: Handel Architects

- Use careful building form and siting to limit the over-shading of public spaces and other buildings, and to minimise wind downdrafts that may cause pedestrian discomfort.

- Residential towers in these climates have an intrinsic energy benefit due to their compact form and low surface-area-to-volume ratio, reducing heat loss in the winter. This provides the designer with the

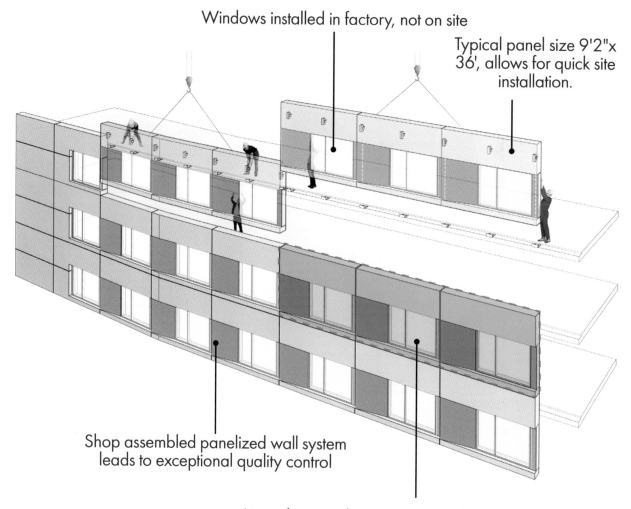

Windows installed in factory, not on site

Typical panel size 9'2"x 36', allows for quick site installation.

Shop assembled panelized wall system leads to exceptional quality control

Air seal at panel joints at interior face of exterior wall

Figure 4.12   The House at Cornell Tech. Prefabricated façade installation minimises joints on-site, thereby improving air-tightness
Source: Handel Architects

flexibility to create undulating and complex shapes, without significantly impacting heat demand.
- Design façade systems to allow for passive solar gain in winter months, but provide shading in the summer.
- Optimise window size and location for programme and orientation. This may involve, for example, larger windows on the south for passive solar gain and smaller areas of glazing on the north (in northern hemisphere sites).
- Use thick insulation and high-performance glazing systems. However, these do not have to be as substantial as those used in sustainable detached houses and low-rises, due to towers' compact form inherently minimising heat losses.

- Minimise thermal bridges, especially at projecting balconies.
- Integrate natural ventilation or mixed-mode systems to provide passive cooling and fresh air in residential, office and other programmes. Design strategies to foster this may include double-skin façades, the use of atria with the stack effect and thin floor plates to facilitate cross ventilation.
- Consider night-flush ventilation in office spaces to remove excess heat built up during the day.
- Capture additional sources of free heating where available. This can include MVHR and heat-sharing systems – e.g. where excess heat from internal gains in office spaces or computer rooms

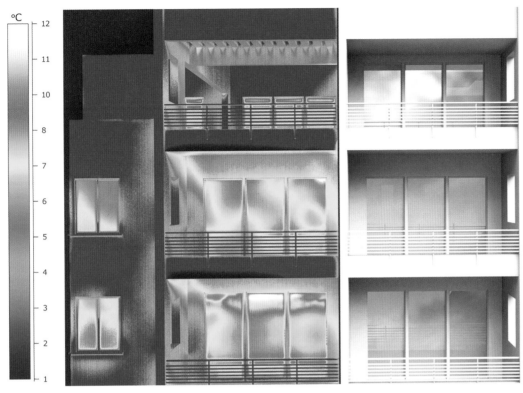

Figure 4.13   Thermal image of a residential building, with higher temperatures highlighting heat loss at the windows and through thermal bridges at the interface between the balcony and the wall
Source: Courtesy of Schoeck Bauteile GmbH

Figure 4.14   Schöck Isokorb® structural thermal break at the balcony/wall interface
Source: Courtesy of Schoeck Bauteile GmbH

is captured and used to space-heat residential programmes.
- Consider geothermal heating systems to capture free heat from underground.
- If integrating vertical greenery, consider deciduous planting that will provide shade in the summer, but allow for greater transmission of solar energy to the interior spaces in the winter.

The 'tropical' skyscraper

Tropical climates (Köppen climate classification 'A') are characterised by consistently high temperatures throughout the year, with every month having an average temperature above or equal to 18°C (Peel *et al.*, 2007). Typically, these climates have high humidity levels, sunpaths that move in a near-vertical trajectory, and only small changes in solar angle seasonally, due to their location in regions around the equator. Such climates include the skyscraper cities of Miami, Mumbai and Singapore. With high external temperatures and humidity levels, the primary aim of passive design in tropical skyscrapers is to minimise heat gain and maximise free cooling, particularly through ventilation. As

such, factors we look to avoid in tall building design in other climates – such as increasing wind speeds and downdrafts and casting large shadows on open spaces – are welcomed, and can contribute to improved thermal comfort in the tropical context (Wong & Hassell, 2009).

As with other climates, response to sunpath is vital. Solar radiation in tropical regions is very high, particularly from the east and west. To avoid this, skyscraper design requires careful orientation on site. A rule of thumb is to organise high-rise buildings with their longest façades facing north-south, minimising east-west elevations. Research shows that such a move can reduce the energy required for cooling by between 8.6% and 11.5% in a typical residential tower in Singapore (Wong & Li, 2007) (Figure 4.15). Other opportunities include the strategic placement of the building service cores on the east and west façade, acting as a solar buffer, or the use of significant solar shading devices on these sides of the building. Of course, designers need to carefully balance the often-competing factors of view, prevailing wind direction and sunpath in orientating a tall building; there is little point in designing a tower facing north-south, if there are fantastic views to

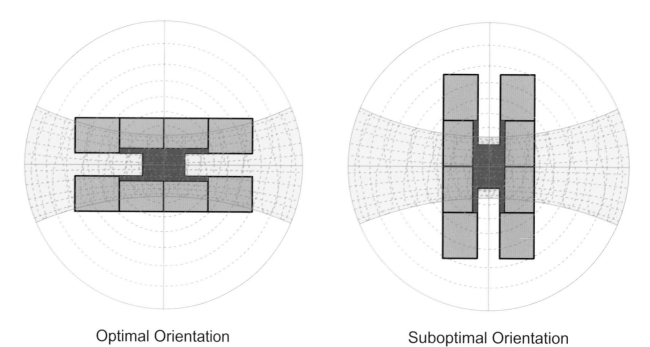

Optimal Orientation   Suboptimal Orientation

Figure 4.15   Orientating tropical residential towers with long façades facing north-south (left) can reduce the energy required for cooling as compared to long façades facing east-west (right)
Source: Philip Oldfield

the west. We can see just such a conundrum in Mumbai. Built on a peninsula, the city has its best views of the Arabian Sea and the harbour to the east and west. Prevailing sea breezes also move east-west, which can be captured to provide free cooling. However, as noted, these directions suffer the highest solar gain in tropical regions, and in Mumbai, also the direction of driving monsoon rains (Correa, 1996). To solve this, Charles Correa's Kanchanjunga Apartments, completed in 1983, makes an environmental compromise. The largest openings are orientated east-west, facing the sun, but are protected by deep terraces cut into the tower's orthogonal form (Figures 4.16 and 4.17). These, according to Correa, are inspired by the verandas that shade the interior of bungalows in the region. The terraces protect a series of complex interlocking apartments, that span the full width of the tower,

allowing for sea breezes to cross ventilate from east to west and vice versa (in a similar manner to Le Corbusier's interlocking apartments at Unite d'Habitation – see also Chapter 5). The terraces become extended living spaces, shaded by the nature of their depth, yet benefitting from increased wind speeds at height for cooling and striking views across the peninsular. It is a shame that these climatically responsive principles, many decades old, have yet to truly inspire Mumbai's contemporary skyscrapers.

In the tropics, one of the key factors in achieving thermal comfort without artificial conditioning is natural ventilation – the tropical tower needs to *breathe*. This is especially true in residential buildings, since at home one can adapt to a wider range of temperatures and humidity that comes with natural ventilation (by changing clothing and activities, for example). In office

Figure 4.16 Kanchanjunga Apartments, Mumbai
Source: Antony Wood/CTBUH

Figure 4.17 Kanchanjunga Apartments. External terraces cut into the tower's orthogonal form creating shaded spaces with access to breezes
Source: Antony Wood/CTBUH

towers in hot tropical climates, it is far more challenging to provide thermal comfort through natural ventilation alone, since there are much tighter comfort parameters, fewer opportunities to adapt to changing conditions and more emphasis on a consistent indoor environment to maintain productivity and work focus. Given this, the vast majority of office towers in tropical regions are air-conditioned. However, in residential apartments, natural ventilation is often sufficient and even preferable for occupants. In Singapore, while domestic use of air-conditioning is increasing,[5] many people live in apartments with only natural ventilation, using operable windows for cooling and drying yards for drying clothes (Wong & Hassell, 2009). In sub-tropical Brisbane, a study of 636 apartment residents found that most have a general preference for natural ventilation over air-conditioning, with 83% choosing to open a window or door to provide cooling in the summer,

compared to 63% using air-conditioning (Buys *et al.*, 2008).

However, optimising tall building design for natural ventilation is not merely a case of providing openable windows; instead, it has a significant impact on building form, planning, organisation and façade design. For example, cross ventilation in buildings is only effective when the depth of the space is shallower than a maximum of five times the height of the room. That is, the space meets the 'rule of thumb' of *W/h* < *5*, where *W* = width and *h* = height to ceiling. Single-sided natural ventilation is only effective where *W/h* < *2.5* (Etheridge & Ford, 2008) (Figure 4.18). So, assuming a typical ceiling height of 2.8 metres, cross ventilation is only effective to a depth of around 14 metres. Although a 14-metre-deep building is commonplace in the low-rise realm, towers tend to be wider to provide the structural stability required to withstand lateral loads. For

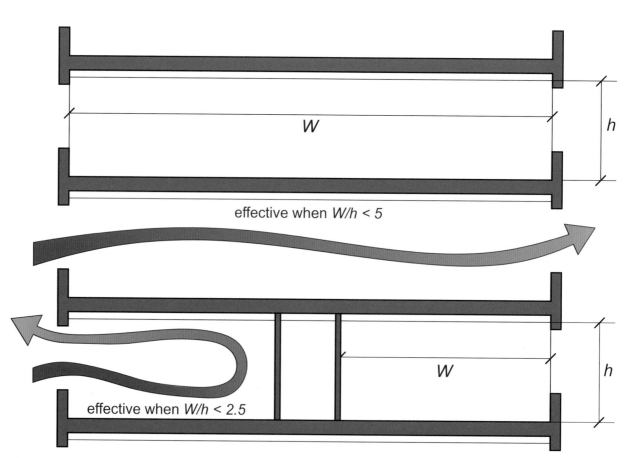

Figure 4.18   Rules of thumb for effective single-sided and cross ventilation
Source: Philip Oldfield

example, it is generally considered structurally efficient for tall buildings to have a slenderness ratio of less than 1 in 10; that is, the height of the building is not more than 10 times its width.[6] Given our theoretical maximum depth of 14 metres for natural ventilation, a tower this width would only really be efficient up to a height of 140 metres. In addition, the cellular nature of high-rise planning, with apartments accessed from dual-loaded corridors, can limit the opportunities for cross ventilation, as some units are left with only one effective façade with access to the wind.

How to overcome these challenges? A common design move to foster natural ventilation in tropical towers is creating a permeable building form; that is, shaping the building mass to increase the surface-area-to-volume ratio, creating open voids and perforations to channel breezes through multiple spaces and effectively reduce the width of spaces. Evidence suggests that such a strategy can reduce energy use and improve thermal comfort in tropical climates. Hirano *et al.* (2006) simulated two different building forms in the hot, humid city of Naha, Japan. The first was a compact block, with apartments fixed close together, typical of European and North American tower arrangements. The second was a permeable form, where 50% of its bulk was made up of voids. Their results demonstrated the permeable form benefited from a more effective air-change rate, with enhanced natural ventilation. In total, they found this move to increase permeability reduced the sensible heat load for cooling by more than 20% and latent heat load by 10%.

In completed skyscrapers, WOHA, perhaps more than any other architects, have embraced this strategy of permeability to create tropical skyscrapers that use passive design and natural ventilation. One of the best examples is The Met, built in Bangkok in 2004 (Figure 4.19). The city's climate is consistently hot and humid, with monthly average temperatures above 26°C and average high temperatures up to 35°C (Figure 4.20). Verticality and living at height in this climate can provide many benefits, including increased wind speeds and reduced pollution, thus the potential to harness natural ventilation for cooling is attractive. The Met consists of a rectilinear residential tower, orientated with its long façades facing north and south, thus minimising unwanted solar gain from the east and west. Structural sheer walls at 4.5-metre centres and

deep balconies with lush planted greenery provide additional shade on the north and south sides. Rather than a compact form, the tower's mass has been cut away, creating a staggered arrangement of apartments in plan, giving the impression of three separate, but interlinked, towers. The voids funnel breezes through the building, allowing for cross ventilation in more rooms and providing access to light and air for the core in the centre (Figure 4.21). It also means every apartment has at least three external façades, increasing the surface area for openings and effective ventilation. The voids between apartments are bridged every six storeys, accommodating community facilities such as skygardens and pools, creating shaded outdoor spaces with greater access to cooling breezes at height (Figures 4.22 and 4.23). Despite residents having access to air-conditioning, as would be expected in luxury high-rise apartments,

Figure 4.19 The Met, Bangkok
Source: Kirsten Bucher

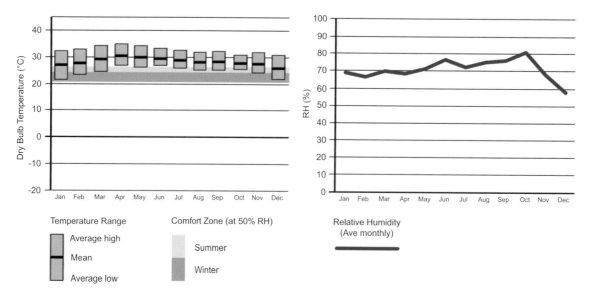

Figure 4.20 Bangkok temperature, comfort and humidity data
Source: Philip Oldfield, data from Climate Consultant, 2018

Figure 4.21 The Met, view looking down a void between apartments, providing opportunities for cross ventilation
Source: Patrick Bingham-Hall

interviews suggest natural ventilation can be sufficient for comfort. One resident noted: "[There is] not much need for air-conditioning. Daytime is fine with natural ventilation. Sometimes when it is very hot, I turn the air-conditioning on during night. It's very breezy most of the time" (Ali, 2013, p. 15). Here is a tall building design then that celebrates both shade and breezes for comfort; The Met is a true prototype for a sustainable tropical skyscraper.

We can also take inspiration from vernacular architecture in the search for a tropical skyscraper typology – and here too WOHA's work is at the forefront. Moulmein Rise is a slim 28-storey tower, facing north-south in Singapore. The city has a tropical rainforest climate, with consistently high relative humidity (over 80%) and daily high temperatures of over 30°C throughout the year, with limited seasonal variations (Figure 4.24). However, when it rains in Singapore – which is often – the temperature drops to a more pleasant 24–27°C, providing an opportunity for comfort (Wong & Hassell, 2009). In the comparable climate of Borneo, vernacular Dayak longhouses harnessed this opportunity by incorporating openings on the underside of projecting ledges; thus, when it rained, and breezes were cooler, air could penetrate the building, but rain would be kept out. WOHA's contemporary take on this is the 'Monsoon Window'. Here openable bay windows are supplemented with a

LEGEND

1 LIFT LOBBY
2 FIRE LIFT LOBBY
3 FIRE STAIRCASE
4 LIVING AREA
5 DINING AREA
6 BEDROOM
7 MASTER BEDROOM
8 BATH ROOM
9 KITCHEN
10 UTILITY
11 BALCONY

THE MET
20th FLOOR PLAN

NORTH

0 2 5 10   25 M

1 : 500

WOHA DESIGNS PTE LTD / WOHA ARCHITECTS PTE LTD
OCTOBER 2008

Figure 4.22 The Met, 20th floor plan, typical apartment level
Source: WOHA

perforated grill on the underside, allowing cool air to penetrate the apartments while water is kept out, even in tropical downpours[7,8] (Figures 4.25, 4.26 and 4.27).

Although these projects demonstrate the value of permeability and natural ventilation in hot and humid climates at the *building scale*, similar concepts are also essential at the *urban scale*. Ng (2010) notes how urban ventilation in high-density cities is important for three reasons:

- To provide access to the wind for all buildings using natural ventilation (minimising buildings blocking access to the wind from each other)
- To disperse air pollution in the city
- To maintain urban thermal comfort – that is, exterior spaces in the city that are comfortable and desirable

This requires careful planning and positioning of tall buildings within the urban realm, to allow wind to penetrate the city. High-density cities have a much higher *roughness* than low-density and rural areas, with an undulating terrain of towers slowing down the speed of cooling breezes, reducing their capacity for comfort. A tall building by itself may rise above the cityscape, benefitting from greater access to cooling breezes, but large numbers of towers in close proximity can limit urban ventilation, blocking the wind and creating stagnant or uncomfortable spaces and places, especially at ground level (Ng, 2010). Design moves to overcome this centre on the intelligent arrangement of urban form, mass and permeability in response to local wind conditions. Staggering towers across a site, rather than aligning them in a grid, has been shown to provide better urban ventilation at ground (Yang & Song, 2013). Creating pathways for breezes in the form of streets, parks and landscaped corridors can also funnel wind deep into the cityscape, especially cooling sea breezes.

The need for urban thermal comfort can be extended to external spaces within the building, too.

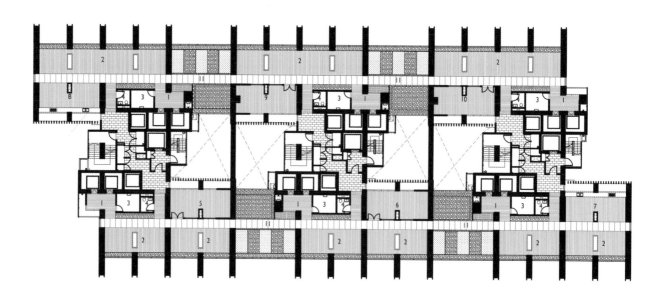

Figure 4.23 The Met, 28th floor plan, communal skyterrace level
Source: WOHA

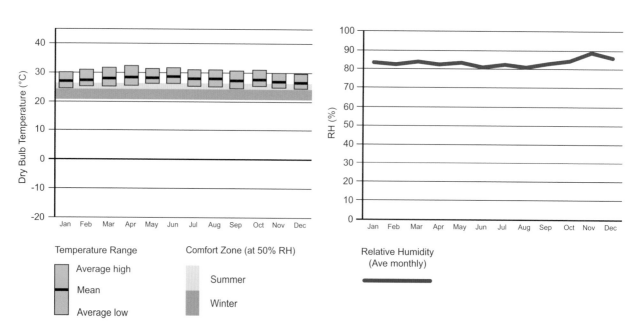

Figure 4.24 Singapore temperature, comfort and humidity data
Source: Philip Oldfield, data from Climate Consultant, 2018

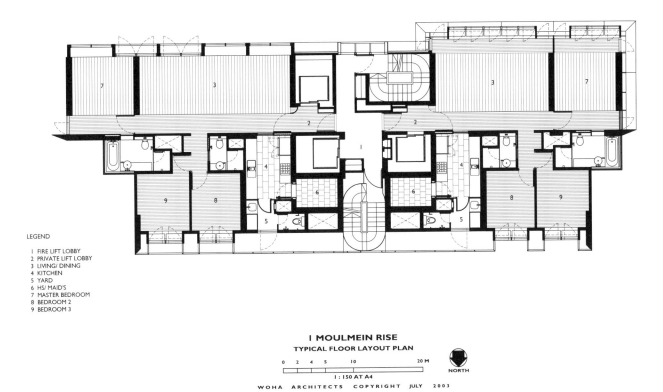

LEGEND

1 FIRE LIFT LOBBY
2 PRIVATE LIFT LOBBY
3 LIVING/ DINING
4 KITCHEN
5 YARD
6 HS/ MAID'S
7 MASTER BEDROOM
8 BEDROOM 2
9 BEDROOM 3

1 MOULMEIN RISE
TYPICAL FLOOR LAYOUT PLAN

0 2 4 5   10   20 M

1 : 150 AT A4

WOHA   ARCHITECTS   COPYRIGHT   JULY   2003

NORTH

Figure 4.25 Moulmein Rise, Singapore, typical floor plan
Source: WOHA

The Singapore National Library (designed by T. R. Hamzah & Yeang and completed in 2005) includes a number of shaded, exterior reading rooms known as *skycourts*. These benefit from access to increased wind speeds at height, but are also shaded by the mass of the building, large projecting louvres and lush planted greenery (Figure 4.28). This can be considered a reinterpretation of the tropical veranda, common in vernacular Kapong housing in South-East Asia. These spaces, shaded by the eaves of the house, were the place where many daily activities occurred: spaces for children to play, daily dining and for receiving guests (Bay *et al.*, 2006). Tropical climates can therefore benefit from this opportunity to create shaded outdoor spaces to accommodate activities that might otherwise take place in an interior air-conditioned environment, thus saving energy consumption. Regular visit to the skycourts at the National Library by the author showed they are frequently used by library-goers for quiet reading and studying, and are comfortable even in the midday heat (Figure 4.29). It is interesting to note too, that studies have shown the National Library

has lower energy needs than typical office buildings in Singapore, with a demand of 172 kWh/m²/annum as compared to the standard 250 kWh/m²/annum (Hart & Littlefield, 2011).

A further design strategy that can provide significant environmental benefits to the tropical skyscraper is the integration of vertical greenery and vegetation. The Urban Heat Island (UHI) effect can be described as the higher temperatures experienced in cities as compared to adjacent suburban or rural areas. While problematic for many cities, and in many climates, its impact is especially prevalent in hot and tropical regions given consistently high ambient temperatures, high solar radiation and the continuous need for cooling. Building integrated greenery can reduce the UHI effect by providing shade, evaporative cooling and filtering breezes to remove heat. Beyond this, vertical greenery can also provide visual delight and an opportunity for psychological escapism from the harsh materiality and lack of nature in the urban realm (for more on this topic, see Chapter 8). Given this potential, in many tropical contexts vertical greenery has

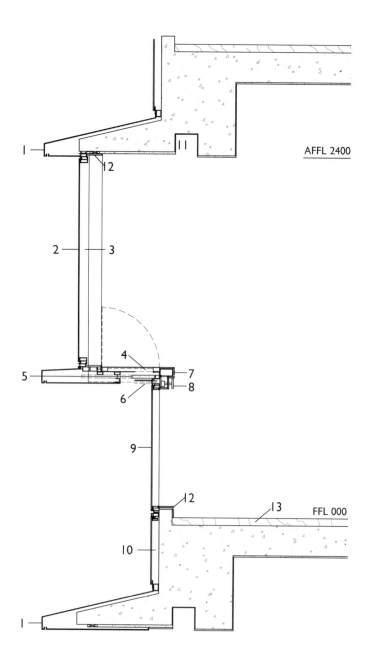

LEGEND

1 ALUCOBOND SHEET FOR HOOD
2 OPEN-OUT CASEMENT SASH FOR
    VENTILATION AND CLEANING
3 STEEL MULLION
4 PERFORATED ALUMINIUM FIXED
    TO HINGED FRAME WITH INSECT
    SCREEN BETWEEN (CLOSED POSITION)
5 MDF BOARD SLIDING (CLOSED POSITION)
6 SAFETY BARS
7 RHS BRACKET
8 HANDLE WINDER
9 FIXED TEMPERED GLASS
10 VENTILATED CAVITY
11 CURTAIN RECESS
12 ASH VENEER PLY WITH EDGE VENEER
13 PARQUETRY FLOORING
    WITH MARINE PLY UNDERLAY

AFFL 2400

FFL 000

BAY WINDOW

1 MOULMEIN RISE
TYPICAL FACADE DETAILS AT WEST APARTMENTS

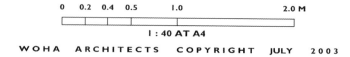

0   0.2 0.4 0.5   1.0   2.0 M

1 : 40 AT A4

W O H A   A R C H I T E C T S   C O P Y R I G H T JULY   2 0 0 3

Figure 4.26 Moulmein Rise, section through a Monsoon Window
Source: WOHA

Figure 4.28   National Library, Singapore
Source: Philip Oldfield

Figure 4.27   Moulmein Rise, photo of the Monsoon Window.
The perforated grill can be opened to allow in cooler air,
without rainwater
Source: Jonathan Lin, CC BY-SA 2.0, https://creativecommons.org/
licenses/by-sa/2.0/

been embraced in contemporary skyscraper design, providing lush spaces of recreation and interaction, but also creating shade and improved thermal comfort (Figure 4.30).

In summary, some potential design strategies for environmentally responsive tall buildings in tropical climates include:

- Orientate the building form to reduce the length of east-west façades where possible, to minimise solar gain. Alternatively, locate cores or major shading devices on the east and west sides of the tower.
- The over-shading of surrounding areas and public spaces can be less of an issue, since shade is desir-

able. However, siting of towers should be planned to maintain sufficient urban ventilation in the city. This could mean staggering towers, creating urban pathways for breezes, etc.

- Design permeable building forms to maximise cross ventilation, thus assisting in thermal comfort in humid conditions. Where possible, orientate the building to face prevailing breezes.
- Consider alternative plan arrangements to the standard double-loaded corridor with apartments on either side, which limits opportunities for cross ventilation. These could include apartments accessed from a single-loaded corridor, the inclusion of atria, interlocking apartments that span two sides of a tower, multiple cores serving apartments without corridors, etc.
- Design shaded external spaces at ground and at height. These can include open void decks at ground and terraces, skycourts and skygardens at height.

Figure 4.29   National Library, open skycourt at level nine
Source: Philip Oldfield

Figure 4.30   Vertical greenery at the Parkroyal at Pickering, Singapore, designed by WOHA. Lush planted vegetation in tropical climates can reduce the UHI effect and provide visual delight
Source: Philip Oldfield

- If artificial conditioning is required for thermal comfort, consider in what spaces this can be eliminated. For example, could lift lobbies, corridors and stairs be semi-outdoor spaces on the building perimeter? These would be subject to a greater range of thermal conditions, but since occupants would only be in these spaces for short durations, this may be acceptable for comfort. Such a strategy could reduce air-conditioned floor area by as much as 20%.
- Optimise window size and location for programme and orientation. Consider larger façade openings to foster natural ventilation of spaces.
- Shading elements should be maximised and celebrated in the building design to reduce unwanted solar heat gain, while allowing sufficient daylight to reach interior spaces.
- Lush vertical greenery can improve thermal comfort, reduce energy demands, provide psychological benefits to occupants and tackle the urban heat island effect in dense cities.

The 'hot desert' skyscraper

Arid climates (Köppen climate classification B) are characterised by a mean annual precipitation lower than a threshold value set according to seasonal variations in rainfall. In this section, emphasis is on a specific type of arid climate, the 'hot desert' climate (Köppen climate classification *BWh*), since such regions are home to growing levels of tall building construction, particularly in the Middle East. The hot desert climate is classified as an arid climate with a mean annual temperature equal or greater than 18°C. It is the most common climate type by land area, making up 14.2% of total global land mass (Peel *et al.*, 2007). As one would expect, such climates are generally dry, hot and sunny and can feature exceptionally hot periods of the year, with record summer highs often above 45°C and occasionally even 50°C. Such climates include the skyscraper cities of Dubai, Jeddah and Las Vegas.

The Middle East is experiencing a rapid period of urban development, characterised by mega-projects and tall building construction. For example, whereas in the year 2000 only 4% of the world's 100 tallest buildings were in the Middle East, by the end of 2017 this figure had grown to 25% (Skyscrapercenter, 2018). Much of this development is being driven by urbanisation and the diversification of the economy away from oil dependency and onto tourism. In addition, many of the tallest skyscrapers in the region are being built as icons to portray technological success, political influence and power to a global audience (Wood & Oldfield, 2008). Think of Dubai, and one of the first things that might come to mind is the Burj Khalifa – the world's current tallest skyscraper at 828 metres tall. However, this will soon be surpassed by the Jeddah Tower in Jeddah, which will stand at over 1,000 metres high.

Vernacular architecture in hot desert climates is typified by thick walls, small windows and the celebration of shade, to protect internal spaces against intense solar radiation (Figure 4.31). However, the availability of cheap energy and the influence of the highly transparent glass skyscraper as a symbol of 'modernity' has allowed for a proliferation of glazed tall buildings throughout the region, with little consideration of climatic or cultural context (Ghabra *et al.*, 2017a). The impact of this is unsurprising: air-conditioning

Figure 4.31   Shibam, Yemen; a sixteenth-century city of mud-brick buildings with small, shaded windows to respond to the harsh desert climate

Source: ©UNESCO, CC BY-SA 3.0 IGO, https://creativecommons.org/licenses/by-sa/3.0/igo/

makes up to 70% of the Gulf Cooperation Council's (GCC)[9] annual peak electricity consumption, with cooling demand in the region expected to triple by 2030 (Strategy&, 2012). Simple design moves, such as a reduction in window-to-wall-ratio (WWR), the use of thermal mass as a solar buffer, and appropriate façade insulation, can play a significant role in improving tall building energy performance in hot desert climates. Research by Ghabra *et al.* (2017b) simulated the cooling energy needed for a theoretical 62-storey residential skyscraper design in Jeddah, with 27 different façade designs, including variations in WWR, U-value, wall construction and glazing type. The findings showed the best-performing iteration had a WWR of 20% (a figure much lower than normal) and high levels of thermal mass and insulation in the façade construction. The worst-performing design consisted of a spandrel panel façade with a much higher WWR of 60%. This worst-case scenario required 77% more cooling energy than the best-performing design.

However, simply reducing the amount of glazing in hot desert skyscraper design is not the only way to improve energy performance. It is also important to balance the often-competing desires to protect from radiative and conductive heat gains, and to maximise natural light and view – no one wants to live and work in a dark concrete box. Design innovation and creativity in the organisation of building plan, form, façade and technology are vital in the realisation of climatically responsive towers, and there are few better examples in the region than the National

Commercial Bank in Jeddah. Designed by Gordon Bunshaft[10] of Skidmore, Owings and Merrill, and completed in 1983, the design represents "a radical shift in Modern architecture, away from universality, towards regionalised Modernism" (Abel, 2000, p. 182). The key design move is almost literally turning the traditional glass skyscraper inside-out as a reaction against the harsh exterior environment of heat, dust and glare; that is, creating an inner glazed core at the centre of the plan, protected by an exterior perimeter of opaque stone cladding. The result is a series of V-shaped plans, with glazing only on the interior façades, self-shaded by the building mass above (Figure 4.32). This creates shaded skygardens which alternate in orientation, with two facing south-east and one facing north (Figures 4.33–4.36). No windows are present on the building exterior, except on the uppermost floor, with the core pushed to the perimeter too, acting as a solar buffer on the hot south-western elevation (Figure 4.37). While fully air-conditioned (as would be expected in a large banking headquarters in most extreme climates), air-conditioning loads are 15% lower than was typical at the time of construction. Shading provided by the building mass and the vertical air movement fuelled by the stack effect in the atrium means the temperature just outside the glass can be up to 10°C lower than the external air temperatures, reducing conductive heat gains into the building (Santelli, 1989).

A more recent example of innovative manipulation of form and envelope in response to the desert climate

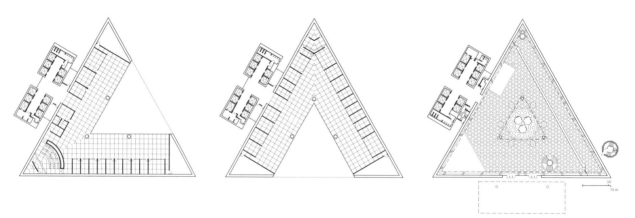

Figure 4.32   National Commercial Bank, Jeddah, typical office floor plans
Source: Image courtesy SOM/©SOM

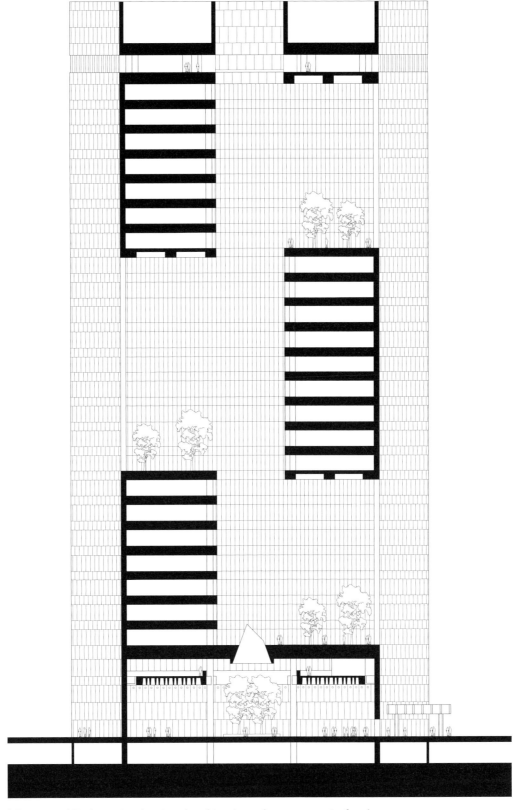

Figure 4.33   National Commercial Bank, section showing glazed interior and opaque exterior façades
Source: Image courtesy SOM/©SOM

Figure 4.34 National Commercial Bank, south-east façade
Source: Noura Ghabra

is the Wind Tower, designed by AGi Architects, completed in Salmiya just outside Kuwait City in 2017. Local temperatures are very high, with clear skies all year round and high levels of solar radiation. Summer temperatures are well above the comfort zone, often reaching 45°C, coinciding with very low humidity (Figure 4.38). In response, the tower design is inspired by vernacular Middle Eastern courtyard housing, with the courtyard translated into a central atrium space. The service core is located on the south side of the plan, with an exterior cladding of light-coloured granite to reflect solar radiation and an exterior WWR of

around 20% (Figures 4.39 and 4.40). While the atrium is shaded by the building mass, it opens up on the north façade at ground level, funnelling prevailing breezes over a swimming pool, which humidifies and cools the air. This cooler air is drawn up the atrium, creating opportunities for natural ventilation in the apartments (Figure 4.41). Larger windows are located inside the atrium, providing access to diffused light and facilitating cross ventilation, but also creating a dramatic space for social interaction and communication at the heart of the building (Figure 4.42).

Changing microclimatic conditions with height can also provide environmental benefits to tall buildings in hot desert climates. As noted in Chapter 1, air temperature, pressure and density all decrease with altitude. Given this, Weismantle (2017) suggests that over a 1,000-metre-tall tower in Jeddah, the climatic change from bottom to top would be equivalent to a shift in climatic region. The climate at the base would be that of hot-arid Jeddah (Köppen climate classification *BWh*), but conditions at the top would be equivalent to the more temperate Sacramento (Köppen climate classification *CSa*). Although such a height is at the most extreme end of tall building construction, changing vertical microclimates can, and should, be taken advantage of in hot desert skyscraper design by changing architectural or technological composition with height. For example, Leung and Weismantle (2008) suggest locating primary air intakes for ventilation in hot desert skyscrapers as high up the building as possible, to take advantage of lower air temperature, moisture and density.

In the design of the desert skyscraper, we should not only be thinking of climate, energy and thermal comfort. Scarcity of rainfall, a high rate of evaporation and a lack of natural potable water resources means water conservation and sustainability is also of paramount importance in many such regions. In the Gulf Cooperation Council (GCC), a lack of natural water resources means potable water is often generated through desalination of sea water, at a significant environmental cost. It is estimated that desalination of water in the United Arab Emirates, for example, consumes between 1.3 and 3 $kgCO_2$ per cubic metre of water – depending on the technology of the desalination plant used (Liu *et al.*, 2015). Beyond carbon emissions, desalinating sea water has caused sea temperature and salinity to

Figure 4.35   National Commercial Bank, view from the office floors, through the shaded skygarden space
Source: Noura Ghabra

Figure 4.36   National Commercial Bank, view up the glazed atrium, from a skygarden
Source: Noura Ghabra

Figure 4.37 National Commercial Bank. The topmost floor has perimeter glazing, but this is shaded by a stone colonnade

Source: Noura Ghabra

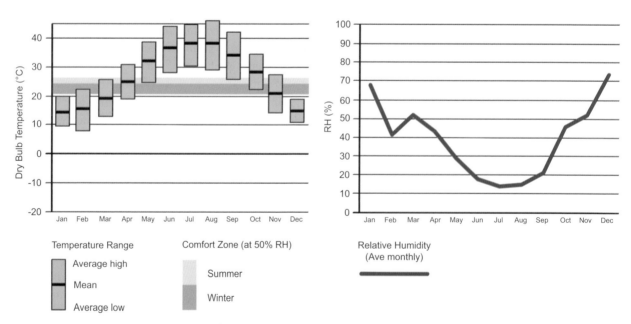

Figure 4.38 Kuwait City temperature, comfort and humidity data

Source: Philip Oldfield, data from Climate Consultant, 2018

Figure 4.39 Wind Tower, Salmiya, Kuwait City
Source: AGi Architects

increase in the last 20 years in the Gulf, at a significant cost to marine life and ecosystems. Despite this cost, GCC countries have a far higher average water use than most other regions, using 816 cubic metres per capita per year, as compared to a global average of 500 (Strategy&, 2014).

Improved water sustainability globally will require economic, lifestyle and regulatory changes, but architectural technologies and design strategies can also play a role. In hot desert climates, with limited potable water resources, every opportunity to reuse, reduce and capture water should be taken advantage of in tall building design. Although there are limited opportunities for rainwater capture, water can be harvested elsewhere. In the Burj Khalifa, for example, the hot and humid exterior air causes a build-up of condensation in the building cooling system. This is collected, saving 15 million litres of water per year, used to irrigate the exterior landscaping (Smith, 2008).

Were this water to come from desalination plants alone, it would create between 19.5 and 45 tonnes of CO_2 per year, depending on the desalination system used. A further opportunity is recycling grey water; this is waste water that comes from baths, showers, basins and washing machines, which can be captured, treated, cleaned and then re-used for toilet flushing or irrigation of landscaped areas.[11] In tall buildings, grey water recycling can be efficient, given the proximity of units and the use of centralised systems. Research by Shanableh *et al.* (2012) found that for a 30-storey residential tower in the UAE, grey water recycling from just the top 14 storeys would be sufficient to serve the entirety of the building's toilet flushing, thus saving 27% of total water needs. The advantage of only capturing grey water from upper floors is to allow for the treatment and pumping plants to be located at height, thus taking advantage of gravity for the distribution of water, minimising the cost of pumping.

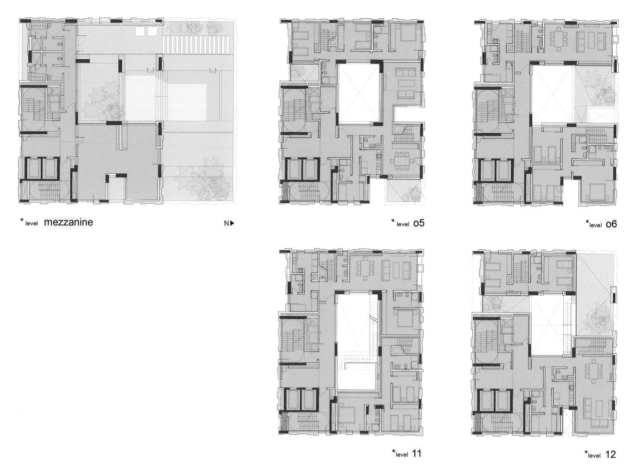

*level **mezzanine**   N▶   *level 05   *level 06

*level 11   *level 12

Figure 4.40   Wind Tower plans
Source: AGi Architects

Water conservation technologies and systems, such as waterless urinals in office buildings, and low-flow taps and highly efficient appliances in residential towers, can also contribute to reduced water demand and thus improve water sustainability and reduce GHG emissions.

In summary, some potential design strategies for environmentally responsive tall buildings in hot desert climates include:

• Orientate the building form to reduce the length of east-west façades where possible, to minimise solar gain. Alternatively, locate cores or major shading devices on the east and west sides of the tower.

• Over-shading of surrounding areas and public spaces can be less of an issue, since shade is desirable.

• It makes sense to use 'inward-looking' or self-shaded building forms, with glazed central atria or courtyards providing views and diffused daylight, and external façades with far more opacity to limit solar radiation.

• The use of external thermal mass as a solar buffer can be beneficial. In tall building design this could mean locating concrete structural shells, cores or framing elements externally, inherently shading interior spaces. Exposed concrete should be light coloured, or painted with a high solar reflectance coating to reduce heat permeating into the building.

• Although very high temperatures can make air-conditioning desirable for much of the year, milder winter months means natural ventilation can still be viable for thermal comfort. Consider orientating towers towards prevailing breezes, and using evaporative cooling of incoming air (e.g. by channelling wind over water features, fountains or pools).

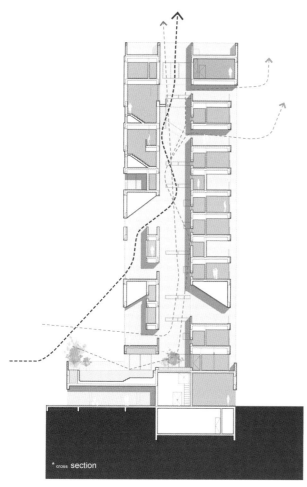

Figure 4.41 Wind Tower, section showing breezes being funnelled over the pool, humidifying and cooling the air, before being drawn up the atrium by the stack effect
Source: AGi Architects

Figure 4.42 Wind Tower, internal atrium as a shaded place for social interaction between levels
Source: AGi Architects

- Façade design should embrace shade and opacity, through low WWRs or external shading systems such as *mashrabiya*, while allowing sufficient daylight to reach interior spaces.
- Supertall towers should take advantage of cooler microclimates at height by locating air intakes for ventilation at upper levels.
- Water sustainability is often critical in these climates. The use of water capture and recycling technologies should be harnessed to reduce the carbon-intensive generation of potable water.
- Clear skies with high levels of solar radiation make building integrated photovoltaic and hot water systems attractive for on-site energy generation (see more in the following section).

The 'net zero' skyscraper

Given the acceleration of climate change, it's vital that future tall building design better responds to the environmental opportunities and challenges that local climate provides. But, if we are to reduce anthropogenic GHG emissions to such an extent as to avoid catastrophic global warming, we need to use every design strategy and technology available to us to reduce the carbon emissions associated with constructing and operating new and existing tall buildings. One target widely recognised as showing the potential to meet these aims is the creation of Net Zero Energy Buildings (NZEB) or Net Zero Carbon Buildings (NZCB). The former can be described as a building where for every unit of energy consumed, at least the same amount of energy is generated on-site from renewable sources such as wind, sun and ground-source energy. Some energy requirements may be delivered by non-renewable sources such as coal, gas or oil from traditional power plants, but this quantity is offset by renewable energy generated on-site, which is fed back to the grid when it is not needed in the building. An NZCB is similar, but effectively means any GHG emissions from the building's operation are offset through renewable energy generated on-site – a scenario often referred to as 'carbon-neutral'. Buildings that are seen to have a very low energy demand and *nearly* meet net zero energy requirements, as defined previously, can be referred to as nearly Zero Energy Buildings (nZEB).

Although some ambiguity remains about these definitions,[12] policies, regulations and guidelines are increasingly emerging identifying these as targets for new and renovated buildings. For example, the European Commission mandates that member national legislation should ensure that all new buildings meet the nZEB standard by the end of 2020, or by the end of 2018 for new buildings occupied and owned by public authorities (European Commission, 2016). Increasing technological innovation and cost effectiveness of on-site energy generation is seeing hundreds, if not thousands, of NZEB and NZCB emerging in the low-rise realm, specifically one-off detached houses, although increasingly multi-storey buildings. However, how do tall buildings fare in their potential to meet these targets? Key to achieving net zero performance is on-site energy generation from renewable sources, and here building vertically can provide both advantages and disadvantages to the designer. These are described across the three categories of wind, solar and geothermal energy in the following sections.

Wind energy

Increasing wind speeds at height are one of the primary challenges to building tall, contributing to higher lateral loads pushing on towers. This often results in the need for more complex structural systems and façade technologies in high-rise buildings, as compared to low-rise (for more details, see Chapter 7). However, wind can also provide an opportunity for renewable energy generation; since power output from a wind turbine is expressed as a function of wind speed cubed,[13] a small increase in wind speed can result in much greater power outputs (Denoon *et al.*, 2008). This means the upper levels of a tall building – where wind speeds are highest – provide a promising location for the integration of wind turbines in the urban realm. However, there remain challenges, too. Turbines are most efficient in low-turbulence environments, and the roughness of dense urban areas – caused by undulating buildings, vegetation and infrastructure – can create increased turbulence as compared to open rural or sea-based locations, where most commercial wind-farms are located.

Despite this challenge, Mertens (2002) suggests there are three promising locations for the installation of wind turbines in tall buildings:

1   Between two aerodynamic shaped towers, which act to funnel the wind using the *Venturi effect*, increasing its speed before it is captured by wind turbines (e.g. Bahrain World Trade Centre, Manama)
2   In a duct through a building, taking advantage of the pressure-differential between the windward and leeward sides to accelerate wind flow (e.g. Pearl River Tower, Guangzhou)
3   On the top of a tower, or along the edges of its form where wind speeds are typically 20% higher than usual (e.g. Strata, London)

One of the most striking built examples to date is the Bahrain World Trade Center, completed in Manama in 2008. Here two aerofoil-shaped towers face the unobstructed prevailing wind of the Gulf coast. Their form is designed to channel the breeze onto three 29-metre-diameter horizontal-axis wind turbines, amplifying wind speeds by an estimated 30% (Figure 4.43). The tapering shape of the towers reduces this effect higher up the building, but this is offset by the increasing wind speeds at height, meaning each turbine benefits from nearly the same typical wind velocity and can therefore be designed to similar specifications. The turbines are mounted onto bridges spanning between the tower's cores, which act as a buffer zone between the noise and vibration of the turbines and the adjacent office space (Figure 4.44). In addition, a wind turbine control system monitors the turbines'

Figure 4.43 Bahrain World Trade Center, Manama. The site benefits from unobstructed breezes from the Gulf coast, providing the opportunity for energy generation on-site
Source: Arunmohanae, CC BY-SA 4.0, https://creativecommons.org/licenses/by-sa/4.0/deed.en

of turbines at height in the city. Turbines can create noise, vibrations and quick moving shadows (known as 'shadow flicker'), which, if not mitigated, can cause significant problems for the occupants in the building or nearby. Who would accept living in a multi-million-dollar penthouse at the top of a skyscraper with turbine noise permeating through the ceiling? Such was the concern about noise in the Strata – a 43-storey London skyscraper completed in 2010 with three turbines at the top (Figure 4.45) – that the project's architect suggested switching the turbines off between 11 pm and 7 am each night (Nicholas, 2010). It can also be difficult integrating large-sized turbines, which are far more effective and generate far more energy than smaller-sized turbines, into tower forms. Given these challenges, built examples of tall building integrating wind turbines remain limited, and many question the effectiveness of current technologies, criticising designs as nothing more than greenwash. It is quite fair to say wind power makes far more sense in open rural and offshore areas, rather than the more turbulent and challenging environment of the high-density urban realm. Yet, this is clearly an emerging technology, and the potential remains to take advantage of clean energy generation through wind at height in future tall buildings.

Solar energy

Solar power is a mature technology that has been widely integrated into low-energy architecture for decades. The use of solar photovoltaic (PV) systems for energy, or evacuated tube solar collectors for hot water generation, has both advantages and disadvantages in high-rise buildings, as compared to low-rise forms. Since towers often rise above the surrounding cityscape, they gain greater access to solar radiation than other buildings, providing an ideal opportunity for energy generation. However, on the flip side, solar panels are generally more efficient when installed on roofs as a horizontal or inclined position allows the panels to be easily tilted towards the sun, thus creating more output. For example, the high levels of solar radiation and clear skies in hot desert climates provide the ideal context for energy generation. However, given that sunpaths in many such climates are typically high for much of the year, photovoltaic panels are

performance, including their position and speed, and can shut them down in extreme weather conditions if required. Overall, simulations prior to construction estimated the turbines would generate between 11% and 15% of the tower's electrical energy needs, for a cost of under 3% of the building value (Smith & Killa, 2007).

This approach seems promising, but there have been few published post-occupancy studies of wind energy generation in tall buildings, meaning actual performance figures are unknown. What's more, there are technical challenges to the successful integration

Unobstructed Prevailing Wind Direction

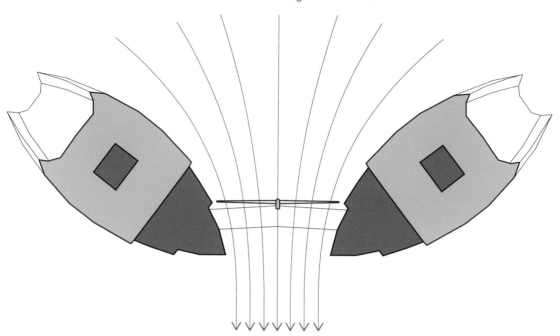

Figure 4.44 Bahrain World Trade Center, plan showing the building form accelerating the prevailing wind and the cores acting as a buffer between turbines and office spaces
Source: Philip Oldfield

Figure 4.45 Strata Tower, London, turbines at the tower's top
Source: Cmglee, CC BY-SA 3.0, https://creativecommons.org/licenses/by-sa/3.0/deed.en

more effective and able to generate more energy when installed at angles close to horizontal, which may pose a challenge for the vertical façade of the tall building. In Abu Dhabi the optimum tilt angle[14] for a photovoltaic panel is 78° from the vertical, facing south, or 22° from the horizontal (Jafarkazemi & Ali Saadabadi, 2013). Aligning panels this way on a large roofscape is relatively straightforward, but vertical panels integrated into a tall building façade would be less effective in terms of energy output. A potential solution could be integrating solar panels as inclined shading devices on a high-rise south-facing façade; such a system would have the dual benefit of renewable energy generation and providing shade to interior spaces.

Solar energy generation systems needn't be opaque and can be integrated into transparent tall building façades. In the Heron Tower, the south-facing façade is built up of PV cells laminated between glass with 38% cell coverage (Figure 4.46). These generate 2.5% of the building's electricity demand (Construction Manager, 2010), but still provide a visual connection to the outside, while allowing light to filter through to service spaces such as elevator lobbies and stairs – areas which rarely benefit from view or natural light (Figure 4.47). Emerging technologies in the field also offer significant promise for higher energy yields, while balancing the needs of view, light and thermal performance in tall building envelopes. The Integrated Concentrating Solar Facade (ICSF) by the Centre for Architecture, Science and Ecology (CASE), for example, proposes multiple solar concentrators on a tracking system, within a double-skin façade. These concentrate solar energy onto a high-efficiency PV cell for energy generation. Much of the remaining solar energy is captured as usable heat via a coolant pipe, while the system's transparency maintains views out to the exterior (CASE, 2016). With such experimental prototypes emerging widely, there is huge potential for state-of-the-art development of solar energy generation in tall building façades in the future.

Geothermal energy

The deep piles and substantive foundation systems required by tall buildings create an opportunity to take advantage of the consistency of the ground's temperature to provide thermal energy for interior heating and cooling. Tall buildings have an inherent advantage in this, given that foundation piles can be transformed into devices for producing power through the addition of geothermal probes (Cangelli & Fais, 2012).

Manitoba Hydro Place, in Winnipeg, Canada (2009), houses a large energy utility company and aims to provide thermal comfort to occupants using low quantities of energy. The building is designed to use just 88 kWh/m^2/annum, some 66% below the local energy code, and far lower than typical office buildings in the region, which require 495 kWh/m^2/annum (Manitoba Hydro Place, 2010). A plethora of sustainable technologies and design strategies are integrated into the tower, with a geothermal system providing 60% of the building's heating requirements – even in a climate with winter months that have average low temperatures below -20°C (Figure 4.48). An array of 280 boreholes, 150mm in diameter and interspersed between the foundation piles, are dug 125 metres into the ground. These circulate glycol, which absorbs the heat underground in the winter, drawing it to the surface. A heat exchanger transfers this heat to a water-based loop, which in turn transfers it to the exposed concrete floor slabs, which act to radiate the heat out into the office spaces. In the summer the reverse happens; excess heat from the building is absorbed by the concrete slabs and transferred into the glycol bores, which return the heat into the cooler ground below (Figure 4.49).

Given these opportunities, how close have we got to the realisation of a net zero or nearly zero energy skyscraper? Table 4.1 outlines published data for energy generation from renewable sources in tall buildings, highlighting the percentage of total or electrical energy generated on-site. Such data needs to be used with a degree of caution, since different published figures may have different boundaries and include or exclude different final energy uses. In addition, most figures are pre-construction simulations rather than empirical measurements taken after occupation and so may over-estimate or under-estimate results. However, we can draw conclusions from this data. Firstly, on-site energy generation from renewable sources in most built towers only contributes a minor proportion of the building's energy needs, often less than 15%. Does this mean these ideas show little promise? Certainly

Figure 4.46 The Heron Tower, London, a glazed south-facing core with PV cells providing 38% coverage
Source: Philip Oldfield

Figure 4.47   The Heron Tower, London, interior view of the lift core and PV façade
Source: Philip Oldfield

not! The integration of renewable energy sources into tall building design is an immature field, with only a handful of completed projects. The emergence of new design strategies and state-of-the-art technologies will no doubt lead to higher energy yields and lower-carbon skyscrapers. What's more, when it comes to energy efficiency, every little bit counts, and a 10% energy savings across multiple towers would make a huge and

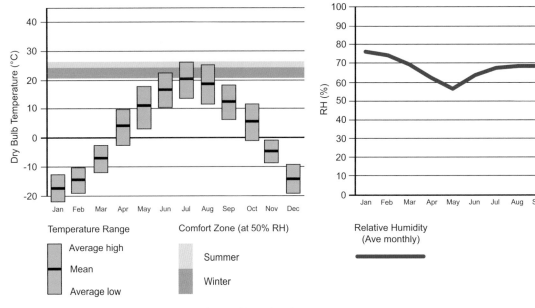

Figure 4.48 Winnipeg temperature, comfort and humidity data
Source: Philip Oldfield, data from Climate Consultant, 2018

valuable contribution to reducing our cities' carbon footprints.

We can also say that given current technologies it is more effective to reduce energy demand in tall buildings though passive measures such as optimal orientation, high-performance façade design, natural ventilation, thermal mass and more, than it is to generate energy on-site. Although wind turbines, solar panels and the like can provide a visual green statement, passive design and energy efficiency, which are often less apparent when walking past a building, are likely to be more cost effective and deliver more significant energy savings. As such, it often makes more sense when designing a high-rise to focus on energy-reduction strategies first, before exploring energy-generation opportunities.

> Renewables are sexy but energy efficiency is not . . . the cheapest watt you can generate is the watt you avoid using.
>
> [Tony Isaacs, from Hannam, 2018]

However, to meet our future climate targets, we cannot just focus on one strategy or the other. And, when intelligently combined, passive design and on-site energy generation can achieve, and even better, net zero energy performance in high-rise buildings. One of the few built examples to demonstrate this is TU Wien's Plus-Energy Office High-Rise Building, in Vienna, Austria, a city with a temperate climate of warm summers and cold winters, with heating being the main conditioning requirement throughout the year (Figure 4.50). Originally constructed in 1970, the tower was renovated in 2014 using multiple energy-reduction and -generation strategies (Figure 4.51). These include:

- A high-performance building façade, designed and built to Passivhaus criteria, with thick insulation and minimal air-leakage to reduce heat loss in winter months
- A heat recovery system to capture waste heat exhausted by the computer server rooms, which is then used to heat office spaces
- Night-flush ventilation where windows are opened on cool summer nights to allow breezes into the building to remove excess heat from office spaces built up during the day
- Very low-energy appliances and LED lighting
- 2,199 m² of photovoltaic panels installed on the roof, south-east and south-west façades with an annual yield of 248,804 kWh

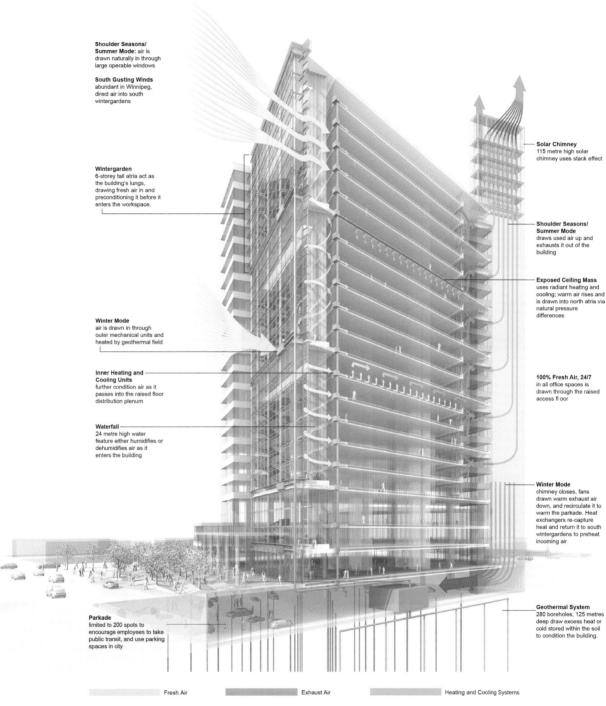

Shoulder Seasons/ Summer Mode: air is drawn naturally in through large operable windows

South Gusting Winds abundant in Winnipeg, direct air into south wintergardens

Wintergarden 6-storey tall atria act as the building's lungs, drawing fresh air in and preconditioning it before it enters the workspace.

Winter Mode air is drawn in through outer mechanical units and heated by geothermal field

Inner Heating and Cooling Units further condition air as it passes into the raised floor distribution plenum

Waterfall 24 metre high water feature either humidifies or dehumidifies air as it enters the building

Parkade limited to 200 spots to encourage employees to take public transit, and use parking spaces in city

Solar Chimney 115 metre high solar chimney uses stack effect

Shoulder Seasons/ Summer Mode draws used air up and exhausts it out of the building

Exposed Ceiling Mass uses radiant heating and cooling; warm air rises and is drawn into north atria via natural pressure differences

100% Fresh Air, 24/7 in all office spaces is drawn through the raised access floor

Winter Mode chimney closes, fans drawn warm exhaust air down, and recirculate it to warm the parkade. Heat exchangers re-capture heat and return it to south wintergardens to preheat incoming air

Geothermal System 280 boreholes, 125 metres deep draw excess heat or cold stored within the soil to condition the building.

Fresh Air   Exhaust Air   Heating and Cooling Systems

Figure 4.49   Manitoba Hydro Place, Winnipeg, heating and cooling diagram showing the geothermal system
Source: KPMB Architects

Building name	Year	Location	Storeys	Primary function	On-site energy generation technology	Percentage of energy generated on-site	Source
C.I.S. Solar Tower	2006 (renovation)	Manchester	25	Office	PV	10% of electrical demand	European Commission, 2004
Bahrain World Trade Center	2008	Manama	45	Office	Wind turbines	11–15% of electrical demand	Smith & Killa, 2007
Power Tower	2008	Linz	19	Office	PV	13%	Kaufmann, 2009
Strata	2010	London	43	Residential	Wind turbines	8% of total energy	Bogle, 2011
Heron Tower	2011	London	46	Office	PV	2.5% of electrical demand	Construction Manager, 2010
Federation of Korean Industries Tower	2013	Seoul	50	Office	PV	3%	Betancur, 2017
Pearl River Tower	2013	Guangzhou	71	Office	PV and wind turbines	8%	Freechette & Gilchrist, 2008
RWH.2	2013	Vienna	20	Office	PV and biogas trigeneration	61% primary electrical demand (1% PV and 60% trigeneration)	Leigh, 2013
TU Wien Plus-Energy Building	2014 (renovation)	Vienna	11	Office	PV	109% of total energy including appliances	Schöberl et al., 2014

Table 4.1 Published data for on-site energy generation from renewable sources in tall buildings
Source: Various

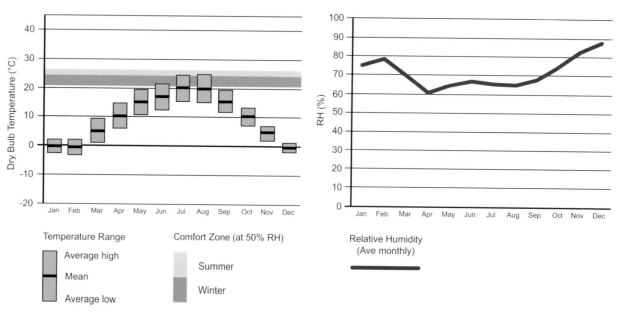

Figure 4.50 Vienna temperature, comfort and humidity data
Source: Philip Oldfield, data from Climate Consultant, 2018

Figure 4.51   TU Wien Plus-Energy Office High-Rise Building, Vienna
Source: Schöberl & Pöll GmbH

- A regenerative elevator system where the lift motor also acts as a generator, converting the kinetic energy of the elevator cab descending into electrical energy that can be used elsewhere in the building

Combined, these strategies result in a building with an operating energy of just 56 kWh/m²/annum, including not only heating, cooling, lighting and ventilation needs, but also appliances such as computers, too. However, through the photovoltaic panels and regenerative elevator drive, it generates 61 kWh/m²/annum, meaning the building achieves 'plus energy' performance, generating more energy on-site from renewable technologies than it uses (Figure 4.52).[15] In this instance, the excess energy generated is not returned to the grid, but is distributed to adjacent buildings (Schöberl *et al.*, 2014).

At 11 storeys, TU Wien's Plus-Energy Building is at the shorter end of the definition of a skyscraper, but taller NZEBs are also possible. A study by environmental consultancy firm Pitt & Sherry (Harrington, 2016) found that net zero energy residential towers in Sydney and Melbourne are technologically feasible and cost effective. The study examined a 25-storey tower in Sydney and a 65-storey tower in Melbourne, both based on real proposed buildings, to determine what was needed to get their energy performance down to zero. The results found that significant reductions in energy demand were possible through improving façade performance to reduce heating and cooling loads. Key moves include reducing the WWR (to 50% in Sydney and 30% in Melbourne), installing high-performance double-glazed windows with a U-value of 1.2 W/m²K, increasing façade air-tightness, using Mechanical Ventilation and Heat Recovery (MVHR), and adding very high-efficiency appliances and lighting systems and high-efficiency heat pumps for domestic hot water. To offset the energy demand that remained,

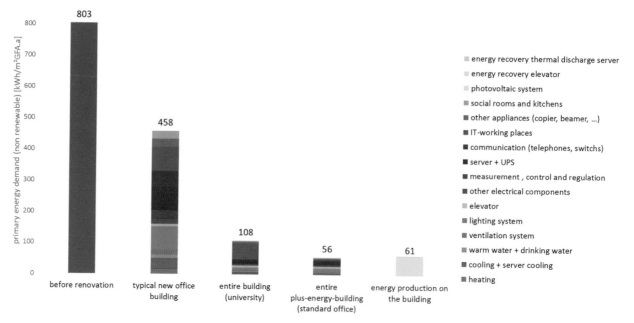

Figure 4.52 TU Wien Plus-Energy Office High-Rise Building, comparison of the primary energy demand of the pre-renovated tower, a typical new office building, the actual building with high-performance computers and the building using standard computers and the energy generated on-site
Source: Schöberl *et al.*, 2014

the Sydney scenario would require photovoltaic panels on the rooftop and integrated into the top 12 storeys of the façade, thus meeting net zero energy performance. The Melbourne scenario requires photovoltaic panels integrated into the upper 44 storeys of the façade to meet the remaining energy demand (Harrington, 2016). Compared to the original buildings, additional construction costs required to achieve net zero energy performance were estimated to be 7.8% in the Sydney scenario and 8.2% in the Melbourne building, but these would be offset by energy savings (and thus reduced energy bills) over the buildings' lifetimes, along with reduced energy infrastructure costs in construction. Interestingly, when considering indirect benefits, such as the financial benefit to society of reduced GHG emissions from the towers, both net zero energy scenarios were found to generate societal cost benefits in the millions of dollars, as compared to typical towers (Harrington, 2016).

One of the best built examples of a supertall[16] building harnessing on-site energy generation is the Pearl River Tower in Guangzhou, designed by Skidmore, Owings and Merrill and completed in 2013. Through a mixture of demand-reduction technologies and on-site

energy generation, the tower is estimated to use 30% less energy than a comparable building constructed to China energy codes. Its dramatic form, with a sculpted concave south façade, is designed to accelerate the prevailing wind into four strategically located voids, housing vertical-axis wind turbines (Figure 4.53). This strategy, it is estimated, will increase the wind speed by a factor of 2.5, resulting in a greater power output, as compared to similar-sized turbines in an open field (Tomlinson *et al.*, 2014). However, while visually dramatic, simulations by the University of Hong Kong and Changsha University of Science & Technology suggest that the actual energy output of the turbines will be relatively low due to weak wind speeds in the urban area to start with, with expected output in the region of 10,000 kWh/year (Li *et al.*, 2015). The tower also makes use of photovoltaic panels integrated into the sloping areas of the building façade and roof, generating an estimated 200,000 kWh of clean energy, while also providing shade from the southern sun to interior spaces (Tomlinson *et al.*, 2014). These strategies are no doubt valuable, but it is worth noting that the greatest energy savings in the Pearl River Tower come from energy reduction, rather than generation,

Figure 4.53   Pearl River Tower, Guangzhou
Source: Tansri Muliani/CTBUH

technologies. These include radiant cooling coupled with underfloor ventilation, a double-skin façade with void integrated blinds, and high-efficiency lighting and equipment.

In conclusion, we can say it is a huge challenge to achieve NZEB performance in high-rise architecture, and certainly more difficult than in low-rise and detached homes, where the target is more regularly met. High-rise buildings have more stacked-up energy-consuming floor area than other typologies, and have to generate much higher quantities of energy per unit site area to achieve net zero status. They also have proportionally less roof space for the optimal orientation of photovoltaic systems. What's more, in dense clusters of towers, as found in many central business districts, access to unobstructed wind and solar energy may be limited, minimising energy-generation opportunities, as compared to less-dense settings. Yet, despite the challenges, net zero energy performance in tall buildings is achievable with current technologies, especially if design emphasis is given to reducing energy demand in the first instance.

However, is net zero energy, or net zero carbon, the best performance target for the tall building designer? Could a net zero energy tower actually be inherently selfish? Consider the design of a sustainable tower in a dense urban setting where a large façade surface area facing the predominant sun direction is used to generate energy with a photovoltaic array. In such an instance, a large amount of clean energy may be generated on-site, but it could result in localised shading of adjacent buildings, limiting their access to the sun and subsequently their capability to generate energy. Thus, the energetic benefit to the tower could be at the expense of the energy demand of the surrounding context.

What's more, we must remember the city is not a static entity, but has a dynamic morphology, with changes to zoning laws and construction levels facilitating increasingly vertical skylines over time. A tower relying on unobstructed solar or wind access for energy generation may suffer reduced performance if a taller building as part of a future development blocks this access. For example, Futcher (2014) demonstrates how the south-facing photovoltaic array in the Heron Tower (Figure 4.46) is set to lose an estimated 40% of its output due to the construction of 100 Bishopsgate,

a 40-storey office building, on the site directly to its south. Interestingly, there will be other impacts, too; the increased shading from the new adjacent tower will reduce the cooling demand in the Heron Tower by 30%, which may go some way in compensating for the lost PV output.

It is clear then that net zero performance in high-rise design should not be considered in isolation, and energetic performance needs to consider the potential impact on the surrounding urban realm, including not only current buildings but anticipated future development, too – as challenging as this may be. Given this, a more appropriate target for high-rises is net zero energy *precincts* rather than buildings, where a larger collection of buildings strives to achieve sustainable performance in a collaborative manner. Such a strategy would allow for interdependencies between building designs and programmes to be harnessed; for example, benefitting from district heating or cooling systems, or energy sharing where excess heat from offices is captured and used to heat residential buildings. It would also allow for on-site energy generation to be optimised at an urban scale, such that buildings were not competing for natural resources, with energy harvested based on local position, microclimate and impact on surroundings. Such an ideal would not be without challenge and would require significant cooperation among building owners, developers and design teams across multiple sites. Local government leadership in achieving such ideals is vital. For example, the City of Sydney aims to reduce GHG emissions by 70% in 2030, as compared to 2006. To achieve this goal, the City's 2030 masterplan proposes to link together 65% of all commercial floor space, 50% of all retail floor space and 30% of all residential floor space to a low-carbon electricity, heating and cooling network (Kinesis, 2012). The energy-generation technology proposed is a series of trigeneration plants located throughout this network, where electricity, heating and cooling is generated simultaneously, contributing to reduced carbon emissions as compared to centralised energy generation in traditional power plants.[17] The system proposes using natural gas as a fuel to begin with, which as a fossil fuel would still contribute to some GHG emissions. However, by 2030, the City aims to utilise renewable gas sources captured from municipal waste, sewage and landfill sources, effectively making the system carbon neutral.

The tall building designer also needs to be aware of the current limitations of most net zero energy and carbon definitions. As noted, typically these only consider the energy used, or carbon emitted, *in operation*; that is the energy needed for day-to-day usage of the building – the lighting, heating, cooling, ventilation and occasionally the appliances. Typically, definitions do not include embodied energy and carbon, from the building's materials, construction, renovation and eventual demolition. In this sense, a net zero energy tower would still contribute to significant GHG emissions through its materials and construction. In fact, the embodied energy of a net zero energy tower would likely be significantly higher than that of a typical tall building, due to the increased use of materials and technologies needed to reduce operating energy needs.

It is important to recognise this issue because highly effective strategies that can improve the environmental performance of a skyscraper may not be captured in the traditional net zero energy framework. For example, using a mass timber structure and reducing the quantities of steel and concrete in a tall building would contribute to significantly reduced GHG emissions across its lifespan, but would not contribute towards NZEB performance. Targeting NZEB as a performance goal for future skyscrapers then could lead the designer to focus only on operational performance, neglecting the large emissions from materials and construction – and the potential strategies to reduce these (see also Chapter 7). Fortunately, more nuanced NZEB definitions are starting to emerge that capture the full lifecycle of environmental impacts of a building. In Norway, six definitions have been proposed ranging from 'ZEB-O÷EQ', which considers all emissions related to the building's operational energy excluding appliances, to the more holistic 'ZEB-COMPLETE', which considers all building emissions across the entirety of its lifecycle, including materials, construction, operation and demolition (Fufa *et al.*, 2016). Such thinking is vital if the true breadth of environmental impacts of our future high-rises is to be considered in sustainable design.

Conclusion

This chapter makes the case for climate to have a far greater influence on tall building design to tackle the pressing challenge of global warming. No longer can we consider the tall building as an 'object' in the city, divorced from its context. Instead, we must use the characteristics of local sunpath, wind, water, temperature, humidity, topography and more to act as major design drivers, influencing high-rise form, planning, façade, systems and technologies. Such strategies will not limit architectural freedom, nor temper the iconic nature of high-rises. On the contrary, a greater response to climate can provide vast opportunities to the tall building designer, generating architecture that is dramatic, comfortable and high performance in terms of carbon emissions. The chapter explores three broad climates: 'cold and temperate', 'tropical' and 'hot desert'. For each a list of potential design strategies is presented. These are purposely broad and general, and in reality, the unique qualities and characteristics of each city, site and microclimate will define a more nuanced set of design opportunities and challenges for the tall building design team.

The chapter finishes by exploring the opportunities for net zero energy and net zero carbon skyscrapers. For many in the built environment community, these represent the ultimate aim in the battle to mitigate climate change, creating buildings that effectively generate all their energy on-site from renewable sources. However, while there is little doubt a high-rise NZEB would have a hugely beneficial impact as compared to a conventional tower, in the author's opinion, NZEB and NZCB are not the best performance targets for the high-rise designer. This is because their definitions typically exclude embodied energy and carbon – a huge contributor to tall buildings' environmental impact, often making up to one-third and more of total lifecycle carbon emissions. What's more, a high-rise NZEB or NZCB may have a detrimental impact on its surroundings if it limits adjacent buildings' access to solar, wind or other free energy sources, and thus their capability for high performance. In this sense, a more appropriate target in the high-density urban setting is that of net zero energy or carbon precincts, generating and sharing energy among multiple buildings at the urban scale.

Notes

1 The Passivhaus concept was initially developed as an approach to provide indoor thermal comfort with very low energy requirements in the cold northern hemisphere climates of Central Europe. Given this history, most Passivhaus buildings are still constructed in colder climates, often in Central Europe or the USA. However, it is worth noting that the Passivhaus strategy of controlling heat flows across the building envelope can be successfully achieved in other climates, including tropical and hot regions, by adapting the shape, orientation, building fabric and shading systems to the local environmental conditions. For example, Schnieders *et al.* (2015) show that it is possible to realise residential Passivhaus construction in cities as varied as Singapore and Abu Dhabi. Despite this, the most obvious application of Passivhaus thinking is in cold and temperate climates, and hence it is included in this section of the chapter.

2 Primary energy refers to the energy contained in the raw fuel (such as coal, crude oil, or natural gas), sometimes also called source energy. It must go through multiple processes to be converted into useful energy (known as delivered energy, or site energy) that can be used in a building.

3 Window-to-wall-ratio (WWR) refers to the quantity of glazing within a building façade. A WWR of 30% means a façade is 30% glazed and 70% opaque.

4 In 2018, an 88-metre-tall Passivhaus tower called '361Bolueta' was completed in Bilbao, Spain. Designed by Varquitectos, it became the tallest Passivhaus in the world at the time.

5 A 2012 Household Energy Consumption Study in Singapore found that air-conditioning was the greatest contributor to energy usage in a typical household, being responsible for 36.7% of delivered energy. Interestingly, when questioned, residents' perception was that refrigerators were the greatest contributor (NEA, 2012).

6 Although a slenderness ratio of below 1:10 is considered common and efficient, an increasing number of 'super skinny' towers are emerging that are far slenderer. These include 111 West 57th Street in New York, measuring in at an incredible 1:23

ratio (19 metres wide and 438 metres tall). For more on this trend, see Willis (2016).

7 Sri Lankan architect Geoffrey Bawa used a similar concept in the 12-storey State Mortgage Bank building in Colombo. Here precast concrete ventilation grills provided access to natural breezes, but were protected from driving rain by overhanging solar shading. However, this system was never truly used; air-conditioning was installed as soon as expatriate occupants moved in, demonstrating the challenges of harnessing natural ventilation for comfort in hot tropical climates (Kiang & Robson, 2006).

8 It should be noted that there is also an economic value to this strategy. In Singapore, bay windows are included in floor area calculations but exempt from development tax (Wong & Hassell, 2009). The Monsoon Window then maximises profit for the developers, but also provides the environmental benefit of access to light and air.

9 The Gulf Cooperation Council (GCC) is made up of Bahrain, Kuwait, Oman, Qatar, Saudi Arabia and the United Arab Emirates.

10 Interestingly, Bunshaft also designed one of the world's first fully glazed skyscrapers, Lever House, New York, completed 30 years prior to the National Commercial Bank in 1952. (See also Chapter 3.)

11 This is as opposed to *blackwater*, which is waste water from toilets, requiring far greater levels of treatment before reuse.

12 For example, a survey carried out in 2008 identified 17 different terms used to describe 'low-energy' buildings in Europe, including 'zero carbon house', 'zero energy house', 'energy positive house' and more (European Commission, 2009). Different definitions of NZEB also focus on different scopes and boundaries, with some considering delivered energy to site and others focussing on primary energy from source (Torcellini *et al.*, 2006). Finally, definitions can change geographically; in Austria the maximum primary energy demand of a new-build residential nZEB is 160 kWh/m²/annum, whereas in Denmark the figure is 20 kWh/m²/annum – although the former considers energy needed for household appliances, and the latter does not (BPIE, 2015).

13 The equation that defines power output from a wind turbine is:

$$Pt = \frac{1}{2}\rho U^3 \lambda A$$

Where:
Pt = Power output
ρ = Air density
U = Wind speed
λ = Turbine efficiency
A = Area of the turbine perpendicular to the wind
(Denoon *et al.*, 2008)

14 Optimum tilt angle refers to the optimum angle to position a photovoltaic panel, or other solar energy–generating surface, in order to maximise energy generation.

15 The figure of 56 kWh/m²/annum refers to building energy use including standard computers in the office spaces. However, given its university programme, the building uses a large number of high-performance computers for research purposes, which are uncommon in standard offices. If we include these, the operating energy would be 108 kWh/m²/annum, more than is generated on-site from renewables, meaning the tower would not achieve net zero energy status (Schöberl *et al.*, 2014). However, it is also worth noting that most definitions of net zero energy or plus-energy performance do not include the energy used by appliances such as computers. If we consider only the energy used for conditioning the building, on-site generation from the photovoltaic panels and regenerative elevator system would far outweigh demand.

16 A supertall building can be defined as one which is taller than 300 metres in height.

17 In a traditional centralised power station, fossil fuels are used to heat water to create steam that drive turbines to generate electricity. However, the heat from this process is often lost, making the power station inefficient. By creating a small-scale power station for a single building, or group of buildings on site, the excess heat can be captured and used for space conditioning and water heating. This is known as cogeneration, or CHP – Combined Heating and Power. A trigeneration system is also known as CCHP (Combined Cooling Heating and Power) and utilises some of the excess heat to generate chilled water for cooling via an absorption chiller.

References

Abel, C. (2000). *Architecture & Identity: Response to Culture and Technological Change*. Princeton Architectural Press, Oxford.

Abel, C. (2006). High-Rise and Genius Loci. In: Abel, C. (ed.) *Norman Foster Works 5*, Prestel, London, pp. 430–441.

Ali, Z. F. (2013). *The Met Tower, Bangkok, Thailand*. On-Site Review Report. https://archnet.org/system/publications/contents/8737/original/DTP101236.pdf?1391602922

Bay, J. H., Wang, N., Liang, Q. & Kong, P. (2006). Social Environmental Dimensions in Tropical Semi-Open Spaces of High-Rise Housing in Singapore. In: Bay, J. H. & Boon Lay, O. (eds.) *Tropical Sustainable Architecture: Social and Environmental Dimensions*. Princeton Architectural Press, Oxford and Burlington, MA.

Betancur, J. (2017). Multitasking Façade: How to Combine BIPV with Passive Solar Mitigation Strategies in a High-Rise Curtain Wall System. *International Journal of High-Rise Buildings*, December, Vol. 6, No. 4, pp. 307–313.

Bogle, I. (2011). Integrating Wind Turbines in Tall Buildings. *CTBUH Journal*, No. IV, pp. 30–34.

BPIE. (2015). *Nearly Zero Energy Buildings: Definitions Across Europe*, April. http://bpie.eu/uploads/lib/document/attachment/128/BPIE_factsheet_nZEB_definitions_across_Europe.pdf

Buys, L., Summerville, J. A., Kennedy, R. J. & Bell, L. M. (2008). Exploring the Social Impacts of High-Density Living in a Sub-Tropical Environment. In: Kennedy, R. J. (ed.) *Proceedings of the 2nd International Subtropical Cities Conference Subtropical Cities 2008: From Faultlines to Sightlines – Subtropical Urbanism 20–20*. Queensland University of Technology, Centre for Subtropical Design, Brisbane.

Cangelli, E. & Fais, L. (2012). Energy and Environmental Performance of Tall Buildings: State of the Art. *Advances in Building Energy Research*, Vol. 6, No. 1, pp. 36–60.

CASE. (2016). *High Efficiency Solar Energy Systems*. www.case.rpi.edu/page/project.php?pageid=1

Climate Consultant. (2018). *Version 6*. ©UCLA Energy Design Tools Group.

Construction Manager. (2010). Put It to the Panel. *Construction Manager*, 18 January. www.construc tionmanagermagazine.com/onsite/put-it-panel/

Correa, C. (1996). *Charles Correa*. Thames & Hudson, Ltd., New York.

Denoon, R., Cochran, B., Banks, D. & Wood, G. (2008). *Harvesting Wind Power from Tall Buildings*. Proceedings of the CTBUH 8th World Congress, "Tall & Green: Typology for a Sustainable Urban Future", Dubai, 3–5 March, pp. 320–327.

Etheridge, D. & Ford, B. (2008). *Natural Ventilation of Tall Buildings: Options and Limitations*. Proceedings of the CTBUH 8th World Congress, "Tall & Green: Typology for a Sustainable Urban Future", Dubai, 3–5 March, pp. 226–232.

European Commission. (2004). *State Aid N 543/2003 – United Kingdom: CIS Photovoltaic Re-Cladding Project, Manchester*. http://ec.europa.eu/competition/ state_aid/cases/136460/136460_487488_25_2.pdf

European Commission. (2009). *Low Energy Buildings in Europe: Current State of Play, Definitions and Best Practice*. Brussels, 25 September.

European Commission. (2016). *Commission Recommendation (EU) 2016/1318 of 29 July 2016 on Guidelines for the Promotion of Nearly Zero-Energy Buildings and Best Practices to Ensure That, by 2020, All New Buildings Are Nearly Zero-Energy Buildings*. http://eur-lex.europa.eu/legal-content/EN/ TXT/?uri=CELEX:32016H1318

Freechette, R. E. & Gilchrist, R. (2008). *"Towards Zero Energy": A Case Study of the Pearl River Tower, Guangzhou, China*. Proceedings of the CTBUH 8th World Congress, "Tall & Green: Typology for a Sustainable Urban Future", Dubai, 3–5 March, pp. 252–262.

Fufa, S. M., Schlanbusch, R. D., Sørnes, K., Inman, M. & Andresen, I. (2016). *A Norwegian ZEB Definition Guideline*. ZEB Project Report 29–2016, SINTEF Academic Press, Oslo.

Futcher, J. (2014). Shadowlands. *CIBSE Journal*, July, pp. 4–7.

FxFowle. (2017). *Feasibility Study to Implement the Passivhaus Standard on Tall Residential Buildings*, 30 March. Report for the New York State Research and Development Authority. www.fxcollaborative. com/projects/182/feasibility-study-to-implement-the-passivhaus-standard-on-tall-residential-buildings/

Gang, J. (2008). *Wanted: Tall Buildings Less Iconic, More Specific*. Proceedings of the CTBUH 8th World Congress, "Tall & Green: Typology for a Sustainable Urban Future", Dubai, 3–5 March, pp. 496–502.

Ge, H., McClung, V. R. & Zhang, S. (2013). Impact of Balcony Thermal Bridges on the Overall Thermal Performance of Multi-Unit Residential Buildings: A Case Study. *Energy and Buildings*, Vol. 60, pp. 163–173.

Ghabra, N., Rodrigues, L. & Oldfield, P. (2017a). Improving Energy Performance in Gulf-Region Residential High-Rises. *CTBUH Journal*, No. III, pp. 38–43.

Ghabra, N., Rodrigues, L. & Oldfield, P. (2017b). The Impact of the Building Envelope on the Energy Efficiency of Residential Tall Buildings in Saudi Arabia. *International Journal of Low Carbon Technologies*, 1 December, Vol. 12, No. 4, pp. 411–419.

Gonçalves, J. C. S. & Umakoshi, E. M. (2010). *The Environmental Performance of Tall Buildings*. Earthscan, Washington.

Handel Architects. (2016). *The House at Cornell Tech*. www.handelarchitects.com/projects/project-main/ cornell-res-main.html

Hannam, P. (2018). The Real Cost of McMansions. *The Age*, 3 February. www.smh.com.au/environ ment/climate-change/the-real-cost-of-mcmansions-20180131-h0qy5w.html

Harrington, P. (2016). *Accelerating Net-Zero High-Rise Residential Buildings in Australia*. Final Report. Pitt & Sherry, Melbourne.

Hart, S. & Littlefield, D. (2011). *Ecoarchitecture: The Work of Ken Yeang*. Wiley, London.

Hirano, T., Kato, S., Murakami, S., Ikaga, T. & Shiraishi, Y. (2006). A Study on a Porous Residential Building Model in Hot and Humid Regions: Part 1 – The Natural Ventilation Performance and the Cooling Load Reduction Effect of the Building Model. *Building and Environment*, Vol. 41, pp. 21–32.

Isaac, M. & Vuuran, D. P. V. (2009). Modelling Global Residential Sector Energy Demand for Heating and Air Conditioning in the Context of Climate Change. *Energy Policy*, Vol. 37, pp. 507–521.

Jafarkazemi, F. & Ali Saadabadi, S. (2013). Optimum Tilt Angle and Orientation of Solar Surfaces in Abu Dhabi, UAE. *Renewable Energy*, Vol. 56, pp. 44–49.

Kaufmann, W. (2009). Power Tower, Konzernzentrale Energie AGLinz, Austria. *Building with Aluminium: Sustainability in Architecture*, Linz, 9 September. www.initiative-metallbautechnik.at/rte/upload/im_day_090909/im-day_vortrag_kaufmann_der_power_tower.pdf

Kiang, T. B. & Robson, D. (2006). *Bioclimatic Skyscraper – Learning from Bawa*. PLEA2006 – The 23rd Conference on Passive and Low Energy Architecture, Geneva, Switzerland, 6–8 September.

Kinesis. (2012). *City of Sydney Decentralised Energy Master Plan – Trigeneration*. www.cityofsydney.nsw.gov.au/__data/assets/pdf_file/0007/193057/Trigeneration-Master-Plan-Kinesis.pdf

Kong, L. (2007). Cultural Icons and Urban Development in Asia: Economic Imperative, National Identity and Global City Status. *Political Geography*, Vol. 26, pp. 383–404.

Leigh, R. (2013). *High Rise Meets Passive House Standards in Vienna*. Urban Green Council, 11 September. https://urbangreencouncil.org/content/news/high-rise-meets-passive-house-standards-vienna

Leung, L. & Weismantle, P. (2008). *How Supertall Buildings Can Benefit from Height*. Proceedings of the CTBUH 8th World Congress "Tall & Green: Typology for a Sustainable Urban Future", Dubai, 3–5 March, pp. 328–335.

Li, Q. S., Shu, Z. R. & Chen, F. B. (2015). Performance Assessment of Tall Building-Integrated Wind Turbines for Power Generation. *Applied Energy*, Vol. 165, pp. 777–788.

Liu, J., Chen, S., Wang, H. & Chen, X. (2015). Calculation of Carbon Footprints for Water Diversion and Desalination Projects. The 7th International Conference on Applied Energy – ICAE2015. *Energy Proceedia*, Vol. 75, pp. 2483–2494.

Manitoba Hydro Place. (2010). *Energy Performance and Sustainable Design*, 13 January. http://manitobahydroplace.com/Post-Occupancy-Performance/Performance/Detail/?rid=42

McLeod, R., Mead, K. & Standen, M. (2011). *Passivhaus Primer: Designer's Guide – A Guide for the Design Team and Local Authorities*. BRE Trust, Watford.

Mertens, S. (2002). Wind Energy in Urban Areas. *Refocus*. March–April, pp. 22–24.

Nagengast, B. (1999). Early Twentieth Century Air-Conditioning Engineering. *ASHRAE Journal*, March, pp. 55–62.

NEA. (2012). *Household Energy Consumption Study 2012*. Singapore.

Ng, E. (2010). Designing for Urban Ventilation. In: Ng, E. (ed.) *Designing High-Density Cities for Social and Environmental Sustainability*. Earthscan, London.

Nicholas, D. (2010). Noise Fears Could Stall Strata Turbines. *Londonist*. http://londonist.com/2010/03/noise_fears_could_stall_strata_turb

Oldfield, P. (2017). A "Fabric-First" Approach to Sustainable Tall Building Design. *International Journal of High-Rise Buildings*, Vol. 6, No. 2, pp. 177–185.

Oldfield, P., Trabucco, D. & Wood, A. (2009). Five Energy Generations of Tall Buildings: An Historical Analysis of Energy Consumption in High-Rise Buildings. *Journal of Architecture*, Vol. 14, No. 5, pp. 591–614.

Passipedia. (2017). *What Is a Passive House?* www.passipedia.org/basics/what_is_a_passive_house

Peel, M. C., Finlayson, B. L. & McMahon, T. A. (2007). Updated World Map of the Köppen-Geiger Climate Classification. *Hydrology and Earth System Sciences*, Vol. 11, pp. 1633–1644.

Santamouris, M. (2016). Cooling the Buildings – Past, Present and Future. *Energy and Buildings*, Vol. 128, pp. 617–638.

Santelli, S. (1989). *National Commercial Bank, Jeddah, Saudi Arabia*. Technical Review Summary. https://archnet.org/system/publications/contents/736/original/FLS0746.pdf?1384748560

Schnieders, J., Feist, W. & Rongen, L. (2015). Passive Houses for Different Climate Zones. *Energy and Buildings*, Vol. 105, pp. 71–87.

Schöberl, H., Hofer, R., Leeb, M., Bednar, T. & Kratochwil, G. (2014). *Österreichs größtes PlusEnergie-Bürogebäude am Standort Getreidemarkt der TU Wien*, June, Vienna. http://schoeberlpoell.at/files/projekte/forschung/Endberichte/Plusenergie/PUBLIKATION_Endbericht_Getreidemarkt_2015-07-24-1.pdf

Shanableh, A., Imteaz, M., Merabtene, T. & Ahsan, A. (2012). A Framework for Reducing Water Demand in Multi-Storey and Detached Dwellings in the United Arab Emirates. In: *WSUD 2012: Water*

Sensitive Urban Design; Building the Water Sensitive Community. 7th International Conference on Water Sensitive Urban Design, Engineers Australia, Barton, ACT, pp. 647–657.

Skyscrapercenter. (2018). *The Skyscraper Center – The Global Tall Building Database of the CTBUH.* www. skyscrapercenter.com/

Smith, A. (2008). *Burj Dubai: Designing the World's Tallest.* Proceedings of the CTBUH 8th World Congress, "Tall & Green: Typology for a Sustainable Urban Future", Dubai, 3–5 March, pp. 35–42.

Smith, R. F. & Killa, S. (2007). Bahrain World Trade Center (BWTC): The First Large-Scale Integration of Wind Turbines in a Building. *The Structural Design of Tall and Special Buildings*, Vol. 16, pp. 429–439.

Strategy&. (2012). *District Cooling: GCC States Have an Opportunity to Reap Great Benefits from District Cooling*, 16 July. https://arabiangazette.com/district-cooling-gcc-states-opportunity-reap-great-benefits-district-cooling/

Strategy&. (2014). *Achieving a Sustainable Water Sector in the GCC Managing Supply and Demand, Building Institutions.* www.strategyand.pwc.com/media/file/Achieving-a-sustainable-water-sector-in-the-GCC.pdf

Tomlinson, R., Baker, W., Leung, L., Chien, S. & Zhu, Y. (2014). Case Study: Pearl River Tower, Guangzhou. *CTBUH Journal*, No. II, pp. 12–17.

Torcellini, P., Pless, S. & Deru, M. (2006). *Zero Energy Buildings: A Critical Look at the Definition.* Conference Paper NREL/CP-550–39833. US Department of Energy.

Weismantle, P. (2017). Architectural Technical Design of the New Generation of Supertall Buildings. *Australian Smart Skyscrapers Summit 2017*, Melbourne, 28–29 March.

Willis, C. (2016). Singularly Slender: Sky Living in New York, Hong Kong and Elsewhere. In: *Cities to Megacities: Shaping Dense Vertical Urbanism.* CTBUH, Chicago, pp. 606–614.

Wong, M. S. & Hassell, R. (2009). Tall Buildings in Southeast Asia – A Humanist Approach to Tropical High-Rise. *CTBUH Journal*, No. III, pp. 24–32.

Wong, N. H. & Li, S. (2007). A Study on the Effectiveness of Passive Climate Control in Naturally Ventilated Residential Buildings in Singapore. *Building and Environment*, Vol. 42, pp. 1395–1405.

Wood, A. (2015). Rethinking the Skyscraper in the Ecological Age: Design Principles for a New High-Rise Vernacular. *International Journal of High-Rise Buildings*, Vol. 4, No. 2, pp. 91–101.

Wood, A. & Oldfield, P. (2008). Global Trends in High-Rise Design. In: *Urbanism and Architecture*, October, No. 49, Heilongjiang Science and Technology Press, Ha'erbin, China, pp. 14–16.

Yang, L. & Song, D. (2013). The Research of Relationship between Architectural Space and Wind Environment in Residential Area. In: Zhang, J. & Sun, C. (eds.) *CAAD Futures 2013, CCIS 369.* Springer-Verlag, Berlin, pp. 233–244.

CHAPTER FIVE

Vertical communities

Introduction: living in high-rise buildings

Ask someone in Europe, or North America, to picture high-rise living, and it's probable that one of two visions will come to mind; firstly, the apparent 'dystopia' of high-rise social housing in the mid-twentieth century, typified by repetitive concrete blocks, interspaced with vacant green parkland. Or alternatively, the fully glazed penthouse: modern, slick and with a price tag making it available only to the uber-wealthy. For few people does high-rise housing conjure up ideas of community, of children playing together, or of neighbourly interaction. But is this really the case? What is it like to live in a tall building?

One of the most comprehensive reviews of the social and psychological impacts of living in high-rise buildings was conducted by Robert Gifford in the journal *Architectural Science Review* (2007). Gifford's work paints a generally negative picture of the experience. Firstly, he suggests high-rise living is less satisfactory than other housing types, especially for parents of small children. There is evidence that children in high-rise housing can suffer more behavioural problems, with potentially delayed development and less opportunities for play. Play can be limited by the lack of appropriate spaces adjacent to the home; instead of the parent-supervised garden or adjacent street available in low-rise and suburban housing, in the tower play is often limited to inside the unit itself, or to a ground-level play area which is likely many storeys from a parent's watchful gaze. In addition, evidence

suggests that although residents in high-rises may encounter more neighbours, there tends to be fewer social interactions and less caring behaviour among them (Gifford, 2007).

> Nowhere is it quite so difficult to create a community as a block of flats. With neighbours above, below and on both sides, the natural tendency is to erect barriers against friendship. People can be too close to be friends, and as prisoners chained together, they come all too easily to hate each other. An even greater deterrent to the growth of community is the fact that the majority of people living in flats do not willingly choose to do so.
>
> [White, 1950, p. 17]

While this may seem damning, it is essential to acknowledge that a variety of factors beyond a building's verticality and architectural design can influence these results. For example, many studies on the experience of living in towers focus on high-rise social housing of the mid-twentieth century. Residents in such buildings often had little choice as to whether to live there, and this may have been the only housing available to them. This lack of choice would have a significant, and likely negative, impact on residents' satisfaction and lifestyle. The build quality and maintenance of such buildings was also often poor. Inner-city areas where many tower blocks were constructed often suffered from a lack of infrastructure, services and jobs necessary to foster satisfaction and community, due to the increasing suburbanisation of society at the time (Graham, 2016). Urban (2012) perhaps captures this best by suggesting these buildings "did not produce the social situations they came to stand for, but acted as vessels, conditioning rather than creating social relations and channelling rather than generating existing polarities" (p. 2). In this sense, the post-war tower block is often used as an architectural scapegoat for a variety of broader socio-economic issues that communities faced at the time.

It is also important to recognise that there are social and community advantages to living in high-rise housing. Higher densities can allow more people to live closer to the city centre, with the cultural and educational facilities on offer. Whitzman and Mizrachi (2012) interviewed children in high-rise housing in Melbourne, Australia and found that many enjoyed the proximity such living gave them to the major public library in the Central Business District, along with local cafes, bookshops, parks and markets. High-rise living can also provide better views and lift residents away from the airborne pollutants and noise of roads. There is evidence, too, that with effective management high-rise social housing projects can prosper. Although the typology is widely considered a failure in the United States, the New York City Housing Authority successfully accommodates 400,000 occupants in high-rise social housing primarily due to strategies developed to continually improve tenant selection, policing, renovation, community affairs and landscape design over time (Dagen Bloom, 2008).

But are towers a desirable place to live? In Singapore, over 80% of its 5.5 million population live in high-rise social housing, most of which is owner occupied. Research by Yuen *et al*. (2006) found that 91% of residents in one such 30-storey development were satisfied with their current floor level. In London, where high-rise living is far less common, and regularly demonised due to perceived historical failures, a survey by Ipsos MORI found that 56% of people would *not* be happy living in a tall building, while only 27% said they would be happy to do so (Ipsos MORI, 2014). Of course, while this shows most people find high-rise living unappealing, this still equates to over one-quarter of the population finding the prospect attractive, which in a megacity such as London, is a number in the millions.

There is a problem though. Living in a tall building may be attractive for some, but having the opportunity to do so is increasingly difficult. Living in a skyscraper in a city like London is inaccessible for most people, due to the tower block shifting from a typology for social or affordable housing to one accommodating luxury apartments. Modern residential towers are often designed for only the wealthy global elite, and they are increasingly seen as "vertical gated communities" (Graham & Hewitt, 2012). Peter Wynne Rees, former City Planning Officer for the City of London, derides such apartments as "safe deposit boxes in the sky" (Wynee Rees, 2015), places where foreign owners will invest their capital but rarely actually occupy. Although it's true there is frequently a shameful lack of affordable housing in many new high-rise developments, there is little evidence to suggest that new towers are mostly vacant. What's more, the trend for the super-wealthy investing in apartments is not limited to tall buildings. In Kensington and Chelsea, areas of low- and mid-rise classical architecture in London, foreign ownership and transient owners is said to have turned some streets into 'ghost towns' (Cumming, 2015; Oldfield, 2015). Millionaire pads aren't only found on top of towers, but across all luxury developments.

We can say the experience of living at height is a complex issue, influenced by a variety of both architectural and non-architectural factors, from the residents' economic status to the level of maintenance the building receives. The generalisation that high-rise social housing projects are vertical ghettos of crime and disorder is unfair and certainly not the experience of tower living everywhere (Graham, 2016). However, what is perhaps more reasonable to argue is that the current crop of high-rise housing internationally is far from optimised to promote community, social interaction, or play, especially for families with children. Their proximity to the city, use of luxury materials and elite views may make them appealing to some, but few factors in the architectural design or planning of the tall building are geared towards fostering successful communities. The contemporary residential tower is designed primarily for economy, rather than humanity or community.

In many western cities, high-rise living is designed primarily for DINKs (dual income, no kids) or empty nesters – middle-age parents for whom the children have left home (Whitzman & Mizrachi, 2012). Yet, despite this situation, the apartment is increasingly becoming home to families with children, especially in cities with rapidly increasing house prices and densification. Drawn by the proximity to employment, and with the traditional detached house being financially out of reach, families are increasingly making up a significant percentage of apartment populations in many cities (Easthope & Tice, 2011). Yet, since apartment blocks are rarely designed with families in mind, they lack the necessary spaces for children of different ages to play and the amenities and infrastructure that families require. One opportunity to overcome this is to include community spaces at height in tall buildings, such as 'streets in the sky' and 'skygardens', to provide areas for children to play, and for escapism and psychological relief from high-density living. Such ideas are becoming increasingly prevalent in high-rise housing propositions around the world. The remainder of this chapter is dedicated to exploring these communal spaces at height, the opportunities they provide and the challenges to their success. In particular, the author calls for their careful and sensitive operation and management to ensure such spaces contribute to positive occupant experiences in vertical communities.

A history of 'streets in the sky'

The idea of creating streets and communal spaces in the sky has a long and chequered history. Within 30 years of the first skyscraper being constructed in Chicago in 1885, visions of future cities with playgrounds and parks at height and towers connected by flying skybridges were being imagined (Wood, 2003). Many of these visions and ideas were influenced by the growing congestion at ground level and the dominance of the motorcar, the aim being to raise the lives of residents away from the chaos of the traffic below (Bansal *et al.*, 2017) (Figure 5.1).

However, it wasn't until the post-war era that actual 'streets in the sky' became a prominent design feature in completed buildings. One of the first examples was Le Corbusier's Unité d'Habitation, built in Marseilles in 1952 (Figure 5.2). This represented the architect's seminal vision for mass housing, seen by many in the field at the time as the ideal prototype for future living (Millais, 2015). The design consists

of over 300 apartments arranged in a 19-storey linear block. Each apartment is L-shaped in section, wrapping around central corridors that provide access to units every third floor. However, more than just apartments were created; Le Corbusier's vision was for the building to act as an 'extended dwelling' – that is, it should be a 'vertical garden city', containing the wide variety of communal spaces and services needed by a diverse community of 1,600 residents to thrive (Jenkins, 1993). These social facilities were created on three public levels. Firstly, the open green space of the ground, with the mass of the building lifted by *pilotis*, creating a parkland for residents and the public alike. Secondly, a public street on levels seven and eight, accommodating a hotel, restaurant, bars, shops, laundry, bakery, butcher and more. Finally, and most recognisably, a public roof terrace, housing a gymnasium, pool and nursery (Figures 5.3 and 5.4). These ideas have only been partially successful. As of the turn of the millennium, the mid-level shopping street was reduced to a small supermarket and bakery, used mostly by the residents rather than the public. Its location, hidden within the middle of the block, limits its visibility to the outside world, while its central-corridor-like design minimises natural lighting, creating what many consider a dull and unappealing space for interaction (Toland, 2001).

Similar ideas were also used in the infamous Pruitt-Igoe public housing development, designed by Leinweber, Yamasaki and Hellmuth and completed in 1954. Designed to accommodate residents who had been displaced by slum clearance, Pruitt-Igoe created 2,700 apartments across a series of high-rise slab blocks in the city of St Louis, Missouri (Figure 5.5). To improve liveability and foster social interaction, the architects proposed two organisational design innovations – skip-stop elevators and glazed 'streets in the sky' (Bristol, 1991). Residents would travel by elevator to the glazed streets, located every third floor. These housed communal facilities such as laundry and storage areas. From here, residents would walk up or down stairs to their individual units. The idea was this would create vertical villages – neighbourhoods of three storeys stacked on top of one another (Figure 5.6). Architects' drawings of the time imagined these glazed streets in the sky as airy spaces full of activity, occupied by parents with prams, bikes, plants and even a child playing

Figure 5.1 'The Wonder City You May Live to See': a vision of the city of 1950, drawn from suggestions made by Harvey M. Corbett, President of the Architectural League of New York

Source: Popular Science Monthly, August 1928

Figure 5.2 Unite d'Habitation, Marseilles
Source: michael1972, CC BY-SA 3.0, https://creativecommons.org/licenses/by-sa/3.0/deed.en

in a playpen out in this communal space. However, this was not to be the case.

Only a few years after the project's completion, it was in decline. Press at the time blamed the design, noting how the streets in the sky had become havens of crime and vandalism. Residents referred to these spaces as "gauntlets", forcing them to pass loitering gangs to reach their doors (Bristol, 1991). Newman (1972) suggests the crime and social issues suffered by Pruitt-Igoe were due to the design of 'indefensible' public spaces, both at ground and at the streets in the sky. He criticised the streets as having no direct relationship with apartments, meaning there was no visibility from the home into the street, allowing crime to prosper away from watchful eyes. This criticism echoed throughout the twentieth century, leading to the denouncement of similar high-rise social housing, and especially brutalist projects incorporating streets in the sky such as Park Hill in Sheffield and the now-demolished Robin

Hood Gardens estate in Poplar, London (Figure 5.7). Today, ideas of streets in the sky are considered a relic of the past – in the west at least (Murphy, 2016).

However, the failure of Pruitt-Igoe, and similar high-rise housing developments of the mid-to-late twentieth century, was about so much more than indefensible space. For example, the excellent work of Bristol (1991), in *The Pruitt-Igoe Myth*, and the later documentary of the same name (Freidrichs, 2011), shows that much wider political, social and economic forces played a huge contribution in the project's demise. For example, the build quality at Pruitt-Igoe was extremely poor, to such an extent that doorknobs and locks broke on their first use (Bristol, 1991). Often when families moved in, fathers couldn't accompany them, since governance stipulated that no able-bodied man could live in a unit where a woman received state support (Freidrichs, 2011). Population and jobs in the city area began to disperse to the suburbs, contributing to the loss of local services and unemployment. Those that could leave Pruitt-Igoe did so, reducing its population, the financial income from rent and subsequently the budget available for maintenance. It fell into a horrific state of disrepair, being eventually demolished, dramatically, by dynamite in 1972. This explosive demolition was widely televised and became seen as an apparent symbol of the end of the high-rise social housing experiment and the ability for architecture to create a more civilised version of the world (Sudjic, 2005). However, these wider societal failures should not let architecture and urban design off the hook. The vastness of the blocks, the oppressive spatial quality of the streets in the sky with their low ceilings and the lack of activation at ground no doubt played a role in the project's demise. But these issues were small compared to the broader challenges Pruitt-Igoe and its residents faced, such as local urban decay and unemployment, lack of maintenance and poor build quality.

The skygarden: an Asian reinvention[1]

Whereas streets in the sky can be seen (somewhat unfairly) to have failed in the west, the idea of creating social and communal spaces at height in tall buildings has more recently been reinterpreted and reinvented in the Asian context. Fuelled by vast urbanisation, many Asian cities are seeing huge levels of skyscraper construction, and thus, increasing amounts of life taking place in the vertical realm. One of the outcomes is that Asia is challenging the standard repetitive high-rise housing block with innovative and ambitious projects. Increasingly, these are including the communal spaces and infrastructure desirable to families and a wider socio-demographic at height in towers. Singapore has adopted these ideas perhaps more than anywhere else. In doing so, the city provides several precedents for how the tall building can provide a socially sustainable and aspirational housing typology.

Like in the west, Singapore's construction of mass public housing began in earnest in the mid-twentieth century, a direct response to the dilapidated conditions of housing at the time. The Housing Development Board (HDB), set up in 1960, was tasked with providing affordable and sanitary dwellings for all. At first, the emphasis was on creating the maximum number of units in the minimum time, with little consideration given to public and communal spaces. However, soon the HDB's focus shifted from mere numbers to creating successful communities. This was achieved primarily in two ways: firstly, through the proactive integration of residents within new high-rise developments, and secondly, through innovative design strategies and the creation of community spaces at ground, mid and upper levels within towers.

Singapore is a multi-cultural country, with residents from a wide variety of ethnic backgrounds. Following race riots in the 1960s, the HDB recognised the need to integrate this diverse population across new high-rise housing developments, to create mixed communities avoiding ethnic and economic polarisation. For example, the HDB assign flats strategically, aiming to create a "good distribution of races" across new towns (Phang & Kim, 2011, p. 134). Beyond this, multi-storey housing is planned with a variety of different unit sizes and tenures throughout, with smaller

Figure 5.3 Unite d'Habitation, roof terrace
Source: pxhere, CC BY 2.0, https://creativecommons.org/licenses/by/2.0/

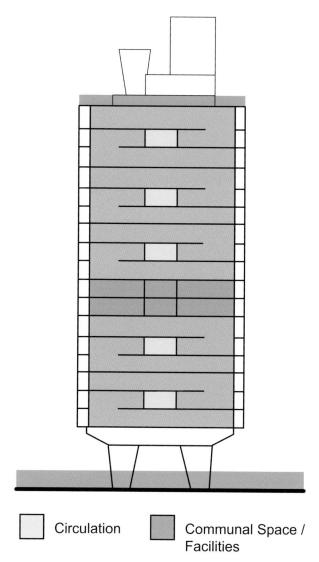

Circulation   Communal Space / Facilities

Figure 5.4   Unite d'Habitation, diagrammatic section of communal/private spaces
Source: Philip Oldfield

external corridors, as it was believed these would be more conducive as spaces for residents to meet and mingle. These corridors were widened to provide more space for interaction, while the floor level of flats was raised to maintain a degree of privacy in the home (Wong & Yeh, 1985). At the ground level, 'void decks' were included in most HDB high-rise projects to provide larger open spaces for communal activities. Void decks are the space beneath tower blocks; sheltered, unplanned areas that accommodate community activities (Cairns *et al.*, 2014). However, as much taller towers became necessary to accommodate Singapore's burgeoning population, the HDB acknowledged that residents living on upper floors would find themselves more and more distanced from the vibrancy of the ground. This fuelled the creation of skygardens – social/communal spaces at height, typically within a garden setting. Such is the popularity of the skygarden that it has now taken over from the void deck as the characteristic communal space in Singaporean towers.

The first major integration of skygardens into a HDB project was the Pinnacle@Duxton, designed by ARC Studio Architecture and Urbanism, completed in 2009. Made up of seven 50-storey towers, the development accommodates 1,848 units and thousands of residents. What separates the Pinnacle from other developments is its dramatic skygardens at levels 26 and 50, joining all seven blocks together. The 26th-storey garden is used by residents only, while the uppermost level is publicly accessible, acting as a hybrid garden and viewing deck, some 150 metres above the ground (Figure 5.8). The skygardens on both levels differ in several ways to the streets in the sky of the past. Firstly, they accommodate a wide mix of functions, including an 800-metre running track, an outdoor gym for the elderly, a playground for children and a residents' community centre all at height (Hadi *et al.*, 2018) (Figure 5.9). Secondly, vegetation is embraced as an integral part of the materiality, as compared to the concrete-dominated designs of the past (Figure 5.10).

However, the most significant difference is how these spaces are operated and managed. Security is extremely high at the Pinnacle. Access to the mid-level skygardens is limited to card-holding residents via metal turnstiles. Access to the 50th floor is restricted to certain opening times, limited numbers of people and an entrance fee, questioning the validity of its apparent

rental units and larger for-sale family flats interspersed. The result is a social, economic and cultural diversity across any HDB development. Singapore's Deputy Prime Minister, Tharman Shanmugaratnam, suggests that this policy of mixing means that while there are poor families in Singapore, there are no longer any poor neighbourhoods (Crabtree, 2017).

High-rise communities have also been enhanced through architectural evolution and progressive urban design. In early Singaporean high-rise housing, internal double-loaded corridors with apartments on each side were phased out and replaced with single-loaded

Figure 5.5   Aerial photograph of Pruitt-Igoe, St Louis, 1974
Source: U.S. Geological Survey

'public' status. A list of rules is posted by the entrances, and includes 'No food or beverages', 'No social events at any part of the Skygardens' and 'No activities such as biking, skateboarding or other similar games'. Keycard access also restricts residents from bringing friends or guests into the skygardens, since turnstiles only allow one person in per card.

Post-occupancy evaluation of these skygardens has been undertaken by researchers from De Montfort University, the University of Nottingham and UNSW Sydney, including this author. We found that despite the high security, the skygardens were regularly used by residents, with on average over 800 uses per day at each level (with a total of 3,541 residents living there at the time). In addition, the skygardens were successful in providing places of escapism and peace in an otherwise high-density setting, where elderly residents would gather to meet and chat at the gym at level 26, and teenagers would retreat for peace to study under a tree in the evening. However, the most common experience in respect to the skygardens was a sense of frustration with the management of the space, with residents upset by the strict rules and security limiting how they use the gardens (Hadi *et al.*, 2018). This is at odds with streets in the sky of the past; whereas in Pruitt-Igoe such spaces were apparently indefensible, at the Pinnacle@Duxton, they are actively defended to such an extent that it is restricting residents' ability to make the most of the wonderful programmes and possibilities they provide.

Despite these challenges, the Pinnacle@Duxton is not a one-off. Instead, a series of innovative vertical designs incorporating skygardens have spawned across Singapore. The Interlace, designed by OMA/Büro Ole Scheeren, is one of the most exciting. The project brief called for the design of over 1,000 apartment units, which would typically be built as a series of 12 orthogonal towers of 24 storeys, laid out across the site, isolated from one another and connected only at ground. Instead, the architect proposed turning the towers

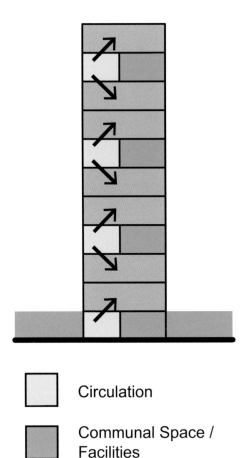

Circulation

Communal Space / Facilities

Figure 5.6 Pruitt–Igoe, diagrammatic section of communal/private spaces
Source: Philip Oldfield

on their side, stacking up horizontal blocks to create a dynamic urban topography, with the form acting as a "generator of space for community, and communal living" (Scheeren & Eng, 2014) (Figure 5.11). The Interlace creates extensive roofgardens and terraces set in multi-storey openings, some sheltered, some open, with a range of scales and views (Figures 5.12 and 5.13). Unlike Pruitt-Igoe, where the social spaces at height were not overlooked, here communal garden terraces sit adjacent to private balconies, providing a degree of visibility and security. A thicker slab at the base of each block also means communal gardens are positioned slightly lower than the floor levels of adjacent apartments, providing a degree of privacy to homes.

A further example is WOHA's Oasia Hotel Downtown. Here the brief called for office, hotel and club room programmes set in a single tower. A tight urban site of around 60 by 60 metres provides little opportunity for open space at ground level. The design stacks the different programmes up, but gives each its own skygarden, providing a generous communal space for the occupants at height (Figure 5.14). To achieve this on a small site, the cores are pushed to the four corners of the tower's footprint, allowing the centre of the building to be carved away, creating voids. Floor plates span between three of the four cores, creating urban windows framing previously unimaginable views and sheltering the skygardens from the sun and rain, while also allowing breezes to pass through to offset the tropical heat and humidity (Figure 5.15). Each skygarden is approximately 30 by 30 metres, the size of a small urban park typically found at ground, but here hoisted into the air (Figures 5.16 and 5.17). Vegetation dominates the aesthetic. Through both horizontal skygardens and vertical green walls, the building manages to create a quite incredible 1,100% of the original site area as new greenery – a wonderful piece of urban and environmental generosity, albeit in a private building.

While the skygarden has been embraced across multiple typologies in Singapore – social housing, private apartments, hotels, offices and more – its popularity did not just occur by chance. Instead, it is the result of progressive planning policies and incentives set out by the Singaporean government. While the HDB have pushed the concept of skygardens in social high-rise housing, private projects are encouraged to include such spaces through the Landscaping for Urban Spaces and High-rises (LUSH) planning circular. Fuelled by Singapore's strategic aim of creating a 'City in a Garden', LUSH stipulates that developers must include greenery either at ground level or at height in a new development, equivalent at least to the total area of the site. Developers who include skygardens and landscaped roofs with outdoor refreshment areas also benefit from floor area tax exemptions and bonus plot ratios, allowing them to construct more area than local zoning laws prescribe (URA, 2014). This provides a strong financial incentive for the inclusion of communal spaces and greenery at height. In addition, the Landscape Excellence Assessment Framework (LEAF) provides certification for projects with outstanding use of greenery, creating a level of national recognition and a further incentive for skygardens. Such is the success of LUSH

Figure 5.7 Robin Hood Gardens, London, streets in the sky
Source: Steve Cadman, CC BY-SA 2.0, https://creativecommons.org/licenses/by-sa/2.0/deed.en

Figure 5.8 The Pinnacle@Duxton, Singapore. Continuous skygardens at levels 26 and 50 link together seven towers
Source: Philip Oldfield

Figure 5.9   The Pinnacle@Duxton, children's playground at level 26 spanning between two towers
Source: Philip Oldfield

Figure 5.10   The Pinnacle@Duxton, greenery and trees providing shade for residents and the public on the 50th-floor skygarden
Source: Philip Oldfield

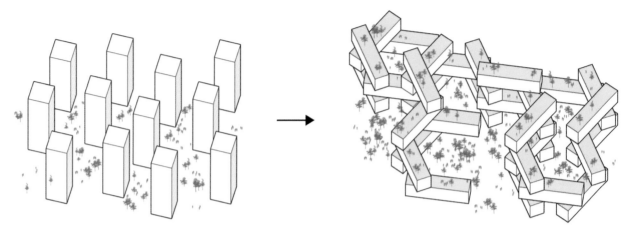

Figure 5.11 The Interlace, Singapore, a traditional site arrangement of high-density towers (left) versus the stacked horizontal blocks of the Interlace with green spaces and terraces at multiple levels (right)
Source: OMA/Ole Scheeren

Figure 5.12 The Interlace, aerial view
Source: Iwan Baan

Figure 5.13 The Interlace, aerial view
Source: Iwan Baan

Figure 5.14 Oasia Hotel Downtown, Singapore
Source: K. Kopter

and LEAF that most new Singaporean high-rises now include significant skygardens and areas of vertical and horizontal greenery, providing not only a unique aesthetic and spaces for community interaction but also shade and mitigation against the urban heat island effect. This has unequivocally changed Singapore's skyline, demonstrating the transformative effect that planning incentives and bonuses can have on a city.

Conclusion

In conclusion, it is important to note that a wide range of socio-political factors influence occupant satisfaction and community interaction in any housing development, be it high, medium or low-rise. Architecture alone cannot create successful vertical communities. The assumption that high-rise social housing is an outright failure is driven, to a large extent, by the generalised experience of a few highly problematic cases which suffered a range of social, political and economic challenges beyond their verticality (Graham, 2016).

> [A]rchitecture can't force people to connect, it can only plan the crossing points, remove barriers, and make the meeting places useful and attractive.
>
> [Denise Scott Brown, from Tamas, 2011]

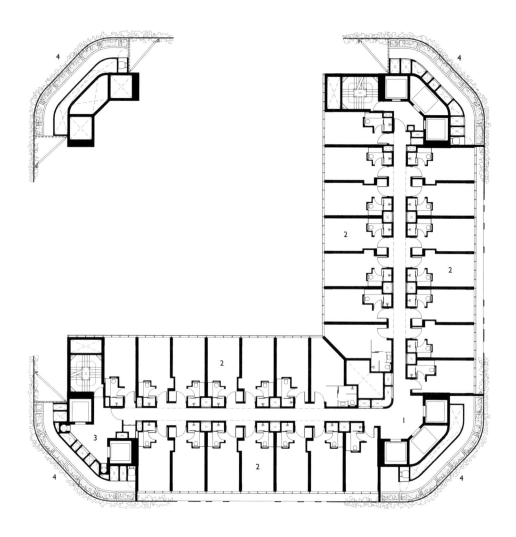

LEGEND

1   GUESTROOM LIFT
2   GUESTROOMS
3   SERVICE LIFT
4   GREEN FACADE

OASIA DOWNTOWN
13TH-20TH STOREY PLAN

0 1 2 3   5   10 M

1 : 400

WOHA ARCHITECTS PTE LTD
APRIL 2016

NORTH

Figure 5.15   Oasia Hotel Downtown, typical plan at levels 13–20
Source: WOHA

However, this does not let the design team off the hook. Our current model of high-rise housing is far from optimised – architecturally, urbanistically or programmatically – to foster community interaction, and especially to accommodate the specific needs of families with children of different ages. One potential opportunity to overcome this situation is to create social and communal spaces at height, providing space and programme for communities in tall buildings. Singapore, perhaps more than anywhere else, has embraced this idea, creating skygardens across both its public and private housing stock. Their designs are a far cry from the streets in the sky of the past, accommodating lush vegetation and recreational programmes suited to a variety of occupants, including sport, play and relaxation. However, the inclusion of skygardens

Figure 5.17 Oasia Hotel Downtown, internal view of a mid-level skygarden. These spaces are the size of small urban parks, but shaded from the harsh Singaporean sun with access to great views and cooling breezes
Source: Patrick Bingham-Hall

protected, but also allowing residents certain freedoms as to how skygardens are used and operated as places of community and social interaction.

Note

1 A version of this chapter was originally published in the *Urban Design Group Journal* – see Oldfield, 2016. It has been significantly extended and adapted for inclusion in this publication with permission.

References

Bansal, K., Varshneya, H. & Oldfield, P. (2017). *The History of the Skygarden: A Chronological Analysis of Socio-Communal Spaces at Height in Tall Buildings*. Proceedings of the 5th Annual International Conference on Architecture and Civil Engineering (ACE 2017), pp. 25–32.

Bristol, K. G. (1991). The Pruitt-Igoe Myth. *Journal of Architectural Education*, Vol. 44, No. 3, pp. 163–171.

Cairns, S., Jacobs, J. M., Yingying, J., Padawangi, R., Siddique, S. & Tan, E. (2014). Singapore's Void Decks. In: Lim, W. S. W. (ed.) *Public Spaces in Urban Asia*, Asian Urban Lab, Singapore, pp. 80–89.

Figure 5.16 Oasia Hotel Downtown, skygarden creating an urban window in the building's mass
Source: K. Kopter

does not simply result in successful communities or happy residents. In the examples of both Pruitt-Igoe and the Pinnacle@Duxton, built some 50 years and 10,000 miles apart, we can see that how such spaces are operated, maintained and governed is the primary influence on their success, and the feelings and experiences of occupants. In Pruitt-Igoe the streets in the sky were unsecured, and poorly maintained, becoming spaces of crime and vandalism. In the Pinnacle@Duxton the skygardens are accessed through intimidating turnstiles and subject to a wide variety of limiting rules and regulations. The success of high-rise communities is reliant not only on the building design, but puts emphasis on building owners and operators to provide *balance* in how such spaces are governed; that is, providing the necessary security for residents to feel

Crabtree, J. (2017). Commentary: What London Can Learn from Singapore's High-Rise Living. *Channel News Asia*, 12 July. www.channelnewsasia.com/news/singapore/commentary-what-london-can-learn-from-singapore-s-high-rise-9023986

Cumming, E. (2015). "It's Like a Ghost Town": Lights Go Out as Foreign Owners Desert London Homes. *The Guardian*, 25 January. www.theguardian.com/uk-news/2015/jan/25/its-like-a-ghost-town-lights-go-out-as-foreign-owners-desert-london-homes

Dagen Bloom, N. (2008). *Public Housing that Worked: New York in the Twentieth Century*. University of Pennsylvania Press, Philadelphia.

Easthope, H. & Tice, A. (2011). Children in Apartments: Implications for the Compact City. *Urban Policy and Research*, Vol. 29, No. 4, pp. 415–434.

Freidrichs, C. (2011). *The Pruitt Igoe Myth*, 11 February.

Gifford, R. (2007). The Consequences of Living in High-Rise Buildings. *Architectural Science Review*, Vol. 50, No. 1, pp. 2–17.

Graham, S. (2016). *Vertical: The City from Satellites to Bunkers*. Verso, London.

Graham, S. & Hewitt, L. (2012). Getting Off the Ground: On the Politics of Urban Geography. *Process in Human Geography*, Vol. 37, No. 1, pp. 1–21.

Hadi, Y., Heath, T. & Oldfield, P. (2018). Gardens in the Sky: Emotional Experiences in the Communal Spaces at Height in the Pinnacle@Duxton, Singapore. *Emotion, Space and Society*, Vol. 28, pp. 104–113.

Ipsos Mori. (2014). *High Rise in the Capital: Londoners Split on Merits of More Tall Buildings*. www.ipsos-mori.com/researchpublications/researcharchive/3361/high-rise-in-the-capital-londoners-split-on-merits-of-more-tall-buildings.aspx

Jenkins, D. (1993). *Unité d'Habitation, Marseilles*. Phaidon, London.

Millais, M. (2015). A Critical Appraisal of the Design, Construction and Influence of the Unité d'Habitation, Marseilles, France. *Journal of Architecture and Urbanism*, Vol. 39, No. 2, pp. 103–115.

Murphy, D. (2016). Notopia: The Fall of Streets in the Sky. *Architectural Review*, 9 June.

Newman, O. (1972). *Defensible Space: People and Design in the Violent City*. Architectural Press, London.

Oldfield, P. (2015). Don't Fear the Skyscraper – Why London Needs More Tall Buildings. *The Conversation*, 31 July. https://theconversation.com/dont-fear-the-skyscraper-why-london-needs-more-tall-buildings-45029

Oldfield, P. (2016). From Void-Deck to Skygarden. *Urban Design Group Journal*, Summer, Vol. 139, pp. 33–35.

Phang, S. Y. & Kim, K. (2011). Singapore's Housing Polices: 1960–2013. In: *Frontiers in Development Policy: Innovative Development Case Studies*, KDI School of Public Policy and Management / World Bank Institute, Seoul, pp. 124–153.

Scheeren, O. & Eng, T. W. (2014). *CTBUH 13th Annual Awards – Tiang Wah Eng & Ole Scheeren, the Interlace, Singapore*. www.youtube.com/watch?v=uD0xBCG6LSs

Sudjic, D. (2005). *The Edifice Complex: How the Rich and Powerful – And Their Architects – Shape the World*. Penguin Books Ltd, London.

Tamas, A. (2011). *Interview: Robert Venturi & Denise Scott Brown, by Andrea Tamas*. www.archdaily.com/130389/interview-robert-venturi-denise-scott-brown-by-andrea-tamas

Toland, I. (2001). *4 Unités LC: Fragments of a Radiant Dream*. www.architects.nsw.gov.au/download/BHTS/TolandIsabelle_4_unites_LC_BHTS_1999.pdf

URA. (2014). *Circular Package: Landscaping for Urban Spaces and High- Rises (LUSH) 2.0 Programme*, 12 June. www.ura.gov.sg/Corporate/Guidelines/Circulars/dc14-lush20

Urban, F. (2012). *Tower and Slab: Histories of Global Mass Housing*. Routledge, London and New York.

White, L. E. (1950). *Community or Chaos: Housing Estates and their Social Problems*. National Council of Social Service, London.

Whitzman, C. & Mizrachi, D. (2012). Creating Child-Friendly High-Rise Environments: Beyond Wastelands and Glasshouses. *Urban Policy and Research*, Vol. 30, No. 3, pp. 233–249.

Wong, A. K. & Yeh, S. H. K. (eds) (1985). *Housing a Nation*. Maruzen Asia, Singapore.

Wood, A. (2003). "Pavements in the Sky": Use of the Skybridge in Tall Buildings. *Architecture Research Quarterly*, Vol. 7, No. 3–4, pp. 325–332.

Wynee Rees, P. (2015). London Needs Homes, Not Towers of "Safe-Deposit Boxes". *The Guardian*, 25 January. www.theguardian.com/commentisfree/2015/jan/25/planners-must-take-back-control-of-london

Yuen, B., Yeh, A., Appold, S. J., Earl, G., Ting, J. & Kwee, L. W. (2006). High-Rise Living in Singapore Public Housing. *Urban Studies*, Vol. 43, No. 3, pp. 583–600.

CHAPTER SIX

Mixed-use and emerging vertical programmes

Introduction: the sustainability of mixed-use

Mixed-use is widely seen as an integral component of the compact city ideology, providing different functions and activities in close (often walkable) proximity, while creating vibrant and exciting cities that are used throughout the day. There are many definitions for what constitutes 'mixed-use', but in the vertical realm the Council on Tall Buildings and Urban Habitat defines a mixed-use skyscraper as one which contains two or more functions where each occupies a "significant proportion" of the building floor area or height, typically judged at 15% or greater (CTBUH, 2018). What this means is that a residential tower with a few shops at the base does not constitute mixed-use, nor does an office tower with an observation deck at the top. Support areas, such as carparks and mechanical plant space, are also not considered as mixed-use functions.

The creation of mixed-use buildings can provide social, economic and environmental benefits. Fundamentally, by providing a mix of residential, employment, civic and service functions in proximity to each other, daily travel distances can be reduced, along with GHG emissions from transportation (see also Chapter 2). In the vertical realm, however, this is sometimes misconstrued as living and working in a single

tower. Over a century ago, architect Raymond Hood suggested "every businessman in the city must have realised what an advantage it would be to live in the building where his office is located. It is toward this ideal that real estate firms and architects should work" (Koolhaas, 1994, p. 174). Of course, such an idea is unappealing to many.[1] The social and psychological impacts of living and working in the same building and rarely needing to venture outside are surely detrimental. More attractive, however, would be the opportunity to live in a mixed-use tower that is active for much of the day, and being able to walk or cycle to another mixed-use tower for work within the same district.

Mixed-use can also contribute to greater city vitality and security. Mono-functional districts and buildings are often only used for short periods of the day: office in the daytime and residential in the early morning and evening. The City of London, for example, accommodates mostly office programmes with a residential population of less than 10,000, giving it a density of around 3,000 people/km². However, its daytime population density peaks at around 140,000 people/km² due to the intensity of employment in the area (Urban Age, LSE Cities, 2012). The vitality this density brings is temporal, limited to weekdays, nine till five, meaning in late evenings and at weekends the City can be relatively barren, providing little benefit to Greater London in terms of space, infrastructure or activity. Mixed-use (specifically live/work) can extend the operating hours of a building or district to at least 16 hours a day, providing more 'eyes on the street' and potentially improving urban safety and security (Jacobs, 1961).

> The district, and indeed as many of its internal parts as possible, must serve more than one primary function; preferably more than two. These must insure the presence of people who go outdoors on different schedules and are in place for different purposes, but who are able to use many facilities in common.
>
> [Jane Jacobs, 1961, p. 152]

Historically, mixed-use towers were seen as risky ventures by developers, due to the complexity of their design, approval and construction processes. However, more recently they are seen as financially attractive, since they provide diversity of risk; if housing demand falters, office demand may still be strong and vice versa (Marsh *et al.*, 2014). As such, the mixed-use skyscraper is becoming more commonplace in tall building construction trends (Figure 6.1). Environmentally, mixed-use can provide energy sharing and reduction of peak load opportunities; excess heat created by the high internal loads of offices (people, lighting, machinery, etc.) is usually rejected via cooling towers. In a mixed-use tower this waste heat can be harnessed to provide hot water or space heating for apartments above, reducing their energy requirements. Since office and residential spaces have different occupancy periods, they require heating and cooling at different times – office in the day, residential in the evening. This means the building peak load will be reduced, as compared to a single-function tower of the same area, allowing for smaller heating and cooling plant to provide space conditioning. This reduction in plant would save both floor area and the carbon-intensive materials that go into creating mechanical systems (steel, aluminium, copper, etc.).

However, mixed-use skyscrapers do require more complex spatial and technological integration than single-function buildings. Different functions usually require separate vertical transportation systems, meaning mixed-use buildings typically have much larger cores. There is often the need for independent mechanical risers for each programme too, which can further

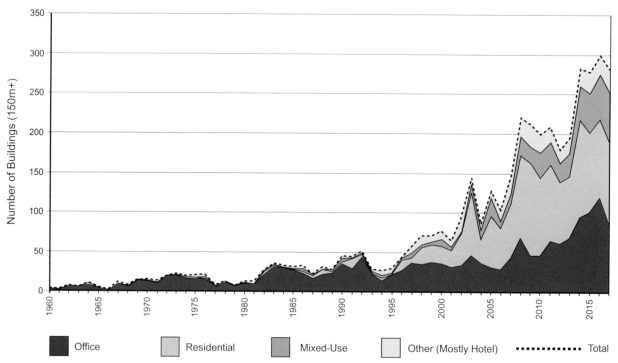

Figure 6.1   Annual tall building construction by function, for heights of 150m+, 1960–2017

Source: Philip Oldfield, data from Skyscrapercenter, 2018

increase core size (Zikri, 2005). Typically, this means that mixed-use towers have lower net-to-gross efficiencies than single-function high-rises (Elnimeiri & Kim, 2004). Each function will likely require a different structural system, or structural grid, which will need to be aligned vertically. In the Shard (London, 2013), office floor plates in the lower 28 storeys use composite steel frames with large spans up to 15 metres. For hotel and residential floors above, post-tensioned concrete slabs are used to reduce floor-to-floor heights for the shorter nine-metre spans. Column spacing is three metres in the hotel and residential areas, and six metres in the office floors, thus requiring mid-level trusses to transfer forces from one grid to the other (Moazami *et al.*, 2008). Such complexities are less necessary in single-function towers and can contribute to extra material and cost requirements. Although there is little research in the field, it would be reasonable to assume that larger cores, reduced efficiencies and more complex structures mean mixed-use towers have a higher embodied carbon than single-function types, given the need for more materials producing less usable space. However, such a small additional carbon cost would go little way to offsetting their wider benefits to the city.

Given these technical challenges, the architectural design of mixed-use skyscrapers requires careful organisation of form and programme. Typically, this involves stacking functions with smaller lease spans above those which require larger ones, resulting in functions ascending from the ground as such – retail, office, hotel and residential[2] – as typified in the Shard (Figure 6.2). Is it possible to accommodate an office and residential split on the same floorplate, rather than through stacking? Such an approach is extremely rare due to the different technical requirements of the functions, such as differing floor-to-floor heights, structural grids, lease spans, etc. Wood (2007) suggests that one of the only buildings to have achieved this is Frank Lloyd Wright's Price Tower, in Oklahoma (1956) (Figure 6.2). Here the office spaces are not large-scale commercial floors but boutique small-scale offices, arranged much like cellular apartments. A more contemporary example is OMA's De Rotterdam (2013), which arranges residential, hotel and office floors across three towers with a common podium; although here, the differing technical requirements of the functions is mitigated by arranging them in separate (albeit touching) towers,

with individual cores (Figure 6.2). While this vertical split of programmes is rare, it could provide potential environmental benefits, due to the complimentary thermal requirements of different functions. In the temperate northern hemisphere, for example, residential units could be organised to face south and office spaces to face north. In such a scenario, apartments would benefit from solar gain for passive heating, but shade the cooling-dominated office spaces beyond.

Emerging vertical programmes

While the mixed-use tall building is a well-established typology, there are growing opportunities for emerging skyscraper programmes in our increasingly vertical cities. They include dramatic ideas such as vertical schools and universities, vertical agriculture and farming and even vertical cemeteries that require a totally new way of thinking and designing high-rise architecture. Rather than being utopian fantasy, such ideas are built and seriously proposed around the world.

In part, the increasing verticality of these traditionally horizontal programmes is being fuelled by urbanisation and density. As cities are growing increasingly dense, and available land diminishes, civic, cultural, educational and other institutions and programmes are having to embrace verticality if they are to remain in the city centre; a three-storey school in downtown New York, Shanghai or Sydney is economically and environmentally unviable. Wherever hyperdensity and verticality have emerged, often the transition of 'horizontal' programmes to the vertical realm has soon followed. One of the first built examples to demonstrate this was the Downtown Athletic Club, completed in 1930 and designed by Starrett & Van Vleck architects. Designed to house recreational facilities for businessmen in Lower Manhattan, a high price of land necessitated a tall building, and a small site dictated that the different functions and facilities of the club be stacked across 35 floors (Landmark Preservation Committee, 2000). These include a swimming pool, gymnasium, squash and tennis courts, barber shop, boxing ring and even a miniature golf course across an entire floor, complete with green meadows and a narrow river – although little in its exterior appearance captured this diversity[3] (Figure 6.3). This stacking of traditionally horizontal functions, superimposed

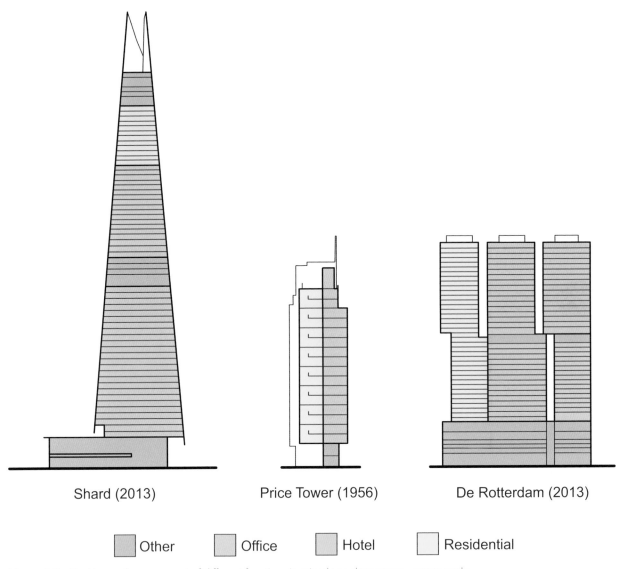

Shard (2013)   Price Tower (1956)   De Rotterdam (2013)

☐ Other   ☐ Office   ☐ Hotel   ☐ Residential

Figure 6.2 Stacking and arrangement of different functions in mixed-use skyscrapers – not to scale
Source: Philip Oldfield

across 35 floors, led Dutch architect and writer Rem Koolhaas to describe the building as "an abstract composition of activities that describes, on each of the synthetic platforms, a different 'performance' that is only a fragment of the larger spectacle of the Metropolis" (Koolhaas, 1994, p. 157). Today we are seeing traditionally horizontal programmes that require much more than this synthetic stacking of different activities atop each other to succeed in high-rise architecture. The sustainable design thinking behind some of these emerging programmes is articulated across the following sections.

Vertical education

There is a vital need for educational facilities to remain in our hyperdense cities. What point is there in encouraging greater residential density in and around city centres, but then forcing families to commute out to suburban areas for access to schools and colleges? The university also plays an important civic role in the city, not only through facilitating public debate around scientific, literary and philosophical subjects, but also increasingly providing publicly accessible facilities such as sports, galleries, libraries and auditoria (Wu &

Figure 6.3 Downtown Athletic Club, New York
Source: Americasroof, CC BY 3.0, https://creativecommons.org/
licenses/by/3.0/deed.en

Oldfield, 2015; Goddard & Vallance, 2011). Maintaining such institutions in the city also provides easier access to mass public transit, reducing students' and teachers' reliance on the automobile, and thus their transit-related carbon emissions.

Current design models for learning and education are changing. Historically, planning of schools and higher education facilities has focussed on spaces for formal learning – that is, traditional classrooms and lecture theatres. However, as lecture-based teaching methods have become less dominant and peer-based and student-centred learning more prominent, new educational facilities have started to include fewer formal teaching areas and more spaces designed for conversation, social interaction and teamworking (French & Kennedy, 2015). There is an increasing

recognition that most learning takes place outside the classroom, in more informal environments, leading education institutes to create a 'learning landscape' of spaces, including the formal and informal, specialised and general, social, communal and eating spaces (Neary et al., 2010). The result is that educational institutions are seeking to provide a multitude of learning experiences, from the traditional 'teacher-led' to less structured peer-to-peer, informal or self-directed learning (Wilson, 2009). In the horizontal campus or school, such informal learning has historically taken place in the courtyard, café or library, but increasingly designers are creating student 'hubs', 'streets' and break-out spaces to facilitate learning and social interaction outside the classroom. Although such spaces are relatively simple to plan in a horizontal building, what does a vertical 'student hub' look like? How can we foster the learning landscape in the vertical dimension, on a small plot of land, at a high density? Such an approach requires a step away from the traditional stacked floorplate model of residential and commercial high-rise design to more volumetric and experiential design thinking.

Perhaps the most exciting interpretation of the learning landscape in the vertical realm is the Roy and Diana Vagelos Education Center at Columbia University Medical Center in Manhattan, designed by Diller Scofidio + Renfro. Housing a 14-storey medical education facility, the design features social and informal learning spaces as a key driver in the building's identity and spatial organisation. The building is arranged around a central core, with more formal classrooms and offices to the north and what the architects term a 'Study Cascade' to the south – a series of vertically linked social and communal spaces, including small auditoria, study spaces, student commons, study lounges and exterior terraces, connected by an open staircase snaking from bottom to top (Figures 6.4, 6.5 and 6.6). "We designed the building to support this informal learning model in which work and social life are blurred, and students have a lot of freedom to select environments with attributes that appeal to them", says Liz Diller, founding partner at Diller Scofidio + Renfro (Giovannini, 2016).

Here verticality does not limit interaction among floors, but is designed to enhance it. In a vertical education building, this is vital as students move between

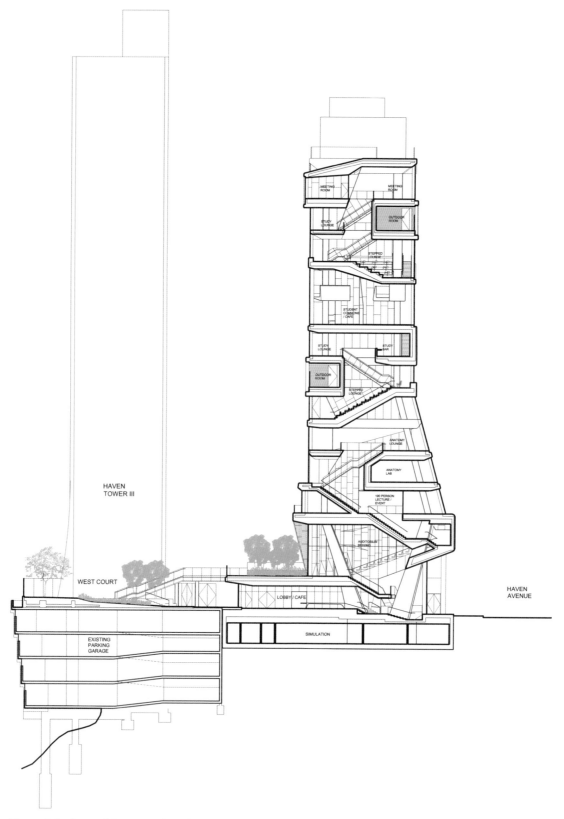

Figure 6.4 Roy and Diana Vagelos Education Center, New York, section through the Study Cascade
Source: Diller Scofidio + Renfro

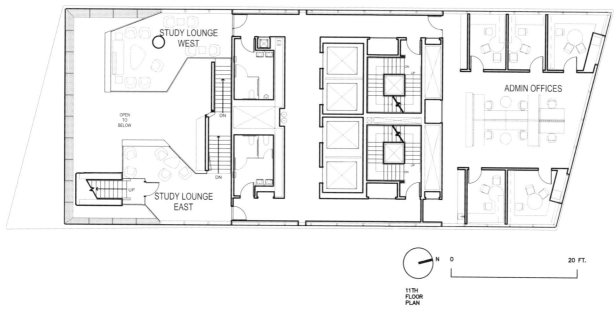

Figure 6.5 Roy and Diana Vagelos Education Center, eleventh-floor plan
Source: Diller Scofidio + Renfro

Figure 6.6 Roy and Diana Vagelos Education Center, exterior view of the Study Cascade and south façade
Source: Iwan Baan

different lectures, study spaces and activities throughout the day. By creating and linking informal and social study spaces along an exposed stairway, the Vagelos Education Center provides a platform for interaction. It provides a place where a student may casually bump into a peer and discuss coursework; where a researcher may look down and see a colleague they have been looking to talk to all morning (Figure 6.7). Of course, there are technical challenges that low-rise buildings wouldn't face. The Study Cascade is actually broken up into four vertical segments, separated by fire doors, for fire enclosure purposes (Giovannini, 2016).Yet there are advantages too, with the spaces benefitting from inspiring views of Manhattan to the south.

In much taller buildings, a vertical street of interlinked learning spaces would likely be more challenging – although far from impossible – to create. The Mode Gakuen Cocoon Tower, designed by Tange Associates and completed in Tokyo in 2008, fosters informal learning through an alternative strategy of *vertical villages*. The building accommodates 10,000 students across three schools – a fashion school, information technology school and medical welfare school – stacked up within a single 50-storey tower (Figure 6.8). The spatial arrangement consists of a central core with three rectilinear blocks of classrooms

Figure 6.7   Roy and Diana Vagelos Education Center. Intersecting stairways ascend to join the Study Cascade and descend to a lower-floor Simulation Suite, comprised of mock clinics, examination rooms and operating rooms
Source: Iwan Baan

Figure 6.8   Mode Gakuen Cocoon Tower, Tokyo
Source: Tange Associates

arranged around the perimeter. So far, so conventional. However, the interstitial spaces between classrooms and core are designed as 'student lounges', three storeys high and each organised around a different view – east, south-west and northwest (Figures 6.9 and 6.10). Considered as "new types of schoolyards" (Tange & Minami, 2009, p. 17), each student lounge creates social space for informal learning and communication among students outside of the classroom environment.

Whereas in the temperate climates of Tokyo and New York both formal and informal learning spaces would tend to be internal, to protect against greater wind speeds at height, external social spaces may be desirable in warmer climates. In the School of the Arts, Singapore, designed by WOHA and completed in 2010, a podium of performing arts theatres sits below seven storeys of academic spaces (Figure 6.11). Due to limited land, the open recreational and social spaces the institute required were not able to be accommodated at ground level, and as such, were lifted up to create an "elevated ground in the sky" (Wong *et al.*, 2014, p. 40). Three linear blocks of classrooms are arranged parallel in plan, with social spaces sandwiched between acting as multi-storey skygardens – spaces for students

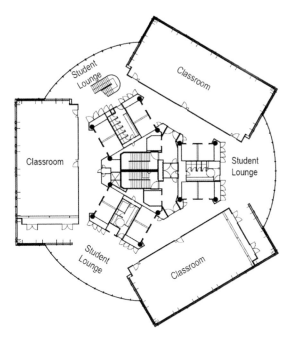

Figure 6.9 Mode Gakuen Cocoon Tower, level 21 plan
Source: Tange Associates

to gather, study and play at height in the city (Figure 6.12). The blocks of classrooms shade these communal areas from the intense Singaporean sun, while their raised nature allows greater access to the city's light breezes for thermal comfort. These terrace spaces are also pocketed with greenery, link bridges and open circulation stairways, linking classrooms and other activities together, thus encouraging spontaneous exchange and collaboration among students (Wong *et al.*, 2014) (Figure 6.13).

Vertical farming

As we strive to improve the sustainability of all aspects of our cities, a strategy increasingly debated is the production of food at height in vertical farms – skyscrapers providing the infrastructure for intensive agriculture, and occasionally even livestock. Interior farming that uses vertical growing technologies to

Figure 6.10 Mode Gakuen Cocoon Tower, three-storey student lounge
Source: Tange Associates

Figure 6.11 School of the Arts, Singapore
Source: Patrick Bingham-Hall

generate intensive agriculture in buildings are already operated around the world, with this market expected to be worth around $4 billion USD by 2020 (Cox, 2016). In this sense, the sustainability and architectural design considerations of the vertical farm are worthy of discussion here.

The case for vertical farming is best made by Dickson Despommier, Emeritus Professor of Microbiology and Public Health at Columbia University, and arguably the godfather of the vertical farming concept. Despommier suggests that the primary advantages of vertical farming in skyscrapers are (2010):

- Reducing land needed for agriculture by stacking this vertically in towers (therefore reducing loss of biodiversity from traditional agricultural spread)

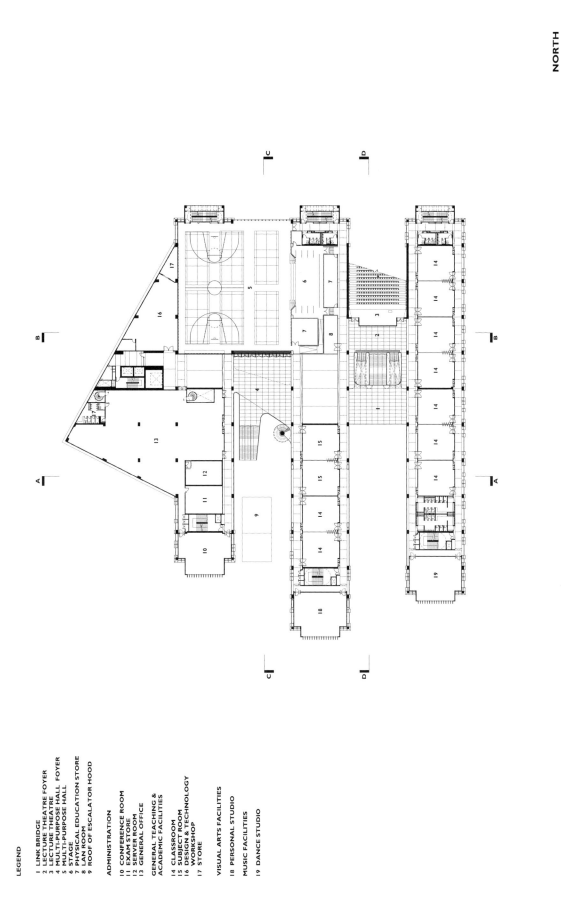

LEGEND

1 LINK BRIDGE
2 LECTURE THEATRE FOYER
3 LECTURE THEATRE
4 MULTI-PURPOSE HALL FOYER
5 MULTI-PURPOSE HALL
6 STAGE
7 PHYSICAL EDUCATION STORE
8 LAN ROOM
9 ROOF OF ESCALATOR HOOD

ADMINISTRATION

10 CONFERENCE ROOM
11 EXAM STORE
12 SERVER ROOM
13 GENERAL OFFICE

GENERAL TEACHING & ACADEMIC FACILITIES

14 CLASSROOM
15 SUBJECT ROOM
16 DESIGN & TECHNOLOGY WORKSHOP
17 STORE

VISUAL ARTS FACILITIES

18 PERSONAL STUDIO

MUSIC FACILITIES

19 DANCE STUDIO

WOHA   .   SCHOOL OF THE ARTS, SINGAPORE   .   6TH STOREY PLAN

Figure 6.12 School of the Arts, level 6 plan
Source: WOHA

Figure 6.13 School of the Arts, the skyterrace as a place of student interaction and collaboration at height
Source: Patrick Bingham-Hall

- Year-round high-yield crop production in controlled environments, with no crop failures due to extreme weather or pests
- Reduced food miles (and subsequent CO_2 emissions) since food is produced in the place it is most consumed – the high-density city
- Reduced water use for agriculture (estimated 70–95% less)

- No need for pesticides, herbicides or fertilises
- More control of food safety and security

Somewhat understandably, others remain sceptical. Stan Cox (2016), for example, suggests that vertical farming would need "extraordinary energy requirements" to provide the necessary lighting for plants inside a building, fuelling their photosynthesis with vast arrays of LEDs. That's not to mention that a skyscraper farm would likely release tens of thousands of tonnes of CO_2 from the embodied carbon needed to create the structure in the first place (see also Chapter 7).

Questions remain about the broader environmental credentials of vertical farming, especially if it is reliant on artificial lighting. However, economic sustainability is the greatest challenge. For example, Monbiot (2010) suggests that the artificial lighting required to grow the 500 grams of wheat that a loaf of bread contains would cost £9.82, as compared to the traditional farm-to-gate price of 6p. More recent research by Banerjee and Adeneuer (2014) on a theoretical 37-storey vertical farm in Berlin found the initial capital cost would be in the order of €200 million, with a €5.3 million annual energy bill. In return, such a facility could produce around 3,500 tonnes of fruit and vegetables and 137 tonnes of tilapia fillets per year at a cost of €3.50–$4.00/kg. This is a figure the authors feel might be economically feasible, but only in resource-constrained nations and cities with substantially high spending power. There are also few incentives for developers to create vertical farms; a penthouse on the fortieth floor offers a far greater return on investment than, say, a lettuce patch.

While seemingly futuristic, the technologies needed to make vertical farming feasible are mature and commercially available. Due to its bulk and weight, soil is an unsuitable growing medium in the vertical realm, with most vertical farms harnessing soil-less cultivation methods for plants. Three systems are commonly proposed:

1 **Hydroponics** involves using a suitable 'fastening method' to hold plants in place such that roots develop in a liquid medium, such as nutrient-infused water, instead of soil (Figure 6.14).
2 **Aeroponics** goes a step further by growing plants in air and spraying exposed roots with a nutrient-filled mist, thus reducing water requirements.
3 **Aquaponics** integrates the hydroponic growing of plants with aquatic foodstuffs such as fish and shellfish in a symbiotic process (Heath *et al.*, 2012). The waste from the fish provides nutrients for the plants through bacteria breaking down ammonia into nitrates. The plants filter the water, providing oxygen for the fish as well as off-cuts of plants proving food-stuff for the fish.

In terms of other technologies, water sustainability would be vital, using closed-loop systems where water used for growing is cleaned and recycled, rather than wasted. Novel energy and servicing strategies would also be necessary. An anaerobic digestion system could provide a source of energy, with food waste consumed in a basement digester to produce methane, which could be burnt for energy and heat. Heath *et al.* (2012) note that in a mixed-use vertical farm with both housing and farming, separate ventilation systems would be needed for growing and living spaces. This is because intensive indoor farming often supplies CO_2 to growing areas at levels three or four times higher than air to accelerate photosynthesis, and therefore growing speeds.

Figure 6.14 Verticrop: a vertical hydroponic growing system
Source: Valcenteu, CC BY-SA 3.0, https://creativecommons.org/licenses/by-sa/3.0/deed.en

In terms of design strategies, vertical farms can be categorised into four types (Figure 6.15):

1 Lighting and conditioning for growing supplied by artificial means
2 Lighting and conditioning for growing supplied by passive means

3 Hybrid servicing, with a mix of artificial and passive strategies for growing
4 Mixed-use, accommodating both vertical farming and another programme (office, residential, etc.)

The first is by far the most common strategy, as it allows for vertical farming to take place anywhere – in

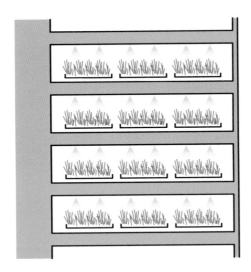

Lighting and conditioning for growing supplied by artificial means

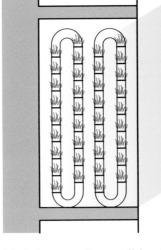

Lighting and conditioning for growing supplied by passive means

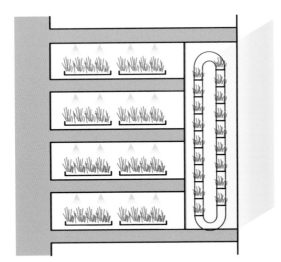

Hybrid servicing, with a mix of artificial and passive strategies for growing

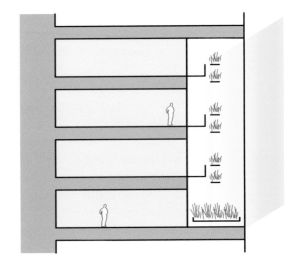

Mixed-use, accommodating both vertical farming and another programme (office, residential, etc.)

Figure 6.15 Vertical farming design and servicing strategies
Source: Philip Oldfield

a warehouse, office, basement, etc. By using LEDs, the precise light wavelength, duration and intensity can be optimised for different crops, maximising yields. In this sense, the artificially lit vertical farm is decoupled from the environment, a 'machine for growing in'. Architecturally, form and orientation are not important, and design is primarily concerned with maximising plot area for growing. Of course, such a strategy would have high carbon emissions if the energy for the vast array of artificial lighting and conditioning was generated from traditional fossil fuel sources, rather than renewables.

The second option, where lighting is provided predominantly by natural means, would use less energy but require much greater architectural innovation. There would be the need to align the lighting quality, duration and intensity and the thermal requirements of selected crops with local weather, temperature and sunpath, through manipulation of architectural form, façade and technology. Whereas deep floor plans would be ideal for the artificially lit vertical farm, much shallower plans and the use of atria would be needed to promote natural light penetration in passive designs. For example, design research conducted by Matthew Humphreys at the University of Nottingham under the supervision of the author with colleague David Nicholson-Cole explored how a naturally lit vertical farm in Singapore might operate. The design consists of a 30-storey tower, lozenge-shape in plan, with the long sides of the building facing east-west to maximise exposure to the equatorial sunpath (Figure 6.16). This is perpendicular to traditional skyscraper orientation in Singapore, which is typically aligned with the long sides to the north-south for minimal solar gain (see also Chapter 4). Multi-storey atria set within a steel mega-frame and a shallow plan form promote natural light penetration deep into the spaces, allowing it to reach aquaponic bays producing fish and leafy vegetables (Figure 6.17). Produce that thrives in warmer conditions would be grown towards the top of each atrium in the tower, where temperatures would be higher due to the stack effect. An inflated ETFE (ethylene tetrafluoroethylene) envelope is specified due to its lightweight properties, thus limiting the structural requirements of the façade and maximising transparency for light penetration. At the northern and southern ends of the plan, apartments are located to provide

accommodation for residents (farmers and scientists), who are mechanically isolated from the growing spaces. At the base, the towers are lifted on mega-structural legs to create an open, permeable ground level for a shaded food market, to facilitate the sale and consumption of the food produced above (Figure 6.18). Such a proposal should demonstrate the radical design thinking across multiple scales that would be necessary to create a passively controlled vertical farm.

It is also worth noting the potential socio-cultural benefits of vertical farming. Growing one's own food has become increasingly popular, fuelled by concerns for healthy, local and organic produce, and a desire to reconnect with nature. While the urban garden provides ample space for a vegetable patch, such opportunities are restricted in the hyperdense and vertical realm (beyond a few potted plants on a balcony). This could be overcome by mixing vertical farming with residential accommodation in hybrid towers. While such an approach would limit yield, with farming becoming more recreational than intensive, 'façade farming' could provide residents an opportunity to grow some of their own food, while providing psychological relief from the concrete and glass city, and act as an enabler of community interaction (Figure 6.19). With greater planted surface area in the summer months, such façade agriculture systems could also provide novel, and beautiful, solar shading.

Vertical cemeteries

> It's a reproduction of what you see . . . We live one above the other. We die one above the other . . . with a view.
>
> [Dominic Fretin, Professor of Architecture – from Noth, 2014]

Perhaps, most challenging of all, it might not be just our lives that are increasingly taking place in the vertical city, but even our deaths. Although rare, the concept of the vertical cemetery is important to discuss here to show just how radical new programmes and morphologies of tall buildings can (and likely will) emerge in the twenty-first century.

The most startling example of this is the Memorial Necrópole Ecumênica in Santos, Brazil. Built in 1983, this 14-storey building houses 14,000 graves, with

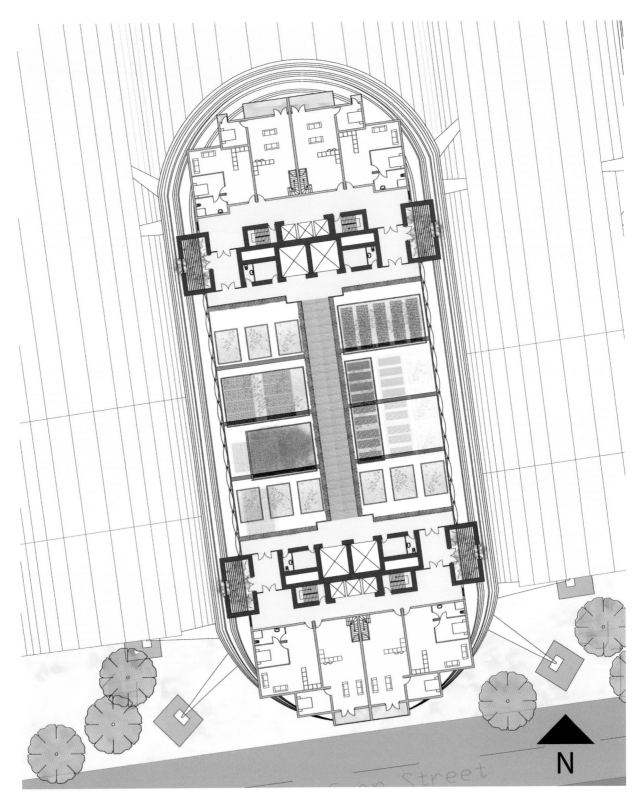

Figure 6.16 Vertical aquaponic farm, Singapore, typical floor plan
Source: Matthew Humphreys

Figure 6.17   Vertical aquaponic farm, section
Source: Matthew Humphreys

Figure 6.18   Vertical aquaponic farm, physical model showing multiple vertical farms above a ground-level market
Source: Matthew Humphreys

plans to expand vertically further still, up to 108 metres tall (approximately 30 storeys) and increase capacity to 25,000 graves (Memorial Necrópole Ecumênica, 2018). Graves are arranged five atop one another per floor and accessed via an open-air perimeter terrace (Figure 6.20). The development also includes other facilities such as an automobile museum, lagoons, a wooded area, chapel, a conservation breeding farm and a restaurant. Such a unique programme is fuelled by two primary mechanisms: density and capitalism. Increasing urbanisation and the price of real estate is forcing alternative programmes to engage with verticality if they are to remain in the city centre. In addition, it is representative of the 'luxification' of height, where a final resting place with a view of the mountains

is amongst the most expensive plots in the building (Noth, 2014; Graham & Hewitt, 2012).

Similar plans are starting to emerge in cities around the world. In Israel, plans have been proposed for thirty 20-metre-tall cemeteries. These are considered necessary since Jewish burial law does not allow cremation, and the land for traditional cemeteries is limited. To comply with Jewish law, which states bodies need to be buried in the earth, the towers have hollow columns filled with soil connected to slabs covered with layers of soil, such that each grave is still essentially connected to the ground (Boyette, 2014). "The source of all this is that there is simply no room", said Tuvia Sagiv, an architect who specialises in high-density burial design in Israel. "It's unreasonable that we will live one on top

Figure 6.19 Agri + Culture, a mixed-use residential tower combining housing with façade-integrated vertical farming for growing, recreation and shade
Source: Jun Loh

of the other in tall apartment buildings and then die in villas" (Associated Press, 2014).

In terms of sustainable performance, it is easy to criticise such proposals. In an age where housing affordability, homelessness and sub-standard living conditions are endemic in many cities, to provide the dead with access to light, view and ventilation above

the city may seem perverse. Yet cemeteries are not only for the dead, but are places of memory, respect, reflection and prayer, which surely deserve such environmental qualities. The alternative is placing cemeteries outside the city proper, where land is more available, but at a cost of transport time and accessibility. Then there is the question of space. Hariyono

The ground floor and public realm

The diversity of programmes emerging at height in towers is, on the whole, a positive thing, helping overcome the vertical monotony common in the skyscraper. Yet, for most tall buildings, regardless of function, the upper floors remain private, out of bounds for the everyday city user. Instead, the ground floor is the most common place where the public can interact, experience and engage with the skyscraper. It is the place that most impacts the vibrancy of the city, the connectivity of its urban spaces and the quality of its streetscape. It is also an area in high-rise design which receives regular criticism, with towers often accused of over-shading streets, creating wind tunnels and replacing diversity of streetscapes with monocultures (Lochhead & Oldfield, 2017). As such, the ground floor interface in any tall building design requires careful attention from urban, programmatic, spatial and environmental perspectives.

Too often, tall buildings take too much away at height, but give too little back at the ground. Office towers tend to create little more than the corporate lobby at ground, transparent and grand, but essentially private in its operation. Residential towers fare worse, often providing little more than car parking access and mechanical areas, with a secure private lobby for residents. The simple inclusion of public facilities and services can go some way to overcoming this divide, creating spaces for cafes, crèches, bars and restaurants at ground, which many towers do provide. Yet, successful ground floor interfaces need to do more than simply provide food and beverage facilities; if a site can accommodate the high densities that towers provide, it must also accommodate urbanistic and programmatic generosity at ground, for the public good. Building vertically does have some advantages in this sense; correctly guided, building up can create higher densities, freeing up more space at ground for the public, adjacent to, or even beneath the tower. For example, the Leadenhall Building (Rogers Stirk Harbour + Partners, 2014), creates a dramatic public space in the heart of the hyperdensity of the City of London. A tight site gives little opportunity for new public realm, thus the tower is lifted up on structural legs, leaving a 28-metre-high, open, yet covered atrium beneath (Figure 6.21). This responds to its context in a number of ways; the

Figure 6.20 Memorial Necrópole Ecumênica, Santos, Brazil, view looking up the central atrium, with open-air terraces providing access to vertically stacked graves
Source: Lucas Grecco

(2015) suggests that if current death rates and burial methods continue, globally we may need additional land area in the region of 6,458 km² to cater for future burials by 2050, an area five times the size of New York City. Building up, as always, can also save open green space. In the Memorial Necrópole Ecumênica, the creation of a vertical cemetery has allowed more than 85% of the 20,000 m² site to be maintained for local fauna and flora, providing memorial goers with access to nature in the heart of the city (Memorial Necrópole Ecumênica, 2018).

Figure 6.21   Leadenhall Building, London, public realm beneath the tower
Source: Paul Raftery, courtesy of Rogers Stirk Harbour + Partners

height relates to the adjacent St Andrew Undershaft Church (constructed in 1532), framing views of it to the east (Figure 6.22). The space provides a half-acre extension to the adjacent St Helen's Square, creating a covered urban place within the city and a permeable link through the building itself. It also responds to sun-path, being south-facing to capture solar gain and thus provide exterior thermal comfort. Public and private functions in the atrium are separated by levels; while the ground level is publicly accessible, private access to the upper floors is via a series of escalators which con-nect to a mezzanine lift lobby suspended above.

But generosity of public realm doesn't have to mean creating large volumes; often simple attention to detail creates popular ground floor interfaces. The design for 1 Bligh Street in Sydney (Ingenhoven Architects and Architectus, 2011) responds to a level change of 4.5 metres across the site by providing a series of sweep-ing stone stairs to the north. These provide access to the lobby and a public route through the building

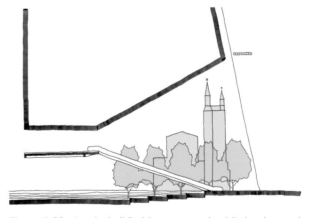

Figure 6.22   Leadenhall Building, recessed public levels reveal the presence of St Andrew Undershaft Church
Source: Graham Stirk/RSHP, courtesy of Rogers Stirk Harbour + Partners

(Figure 6.23). Care has been taken to design the stairs to remain as unobstructed as possible, with minimal handrails, thus essentially turning them into ter-raced seating facing the sun. In the winter, the stairs

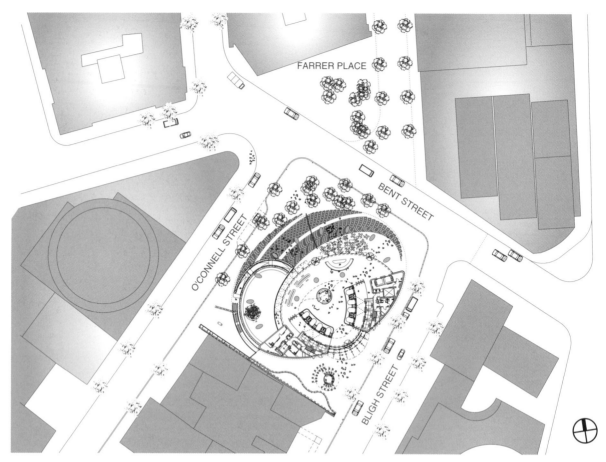

Figure 6.23 1 Bligh Street, Sydney, ground floor plan with curving steps to the north
Source: Architectus + Ingenhoven

are bathed in daylight, providing a degree of warmth, whereas in the summer the projecting floor plates above shade the stairs, providing exterior thermal comfort (Figures 6.24 and 6.25). The result is the steps are hugely popular at lunchtimes, as a place to eat, read or admire views of the city's historic sandstone buildings to the north (Lochhead & Oldfield, 2017).

Different climates also require a different architectural response at ground; whereas a shady, breezy undercroft beneath tall buildings is undesirable in colder regions, in the tropics it can create vibrant and comfortable urban spaces. The Singapore National Library, designed by T. R. Hamzah & Yeang and completed in 2005, consists of two wings of accommodation either side of a linear atrium. These all sit above an open, permeable ground floor realm, shaded by the mass above. The plan form of one of the wings splays out towards the edge of the site, acting to capture and accelerate cooling breezes into the ground floor space, creating an

Figure 6.24 1 Bligh Street, north-facing steps bathed in sunlight
Source: Architectus + Ingenhoven, photographer H.G. Esch

outdoor shaded plaza that is comfortable in the tropical heat and regularly populated, activated by public events, retail spaces, cafes and a library shop (Figure 6.26).

Figure 6.25   1 Bligh Street, north-facing steps as a place to sit
Source: Architectus + Ingenhoven, photographer H.G. Esch

Figure 6.26   National Library, Singapore. The shaded ground floor event space captures incoming breezes to provide thermal comfort, as illustrated by the flags moving in the wind
Source: Philip Oldfield

Conclusion

There is a compelling case that mixed-use tall buildings can provide environmental, social and economic benefits to the city. What's more, we can be sure that as cities' populations and densities grow, we will see previously 'horizontal' functions embracing verticality and emerging in tall buildings. As land prices increase, and available land diminishes, a wider array of programmes including educational, recreational, civic and cultural facilities will need to be accommodated within high-rise design, if they are to stay within the hyperdense city. It is vital that such a diversity of facilities do remain in our city centres, to maintain a proximity of functions and reduce transportation emissions, but also to ensure that our cities stay vibrant and exciting, rather than just regions of high-density commercial space.

There is a huge opportunity for future tall buildings to accommodate a more ambitious mix of functions and spaces, both at ground and at height. The question for the skyscraper developer and designer is: how do we achieve such a mix? Ken Yeang is perhaps the first to propose a framework for this approach, in what he terms a "vertical theory of urban design" (2002). Yeang suggests such is the scale of the skyscraper that it should be looked at as an urban design proposition, rather than architectural form-making. Yeang laments the repetitive stacked homogeneity of many current skyscrapers as providing a demeaning and alienating existence for inhabitants, as they lack the complexity of urban spaces, places and programmatic mixes found on the ground. He encourages future skyscrapers to be "more diverse, less regimented, with networks of plazas, parks and enclosed spaces in the sky" (Yeang, 2002, p. 12). This vision is echoed more recently by Antony Wood (2015), who suggests future skyscraper design should see us bring "ALL aspects of the city up into the sky" (p. 99), including parks, schools, shops, sports and other public and civic functions.

Such visions are starting to come to fruition. As discussed in Chapter 5, many Singaporean high-rises have begun accommodating a mix of publicly accessible and communal activities that are typically found on the ground, at height in towers. However, the Shanghai Tower (designed by Gensler and completed in 2015) is perhaps the closest we have come to the realisation of "vertical urban design". Its height of 128 storeys disguises the fact that the Shanghai Tower is essentially a series of nine separate 12- to 15-storey neighbourhoods of office and hotel stacked above one another. Each neighbourhood has its own 'ground level', known as a skylobby, designed to act as a plaza or square would within a city. Skylobbies sit at the base of multi-storey atria within a generously wide double-skin façade, and they host publicly accessible functions such as gardens, galleries and a museum (Gensler, 2010) (Figures 6.27 and 6.28). Shuttle elevators from the ground only stop at the nine skylobbies, allowing occupants to take a walk in these open spaces at height, grab a coffee and maybe meet a colleague, before jumping into a local elevator serving the intermediate office and hotel floors.

Of course, this is still some way off the suggestions of Yeang and Wood, and we are yet to see the success of such ideas in practice. The biggest barrier to this success is not design nor technology, but instead due to legislation and accessibility. There are many high-rise spaces in towers around the world marketed as 'publicly accessible', but few, if any, of these are as 'public' as the streets, squares and parks we use on a day-to-day basis.

Figure 6.27 Shanghai Tower, Shanghai. Office floors sit inside a wide double-skin façade, which accommodates public skylobbies every 12–15 storeys
Source: Philip Oldfield

Figure 6.28   Shanghai Tower, communal skylobby level at the base of an office 'neighbourhood'
Source: Philip Oldfield

Figure 6.29   The Skygarden, 20 Fenchurch Street, London, a 'publicly accessible', rather than 'public', space at the top of a skyscraper

Source: Henry Cheng

At ground level too, there is an increasing privatisation of public spaces, with many publicly accessible areas now under the ownership of corporate rather than governmental control (Minton, 2012). The Skygarden at the peak of London's 20 Fenchurch Street (often referred to by its moniker, the 'Walkie Talkie') was originally marketed as a 'public park' 150 metres above the city. Yet to access this space requires prior internet booking and then airport-style security to get into the building, leading critics to deride it as a private party space, available only by appointment (Wainwright, 2015) (Figure 6.29).

If we are to create truly diverse mixed-use tall buildings, with a generosity of public spaces at both ground and height, we need to consider better their governance and accessibility. Of course, this is likely to be challenging in a post-9/11 world where security is vital, especially in high-rises (Wood & Oldfield, 2007). Wood (2015) suggests the way to overcome this is to consider future tall buildings as public-private partnerships, where local government takes responsibility for the spatial and public infrastructure in towers, much as they do the streets, parks and squares at ground. There is precedent too, with the skygardens in the Pinnacle@Duxton operated and maintained by the local municipal council (Hadi *et al.*, 2018). While no doubt radical, such an approach could provide a real vertical diversity of both programme and experience in a skyscraper, which exists far too rarely today.

Notes

1 A notable exception to this is the 'officetel', a common typology found in South Korea providing both office space and residential studios for people to live and work in the same building.

2 Although this is by far the most common architectural arrangement, it is by no means obligatory. Interestingly, the world's tallest building, the Burj Khalifa in Dubai, is organised with office spaces on the smallest floors at the top of the building, rather than the larger floors below, which are hotel in programme. This is due to the office floors being 'boutique' in nature, rather than typical open plan commercial layouts.

3 Much of the sport programmes in the Downtown Athletic Club were removed in a 2005 renovation to turn the tower into a predominantly residential programme (Per *et al.*, 2011).

References

Associated Press. (2014). Pressed for Space, Israel Building Cemetery Towers. *Haaretz*, 17 October. www.haaretz.com/jewish/news/1.621256

Banerjee, C. & Adeneuer, L. (2014). Up, Up and Away! The Economics of Vertical Farming. *Journal of Agricultural Studies*, Vol. 2, No. 1, pp. 40–60.

Boyette, C. (2014). Saving Space in Israel with Cemeteries in the Sky. *CNN*, 27 October. http://edition. cnn.com/2014/10/22/world/israel-sky-cemeteries/

Cox, S. (2016). Enough with the Vertical Farming Fantasies: There are Still Too Many Unanswered Questions About the Trendy Practice. *Salon*, 17 February. www.salon.com/2016/02/17/enough_with_ the_vertical_farming_partner/

CTBUH. (2018). *CTBUH Height Criteria*. www. ctbuh.org/TallBuildings/HeightStatistics/Criteria/ tabid/446/language/en-US/Default.aspx

Despommier, D. (2010). *The Vertical Farm: Feeding the World in the 21st Century*. Thomas Dunne Books, New York.

Elnimeiri, M. & Kim, H. (2004). *Space Efficiency in Multi-Use Tall Buildings*. Proceedings of the CTBUH 2004 Seoul Conference: Tall Buildings in Historical Cities – Culture & Technology for Sustainable Cities, pp. 748–755.

French, S. & Kennedy, G. (2015). *The Value of Campus in Contemporary Higher Education*. Melbourne Centre for the Study of Higher Education, Issues and Ideas Paper, October.

Gensler. (2010). *Design Update: Shanghai Tower*. http:// du.gensler.com/vol6/shanghai-tower/

Giovannini, J. (2016). Columbia University Roy and Diana Vagelos Education Center. *Architect*, 24 October. www.architectmagazine.com/project-gallery/columbia-university-roy-and-diana-vagelos-education-center_o

Goddard, J. & Vallance, P. (2011). *The Civic University and the Leadership of Place*. Centre for Urban and Regional Development Studies (CURDS), Newcastle University, Newcastle upon Tyne.

Graham, S. & Hewitt, L. (2012). Getting Off the Ground: On the Politics of Urban Verticality. *Progress in Human Geography*, Vol. 37, No. 1, pp. 72–92.

Hadi, Y., Heath, T. & Oldfield, P. (2018). Gardens in the Sky: Emotional Experiences in the Communal Spaces at Height in the Pinnacle@Duxton, Singapore. *Emotion, Space and Society*, Vol. 28, pp. 104–113.

Hariyono, W. P. (2015). Vertical Cemetery. *Proceedia Engineering*, Vol. 118, pp. 201–214.

Heath, T., Zhu, Y. & Shao, Y. (2012). *Vertical Farming: A High-Rise Solution to Feeding the City?* Proceedings of the CTBUH 9th World Congress, Shanghai, pp. 440–446.

Jacobs, J. (1961). *The Death and Life of Great American Cities*. Random House, New York.

Koolhaas, R. (1994). *Delirious New York*. The Monacelli Press, New York.

Landmark Preservation Committee. (2000). *Downtown Athletic Club Building*. Landmarks Preservation Commission, 14 November, Designation List 319, LP-2075.

Lochhead, H. & Oldfield, P. (2017). The Role of Design Competitions in Shaping Sydney's Public Realm. *CTBUH Journal*, No. IV, pp. 34–39.

Marsh, J., Rupe, E. & Baker, R. (2014). *Vertical Transportation and Logistics in Mixed-Use High-Rise Towers*. Proceedings of the CTBUH 2014 Shanghai Conference, pp. 861–865.

Memorial Necrópole ecumênica. (2018). *The Most Complete Vertical Graveyard in the World*. http:// memorialcemiterio.com.br/

Minton, A. (2012). *Ground Control: Fear and Happiness in the Twenty-First-Century City*. Penguin Books Ltd, London.

Moazami, K., Parker, J. & Giannini, R. (2008). *Steel-Concrete-Steel: Unique Hybrids at London's Tallest*. Proceedings of the CTBUH 8th World Congress, "Tall & Green: Typology for a Sustainable Urban Future", Dubai, 3–5 March, pp. 538–544.

Monbiot, G. (2010). Greens Living in Ivory Towers Now Want to Farm Them Too. *The Guardian*, 16 August. www.theguardian.com/commentisfree/ 2010/aug/16/green-ivory-towers-farm-skyscrapers

Neary, M., Harrison, A., Crellin, G., Parekh, N., Saunders, G., Duggan, F., Williams, S. & Austin, S. (2010). *Learning Landscapes in Higher Education*. Centre for Educational Research and Development, University of Lincoln, Lincoln.

Noth, R. J. (2014). *Rethinking Architecture for the Dead: Views from the World's Tallest Cemetery*. Fifth Town Films. https://aeon.co/videos/rethinking-architec

ture-for-the-dead-views-from-the-world-s-tallest-cemetery

Per, A. F., Mozas, J. & Arpa, J. (2011). *This is Hybrid: An Analysis of Mixed Use Buildings*. A+T Architecture Publishers, Spain.

Skyscrapercenter. (2018). *The Skyscraper Center – The Global Tall Building Database of the CTBUH*. www.skyscrapercenter.com/

Tange, P. N. & Minami, M. (2009). Mode Gakuen Cocoon Tower, Tokyo. *CTBUH Journal*, No. 1, pp. 16–19.

Urban Age, LSE Cities. (2012). *Electric City*, December. https://urbanage.lsecities.net/newspapers/electric-city-1

Wainwright, O. (2015). London's Sky Garden: The More You Pay the Worse the View. *The Guardian*, 6 January. www.theguardian.com/artanddesign/architecture-design-blog/2015/jan/06/londons-sky-garden-walkie-talkie-the-more-you-pay-the-worse-the-view

Wilson, H. (2009). The Process of Creating Learning Spaces. In: Radcliffe, D., Wilson, H., Powell, D. & Tibbetts, B. (eds.) *Proceedings of the Next Generation Learning Spaces 2008 Colloquium*, University of Queensland, Brisbane, Australia, pp. 19–24.

Wong, M. S., Hassell, R. & Yeo, A. (2014). *The Tropical Skyscraper: Social Sustainability in High Urban Density*. Proceedings of the CTBUH 2014 Conference, Shanghai, pp. 39–46.

Wood, A. (2007). Sustainability: A New High-Rise Vernacular. *The Structural Design of Tall and Special Buildings*, Vol. 16, pp. 401–410.

Wood, A. (2015). Rethinking the Skyscraper in the Ecological Age: Design Principles for a New High-Rise Vernacular. *International Journal of High-Rise Buildings*, Vol. 4, No. 2, pp. 91–101.

Wood, A. & Oldfield, P. (2007). Bridging the Gap: An Analysis of Proposed Evacuation Links at Height in the World Trade Centre Design Competition Entries. *Architectural Science Review*, June, Vol. 50, No. 2, University of Sydney, Australia, pp. 173–180.

Wu, X. F. & Oldfield, P. (2015). How the "Civic" Trend Developed in the Histories of the Universities. Open *Journal of Social Sciences*, Vol. 3, pp. 11–14.

Yeang, K. (2002). *Reinventing the Skyscraper: A Vertical Theory of Urban Design*. Wiley Academy, London.

Zikri, M. (2005). Services. In: Strelitz, Z. (ed.) *Tall Buildings: A Strategic Design Guide*. RIBA Publishing, London.

PART III

Sustainable high-rise engineering

CHAPTER SEVEN

Sustainable structures and embodied carbon

Introduction: the premium for height

Designed by William Le Barron Jenny and engineer George B. Whitney, the Home Insurance Building, completed in Chicago in 1885, is generally regarded as the world's first skyscraper where the load-bearing capacity of the façade was liberated by a structural steel frame.[1] Compared to load-bearing high-rise structures, such as the 17-storey Monadnock Building (Figure 7.1), lightweight steel construction provided a number of sustainability benefits. These included freeing up the façade for larger windows to admit more light into the office floors and increasing the efficiency of the structure by reducing column sizes (Willis, 1995). Lighter construction also meant smaller foundations, and therefore less material consumption. The brick piers of the Monadnock Building, for example, are almost two metres thick at ground[2] (Figure 7.2).

> There must be sufficient building material and no more, for it is essential, not only for economy but also to reduce the weights on the foundations, and the construction should be as light as possible consistent with stability.
>
> [William Le Barron Jenny, 1891, p. 41]

Conceptually, we can consider a tall building structure to be a vertical cantilever beam with its base fixed at the ground (Ali & Moon, 2007). Two loads are acting on the building; firstly, gravity loads from the weight of the building, people, machinery, etc., and secondly, lateral loads, from wind and occasionally seismic forces acting perpendicular to the tower. What distinguishes skyscraper structures from low-rise structures is the challenge of resisting the increasing lateral loads with height. Eminent architect and engineer Fazlur Khan of Skidmore, Owings and Merrill (SOM) described this as the *premium for height*; as buildings get taller, the structural material quantities needed to resist gravity loads increase linearly with height. But the structural materials needed to resist the lateral loads increase exponentially, to such an extent that they quickly become the dominant factor in high-rise structural design (Figure 7.3). Khan recognised that to create the world's tallest buildings emerging in the 1970s, alternative structural systems would be needed where wind bracing was placed on the building perimeter, known as 'tube-systems' (Figure 7.4). Khan revolutionised tall building design by recognising that different structural systems would be optimal for different heights,[3] ushering in a new era of structural efficiency and contributing to a significant reduction in materials and embodied carbon.

As we build taller and more slender towers, wind and lateral stability govern structural design, and can have a significant impact on material consumption, tall

Figure 7.1 Monadnock Building, Chicago, 1891
Source: Philip Oldfield

Figure 7.2 Monadnock Building, load-bearing brick piers at the base
Source: Philip Oldfield

building cost and sustainability. At supertall heights, over 300 metres, resisting lateral loads can become the predominant design driver, informing skyscraper form, plan and details. This is less to do with stopping the building from toppling over and more related to occupant comfort and the perception of motion at height. Increased wind speeds at height can cause swirling eddies of wind to occur on the leeward side of the building, known as vortices. These can push and pull the building perpendicular to the wind direction, causing it to oscillate (Figure 7.5). When the frequency of these oscillations occurs at the natural frequency of the building, the effects can be dramatically amplified, causing accelerations and sway to the detriment of occupant comfort (Irwin *et al.*, 2008).

The traditional strategy to reduce these cross-wind oscillations is by stiffening the structure. However, this can involve thousands of tonnes of extra steel and concrete, bringing with it reduced building efficiency (less lettable floor area), increased cost and increased embodied carbon. Alternatively, relatively

subtle changes to plan, form and shape can have dramatic impacts on sway in the world's tallest skyscrapers. In the design of Taipei 101 (508 metres tall, completed in 2004), wind tunnel testing showed that a square plan with sharp corners suffered from significant cross-wind movements. However, chamfered or rounded corners reduced this motion, and a sawtooth design with a double-notch caused a dramatic reduction, which was incorporated into the final design (Poon *et al.*, 2004) (Figure 7.6). In the Burj Khalifa, the world's tallest skyscraper (828 metres tall, completed in 2010), the building form is designed to 'confuse the wind' through the incorporation of set-backs at different heights. Informed by a series of wind tunnel tests, the number and spacing of these set-backs was iteratively optimised to reduce wind forces on the tower. Their alternating nature, changing throughout the height, breaks the rhythm of the vortices, meaning they cannot build significant momentum (Baker *et al.*, 2008) (Figure 7.7).

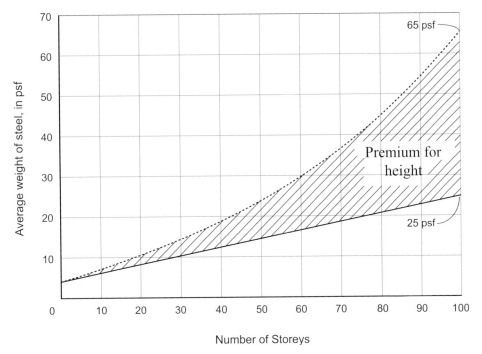

Figure 7.3 The 'premium for height'. The straight line represents the material quantities needed to resist gravity loads, while the curved dotted line represents the additional materials needed to resist lateral forces

Source: Ali & Moon, 2007. Reprinted by permission of the publisher, www.tandfonline.com

Figure 7.4 John Hancock Center, Chicago, designed by Fazlur Khan and Bruce Graham of SOM. It is an example of a 'trussed tube' structural system

Source: Philip Oldfield

Embodied carbon and tall building sustainability[4]

Like all buildings, tall buildings utilise energy and generate greenhouse gas (GHG) emissions not only during their operations but across their entire lifecycle, from the extraction of the raw materials needed for construction to the disposal and recycling of materials after demolition. This complete boundary, encompassing all the activities related to a building's creation, use and removal, is known as *cradle-to-grave* (Figure 7.8). The embodied energy/carbon of a building comprises the energy/carbon required to extract, transport and refine the raw materials (e.g. mining iron ore), manufacture the building components (e.g. creating steel beams) and construct, renovate and maintain the building[5] (Fay *et al.*, 2000). The total embodied carbon of a building can be considered the sum of its *initial embodied carbon* and its *recurring embodied carbon*. The former is the carbon emitted in initially creating the building, whilst the latter is the carbon emitted from maintaining, repairing and refurbishing the building over its effective life (Chen *et al.*, 2001).

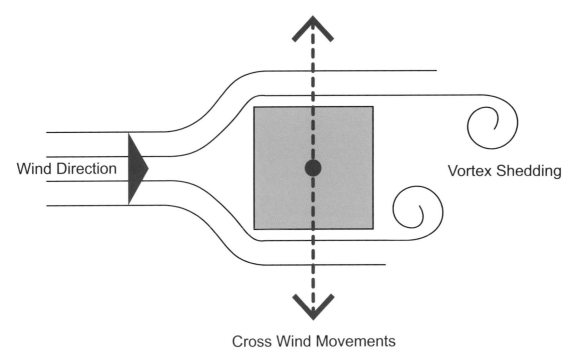

Wind Direction

Vortex Shedding

Cross Wind Movements

Figure 7.5 Plan of cross-wind motion in tall buildings
Source: Philip Oldfield

Figure 7.6 Taipei 101, view from Elephant Peak with details of the 'sawtooth' plan form visible at the corners
Source: Rob Young, CC BY 2.0, https://creativecommons.org/licenses/by/2.0/deed.en

Figure 7.7 Burj Khalifa, under construction in Dubai, 2008. Set-backs at different heights are designed to 'confuse the wind'
Source: Philip Oldfield

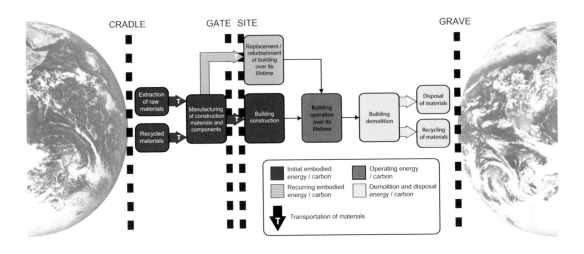

Figure 7.8   The environmental impact of a building over its entire lifecycle, from cradle-to-grave
Source: Oldfield, 2012

The extraction, processing and transportation of construction materials depletes natural resources, pollutes water and the air, requires large quantities of energy and releases CO_2 and other GHGs into the environment. The global production of concrete, for example, increased from 40 million cubic metres in 1900 to 6.4 billion cubic metres in 1997, making it the most widely used construction material in the world, with only fresh water utilised in larger quantities (Aïtcin, 2000). The cement industry alone is responsible for around 8% of all anthropogenic CO_2 emissions (Andrew, 2018), higher than the much-maligned aviation industry (around 3.5%) for just this one material.

Most sustainability thinking is informed by the idea that roughly 20% of a building's total environmental impacts are embodied in the materials, with the remaining 80% due to operations (Kestner, 2009), although research suggests this is becoming closer to 40% embodied and 60% operational for contemporary buildings (Sturgis & Roberts, 2010). There is a growing acknowledgement in both industry and academia that reducing embodied carbon emissions should form an integral part of strategies to improve the environmental performance of the built environment. The UK, for example, has set a legally binding target of reducing total GHG emissions by 80% by 2050, relative to 1990 levels. In the construction sector, such ambitious targets cannot be met by improving the operational

performance of buildings alone. Giesekam *et al.* (2014) suggest that reductions in the order of 80% can *only* be met by also substantially reducing the use of materials with carbon-intensive supply chains.

Understanding and reducing embodied carbon in tall buildings is particularly important given the aforementioned 'premium for height' – that is, that more materials are needed to resist lateral loads the taller we build. The upshot is that tall buildings typically have higher embodied energy and carbon emissions per unit area than low-rise buildings. A widely cited study by Treloar *et al.* (2001) examining initial embodied energy in five office buildings in Melbourne, Australia – 3, 7, 15, 42 and 52 storeys in height – shows the two high-rise buildings have approximately 60% more embodied energy per unit gross floor area than the two low-rise buildings due mainly to increases in structural materials (Figure 7.9). This has led some in the built environment to suggest that alternatives to tall buildings should be sought where possible. However, the author disputes this point of view and suggests that it presents a simplistic and at times inaccurate portrayal of the more complex issues surrounding embodied carbon and tall buildings. For example, changes to the functional unit[6] used to compare the embodied energy of high-rise and low-rise buildings can significantly influence the results. A study by Norman *et al.* (2006) compares the embodied carbon of detached suburban dwellings with

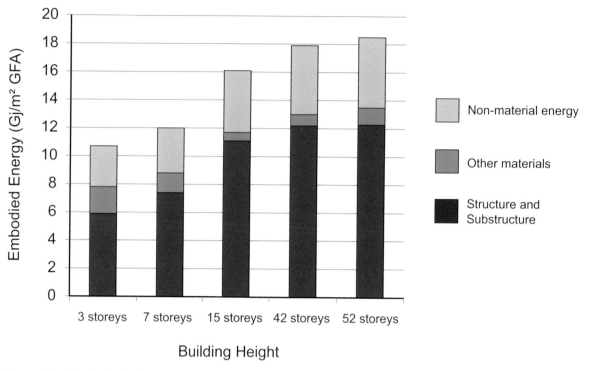

Figure 7.9   Initial embodied energy increasing with height in five buildings in Melbourne

Source: Treloar *et al.*, 2001

15-storey condominiums in Toronto, Canada. The find-ings, presented in Figure 7.10, show that when com-pared in terms of embodied carbon per square metre, the high-rise condominiums do indeed have greater carbon requirements, as we would expect. But when compared per person, the suburban dwellings' embodied carbon is around 1.5 times higher than the 15-storey building. This is due to the apartments accommodating more res-idents per unit floor area than the detached dwellings in this instance. When we consider material sustainability and embodied carbon then, it is not simply a case of low-rise being better or worse than high-rise buildings, and there are a variety of advantages and disadvantages to building tall. These are outlined in Table 7.1.

To quantify the importance of embodied carbon in tall buildings, a study by the author determined the total lifecycle carbon emissions of the '30 St Mary Axe' building in London (often referred to as the 'Swiss Re Tower' or 'Gherkin') (Figure 7.11). The scope of this analysis is cradle-to-end of life, encompassing all CO_2 emissions until the end of the building's effec-tive life, but excluding the demolition and disposal of materials. The analysis boundary includes all major

architectural elements, but excludes fit-out, furniture and the embodied carbon of local infrastructure and landscaping. The analysis is taken over a 50-year period from 2004, when the tower was completed, to 2054, and includes future estimations of the decreasing car-bon intensity of the UK's energy mix in this timeframe (for the full methodology, see Oldfield, 2012).

The results show the initial embodied carbon of 30 St Mary Axe is 61,548 tonnes of CO_2, or 955 $kgCO_2/m^2GFA$ (Figure 7.12). This is equivalent to 12.9 years of building operating emissions. Corresponding with previous research, the structural elements (structural frame, substructure and upper floors) make the largest contribution, being responsible for 56% of the build-ing's initial embodied carbon. The recurring embod-ied carbon is shown in Figure 7.13. The building has a recurring embodied carbon of 13,168 tonnes of CO_2, or 204 $kgCO_2/m^2GFA$, with recurring emissions contributing 17.6% of total embodied carbon. It can also be seen that while the structural elements are the greatest contributor to initial embodied carbon, build-ing services and finishes also have a significant envi-ronmental impact due to their regular refurbishment

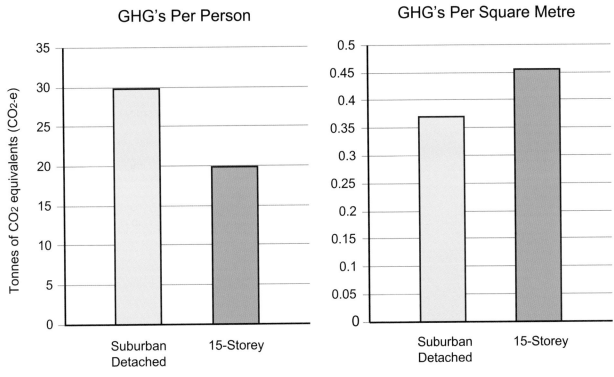

Figure 7.10 Embodied carbon comparison of suburban dwellings and 15-storey apartments, showing the impact of functional unit
Source: Norman *et al.*, 2006, with permission from ASCE

Tall buildings and embodied energy/carbon: *advantages*	Tall buildings and embodied energy/carbon: *disadvantages*
Residential high-rise typically accommodates more occupants per unit area than suburban housing, which can result in reduced embodied energy/carbon per person.	Increased height means increased structural material requirements to provide resistance to wind and lateral loads.
Increased density of cities can reduce infrastructure requirements, thus saving materials for road construction, water and waste supplies, etc.	Construction at height requires lifting materials often hundreds of metres into the sky (energy requirements for craning, pumping concrete, etc.).
Repetition of floor plates, façade and other elements allows for prefabrication, reuse of formwork, etc.	Tall building construction often requires specialist materials/components, which may not be available locally, contributing to transportation emissions.
Tall buildings are generally refurbished or renovated rather than demolished and replaced with entirely new construction.	Net-to-gross efficiencies are reduced as compared to low-rises (i.e. more materials needed for less usable space).
	Due to greater wind speeds at height, natural ventilation strategies often require additional materials such as double-skin façades.
	Timber structural systems, which contribute to far less embodied carbon emissions, are less common in high-rises, which typically rely on steel and concrete (although this is changing).

Table 7.1 Environmental advantages and disadvantages of tall buildings from an embodied energy/carbon perspective
Source: Oldfield, 2012

and maintenance. For the tall building designer then, strategies to reduce embodied carbon in these three areas (structure, services and finishes) would be hugely valuable to the environment.

The total lifecycle carbon emissions of the building over a 50-year lifespan stand at 224,596 tonnes of CO_2, or approximately 3.5 tonnes of CO_2 per metre gross floor area (Figure 7.14). To put this into perspective,

Figure 7.11 30 St Mary Axe, London
Source: Philip Oldfield

224,596 tonnes of CO_2 is equivalent to the annual emissions of 47,442 cars, or the carbon sequestered by almost 6 million tree seedlings grown over 10 years. The total embodied carbon (initial plus recurring) of the building stands at 74,716 tonnes of CO_2, or 1,159 $kgCO_2/m^2GFA$, which equates to 33% of the total lifecycle carbon emissions.

It's important to note that 30 St Mary Axe represents a 'typical' skyscraper of 180 metres in height. In supertall buildings (those over 300 metres in height) or megatall buildings (those over 600 metres in height), embodied carbon contributions are likely to be far more significant. For example, the next tallest building in the world is set to be the Jeddah Tower in Saudi Arabia. Although a final height has not been released to date, the tower is expected to be more than 1,000 metres tall, with some 167 storeys, upon completion in 2021. Given the aforementioned 'premium for height', this will require a vast quantity of materials, some 500,000 cubic metres of concrete and 80,000 tonnes of steel,

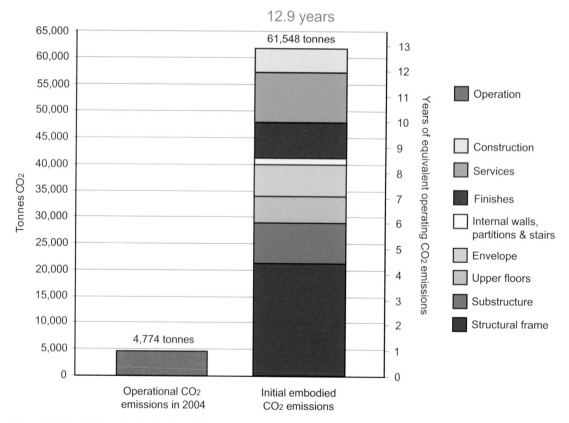

Figure 7.12 Initial embodied carbon of 30 St Mary Axe, in comparison with one year of operating emissions for 2004
Source: Oldfield, 2012

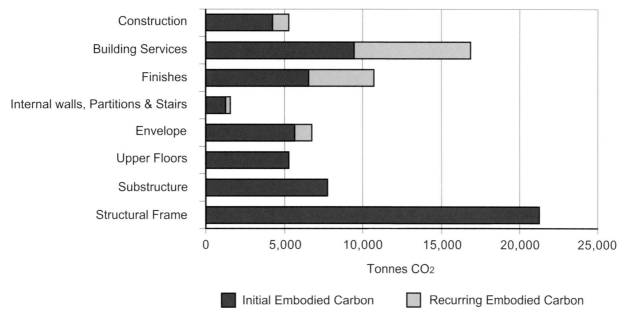

Figure 7.13   Recurring embodied carbon of 30 St Mary Axe
Source: Oldfield, 2012

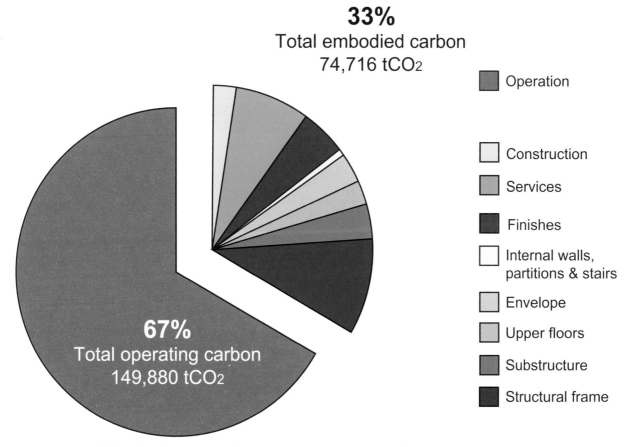

Figure 7.14   Total lifecycle carbon emissions of 30 St Mary Axe, cradle-to-end of life, 2004–2054
Source: Oldfield, 2012

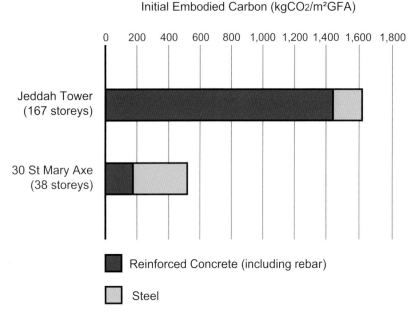

Initial Embodied Carbon (kgCO2/m²GFA)

Figure 7.15   Comparison of the initial embodied carbon (cradle-to-gate) of steel and reinforced concrete in the structural elements of the Jeddah Tower (1,000m+ tall) and 30 St Mary Axe (180m tall)
Source: Philip Oldfield

according to reports (Sophia, 2014). Such figures are no doubt approximations, but we can use these to conduct an estimate of the initial embodied carbon of the Jeddah Tower's structure. Using data from Hammond and Jones (2008), we can say that the aforementioned material quantities would contribute to initial embodied carbon emissions on the order of 393,700 tonnes of CO_2, or 1,614 $kgCO_2/m^2GFA$ for the structural materials alone, within a cradle-to-gate boundary.[7] This is 315% of the cradle-to-gate initial embodied carbon of the structural materials in 30 St Mary Axe, at a mere 512 $kgCO_2/m^2GFA$ (Figure 7.15). Thus, it is clear, in the world's tallest skyscrapers, embodied carbon is likely to be one of the most, if not *the most* significant contributor to carbon dioxide emissions – and thus, the area where greatest environmental savings can be made.

Strategies to reduce embodied carbon in tall buildings

For those involved in the design and construction of skyscrapers, a variety of strategies and technologies can contribute to significant reductions of embodied carbon. These can be categorised under the four R's of *Reduce, Recycle, Reuse* and *Replace*.

Reduce

An obvious opportunity to reduce embodied carbon in tall buildings is to use fewer materials; that is, to *dematerialise* their design and construction. Given the 'premium for height', the identification of an optimal structural system and combination of materials early in the design process is essential. Research by Trabucco *et al.* (2016) has showed that different structural systems and materials can have a significant impact on high-rise embodied carbon emissions. For a hypothetical 60-storey tower in Chicago, an all-concrete structure would use 18% more embodied carbon (around 5,000 tonnes of CO_2-e[8]) than a perimeter steel frame with a concrete core. In a 120-storey tower, a perimeter steel frame with a concrete core would use 18% more embodied carbon than a composite diagrid system (around 20,000 tonnes of CO_2-e). Different building designs, locations and material supply chains could change these results dramatically, meaning the design team, consultants and material suppliers need to optimise structural system and materials for each specific project (Trabucco *et al.*, 2016). Form and shape can be optimised, too. Modern design and analysis tools, along with developments in building materials and structural systems, have liberated the designer from the orthogonal, allowing tall buildings of seemingly impossible shapes and unusual forms to appear on skylines around the world. Although irregular forms may pose challenges to structural engineers in the development of the structural framework, they can assist in reducing wind loads and therefore material quantities (Oldfield & Wood, 2010; Ali & Moon, 2007). A prime example of this is the Shanghai Tower, designed by Gensler and completed in 2017. Its gently twisting form is iconic but also integral to its sustainable credentials (Figure 7.16). To refine the tower's form and reduce wind loads, Gensler, structural engineer Thornton Tomasetti, and wind engineers RWDI conducted a series of wind tunnel tests with different building forms and twists ranging from 60° to 210°. The optimal form was determined to be asymmetrical, with rounded corners and a 120° twist. This reduced wind loads on the building by 24%, thus reducing

Figure 7.16   Shanghai Tower, Shanghai. The building's asymmetrical twisting form reduces wind loads on the building, and thus required structural material quantities

Source: Philip Oldfield

structural materials by 32%, a saving of 20,000 tonnes of steel (Gu, 2014; Gensler, 2010).

It is worth pausing just to consider what a saving 20,000 tonnes of steel has on the economic and environmental performance of a building. When the Shanghai Tower started construction in 2009, average steel prices in China were on the order of USD $600/tonne. Thus, a 20,000-tonne saving would be equivalent to some $12 million – not including expenses for fabrication, transport and installation. Environmentally, the production of steel is a carbon-intensive process, with 2,148 kg of CO_2 emitted per tonne of steel manufactured in China[9] (Hasanbeigi *et al*., 2015). With 20,000 tonnes of steel omitted from the Shanghai Tower, this equates to a saving of 42,960 tCO_2 through structural optimisation. The building also has 270 vertical axis wind turbines located at its peak, which are expected to generate 150,000 kWh/year of zero-carbon electricity (Han & Fan, 2014). In China, 0.8 kgCO_2 is emitted per kWh of delivered electricity (Hasanbeigi *et al*., 2015), meaning these turbines will save 120 tCO_2/year. What all this means is that the process of structural optimisation undertaken in the wind tunnel well before the building made it to site will save the equivalent of 358 years of CO_2 as generated by the wind turbines. There are other benefits too; embodied carbon savings are immediate, and occur before construction even starts, thus reducing CO_2 emissions when we need to the most – right now, in the present. Carbon savings from on-site energy generation can take decades to accumulate, by which time irreversible climate change may have already occurred (Figure 7.17). This comparison is not to downplay the role that energy generation on-site from renewable resources can play because *all* technologies and design strategies to improve the sustainable performance of towers are valuable. Instead, it should highlight the significant and immediate carbon savings possible through the optimisation of tall building form and structure and the close cooperation of the design team early in the design process.

Technological advances can also contribute to structural dematerialisation. The dynamic response of a tall building to wind or seismic loads is governed by a number of factors, including shape, stiffness, mass and damping (Smith & Willford, 2007). If not adjusting the building shape and form, the most common method to reduce wind or seismic-induced building

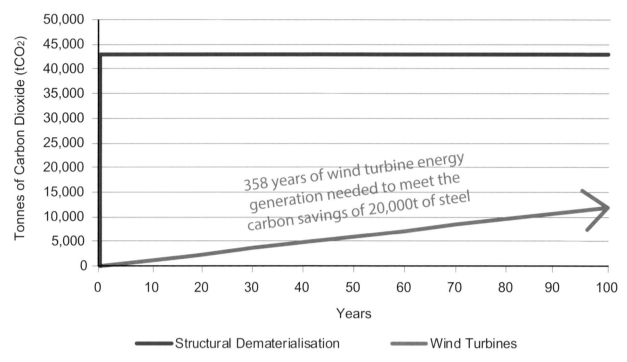

Figure 7.17 Cumulative carbon dioxide savings from the structural dematerialisation of the Shanghai Tower and energy generation from building integrated wind turbines over 100 years
Source: Philip Oldfield

motion is through increasing the stiffness of the structural system. This means adding significantly more material to the structure, meaning a heavier building with a larger foundation. This in turn can increase costs and embodied carbon and reduce lettable floor area. An alternative strategy is to integrate a tuned mass damper (TMD) or tuned liquid damper (TLD) into the top of the building, which can improve occupant comfort by transforming building motion into heat. A TMD typically involves a large mass on a pendulum that swings in response to building motion. The mass is fixed to shock absorbers that dissipate motion into heat. In the Taipei 101, a TMD is used to reduce building motion and ensure occupant comfort in high typhoon winds. This consists of a 726-tonne solid steel ball, suspended between level 88 and 92, and fixed to a series of shock absorbers (Figure 7.18) (Poon *et al.*, 2004). However, the problem with such damping systems is they are heavy, take up prime real estate at the top of the building and can be expensive. What's more, there is often no redundancy if the damper fails, meaning they are only used to reduce occupants' perception of motion, rather than reduc-

ing the building's structural requirements (Smith & Willford, 2007).

An alternative is to integrate multiple viscous dampers across the building structure. For example, Arup's Damped Outrigger concept uses viscous dampers positioned between columns and outriggers[10] to achieve a similar effect as a TMD (Figure 7.19). The difference is that such a system doesn't take up considerable space, and the use of multiple dampers provides inherent redundancy, meaning they can be used to reduce design lateral loads on the building, and therefore structural materials. In the twin 60-storey St Francis Towers in Manila (2009), 16 viscous dampers were used in each building (Figure 7.20). These substantially reduced lateral loads in the building structure, meaning it could be made lighter, reducing concrete quantities by 30%, cost by $5 million USD and increasing the net floor area by 2% (Willford *et al.*, 2008).

It is not just structural systems that can be dematerialised to benefit tall buildings; pursuing passive design strategies can reduce mechanical service provision, which typically has high embodied carbon intensities, due to the need for copper piping, aluminium

Figure 7.18 Taipei 101, tuned mass damper
Source: Armand du Plessis, CC BY 3.0, https://creativecommons.org/licenses/by/3.0/

ducts, etc. The Post Tower in Bonn (2002) incorporates a double-skin façade with internal atria to drive natural ventilation without the need for a central mechanical system (Figure 7.21). Although there is clearly an embodied carbon and financial cost to creating an additional layer of skin over 7,000 m² of building façade, there are also environmental and economic advantages. In the case of the Post Tower, incorporating natural ventilation allows for the elimination of all vertical air distribution shafts and the removal of an entire mechanical floor, saving carbon-intensive materials required for technical building equipment and 1,000 m² of rentable floor space (Jahn *et al.*, 2004).

Recycle

A further strategy to reduce embodied carbon in tall buildings is to use recycled, recyclable or waste materials in their construction. In particular, recycled metals (steel, aluminium, copper, etc.) and cement replacements in concrete, such as fly ash or blast furnace slag,[11] can have a significantly reduced embodied energy and carbon as compared to their virgin/non-recycled equivalents (Table 7.2).

To examine the impact of using recycled materials in tall buildings, an initial embodied carbon analysis is undertaken on the structural materials of 30 St Mary Axe within a cradle-to-site boundary. Three scenarios are considered: 'typical' recycled and waste content of materials in the UK, 'zero' recycled and waste content of materials, and 'maximum' recycled and waste content of materials, including cement replacement materials. Embodied carbon data for these materials is taken from Hammond and Jones (2008). The results, outlined in Figure 7.22, show the dramatic reductions in embodied carbon that recycled and waste materials can generate.

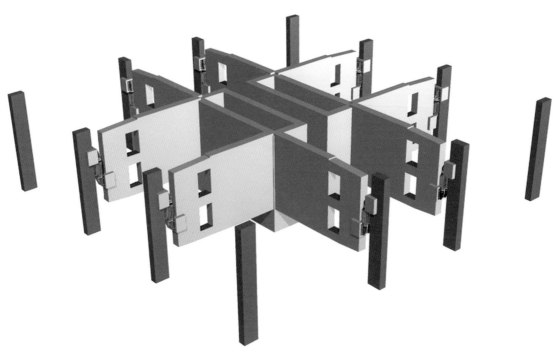

Figure 7.19 St Francis Towers, Manila, isometric of Arup's Damped Outrigger system, with viscous dampers positioned between columns and outriggers
Source: Arup

Figure 7.20 St Francis Towers, installed viscous dampers
Source: Arup

However, while it may be theoretically possible to construct a tower out of 100% recycled steel, in practice there are notable challenges. Firstly, different types of steel typically have different quantities of recycled content. Rebar is often 100% recycled, whereas steel sheet usually comes from primary sources with no recycled content. Even if a skyscraper design somehow specified 100% recycled steel, this approach would be to the detriment of others who also wished to use recycled materials. If a single consumer purchases all of the recycled steel in the marketplace, then remaining consumers are forced to purchase virgin steel at an increased carbon cost (Hammond & Jones, 2011).

There are also alternative methodologies for crediting the value of recycled materials in embodied carbon calculations. The prior analysis (Figure 7.22) uses what's known as a *recycled content method*, where the recycled content of steel, as a percentage, is recognised in the embodied carbon calculation. However, the metals industry suggests this approach is unfair, as it fails to recognise that most metals are recycled at the end of a building's effective life. Instead, they promote a *recyclability method*, which credits the future recyclability of a material. Let's

Figure 7.21   Deutsche Post Tower, Bonn, looking up at the double-skin façade
Source: H005, CC BY-SA 3.0, https://creativecommons.org/licenses/by-sa/3.0/deed.en

Material	Virgin material embodied carbon (kgCO$_2$-e/kg)	Recycled material embodied carbon (kgCO$_2$-e/kg)	Typical recycled content embodied carbon (kgCO$_2$-e/kg)	Estimated recycled content in UK materials (%)
Aluminium	12.79	1.81	9.16	33%
Copper	3.81	0.84	2.71	37%
Steel	2.89	0.47	1.46	59%

Table 7.2   Embodied carbon (cradle-to-gate) of virgin and recycled metals
Source: Data from Hammond & Jones, 2011

imagine a steel frame tower where 40% of the steel used has been recycled. Using the recycled content method, 40% of the steel would be calculated as recycled, with 60% considered as virgin. In the recyclability method, it could be argued that 95% of the steel in the building would be recovered and recycled at the end of the building's life, and therefore 95% of the steel would be credited as recycled. Using the recyclability method can generate results that show

significant embodied carbon and energy benefits to using steel in tall buildings, and for using metals in buildings in general (Trabucco *et al.*, 2016; Kilaire & Oldfield, 2010). However, the problem with using the recyclability of a material is that we are relying on multiple assumptions about the state of the construction industry many years into the future. Who really knows what the market for recycled steel will look like in a hundred years' time or more?

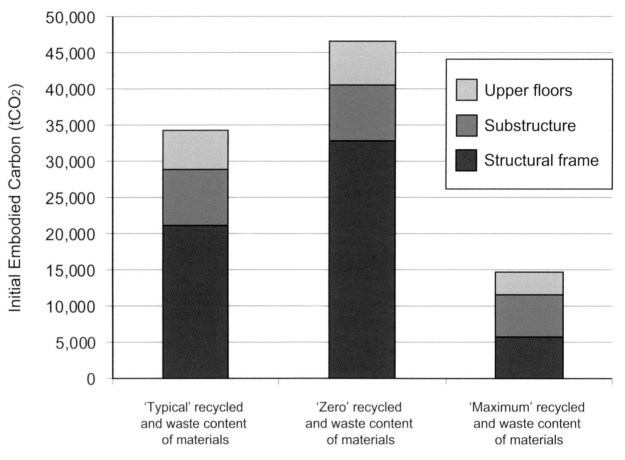

Figure 7.22   Initial embodied carbon of the primary structural elements in 30 St Mary Axe, with different recycled and waste content of materials applied
Source: Philip Oldfield

Reuse

The upgrading and retrofitting of existing structures can also be used to reduce embodied carbon emissions over a tall building's lifetime. Whereas building elements such as the façade, services, finishes, etc. need replacement, a tall building's structure can effectively last for hundreds of years, allowing for a building to be upgraded or improved, without the need for total demolition and replacement at a greater environmental cost.

This strategy is used across all typologies, but tall buildings do have an inherent advantage in this case. Whereas low-rise buildings are regularly pulled down and replaced, tall buildings are rarely demolished due to their iconic stature in cities and the high investment that goes into every project – both financially

and professionally. Looking at the figures, as of the end of 2017 there had been 4,303 tall buildings over 150 metres built and completed globally. However, in the entire history of the typology, only seven buildings over 150 metres have ever been demolished. Figures above 100m are less accurate, but data suggests 9,711 have been completed and only 58 have ever been demolished.[12] Perhaps this is unsurprising, given that many of these towers are relatively modern. However, even if we look at the number of tall buildings which are over 50 years old, only 1.55% of those over 150 metres and 4.63% of those over 100 metres have ever been demolished (Table 7.3). So, while the construction of a tall building may be a significant embodied carbon investment in the first instance, their long lifecycles provide an infrastructural legacy, which can be considered beneficial in terms of embodied carbon.

How can we maximise the environmental benefit of this long lifecycle? Firstly, when designing a tall building we need to recognise that it may well last hundreds of years and plan for ease of adaptation and retrofit in the future. That is, we need to recognise that a tall building is not an object, but a process; one which will likely be adapted programmatically, spatially and technologically across many decades. It is difficult to predict just what technologies and materials will develop in the future, and what retrofits might occur, but opportunities are available. For example, Patterson *et al.* (2012) suggest a modern tall building will likely see three or four façade retrofits during its lifetime. They lament current curtain wall systems as giving little regard to how innovative new glazing systems might be installed in a future retrofit since glass is often structurally glued to framing members, requiring a replacement of the whole façade. Instead, they promote prefabricated cassette-type façade systems that eliminate the need to glue glass panels to the primary frame. We can also plan for future programmatic changes. The conversion of some of our high-rise stock from office space to residential accommodation is likely in the future, as populations swell and technology liberates the 'office' as the predominant place of work. Since office floor plates are generally column free with high ceilings, such conversations are relatively practical. However, deep office floor plates would convert to potentially deep and dark residential units, meaning shallower plans have greater flexibility.

We can also be more radical in what we choose to reuse in new tall building construction. There is perhaps no better example of this than the Quay Quarter Tower in Sydney, by 3XN architects. The design con-

sists of a twisting tower of stacked blocks, organised to orientate office spaces towards the best views at Sydney's Circular Quay at different heights. The result is a series of vertical villages, each with multi-storey atria within, allowing light to penetrate the floorplate, but also fostering visual and physical connections between levels. Although this is dramatic, even more revolutionary is that the project will retain and upcycle two-thirds of the structure of the existing AMP Tower, built on the site in 1976 (Figures 7.23 and 7.24). This includes retaining the existing concrete core, beams, perimeter columns and slabs, but extending the core and floorplate to the north, and then wrapping the whole structure in a new high-performance façade (Cardno, 2015) (Figure 7.25). In this way the design adds 45,000 m² of additional floor space to the city, but also upcycles thousands of tonnes of concrete, reducing embodied carbon and construction waste. In doing so it breathes a new lease of life into a structure which is only 40 years old, but will now last for decades more.

Finally, the long lifecycles of tall buildings should be a warning to the design team that if we get it wrong, if we create poorly performing skyscrapers with high energy requirements today, we will likely be stuck with them for many decades to come (unless we undertake major refurbishments, at an economic and logistical cost). The towers we build today will likely still be standing and functioning well into the architect's great-great-great-grandchildren's lives. During this time, climate change will see temperatures rise and our cooling demands increase, social changes and increased urbanisation, and technological developments we can hardy predict. The need for the next generation of tall buildings to be able to adapt to these future changes is vital.

	Number of buildings completed	Number of buildings demolished	Percentage of buildings demolished
Total buildings 150m or taller (built between 1885 and 2017)	4,303	7	0.16%
Total buildings 100m or taller (built between 1885 and 2017)	9,711	58	0.60%
Total buildings 150m or taller, at least 50 years old (built between 1885 and 1967)	129	2	1.55%
Total buildings 100m or taller, at least 50 years old (built between 1885 and 1967)	561	26	4.63%

Table 7.3   Total number of tall buildings built and demolished as of December 2017

Source: Data from Skyscrapercenter, 2018

Figure 7.23 The existing AMP Tower (rear), Sydney, built in 1976

Source: Hpeterswald, CC BY-SA 3.0, https://creativecommons.org/licenses/by-sa/3.0/deed.en

Figure 7.24 Quay Quarter Tower, Sydney, which upcycles two-thirds of the AMP Tower structure

Source: Courtesy of 3XN

Replace

Another strategy to reduce embodied carbon is to replace carbon-intensive materials with low-carbon alternatives. Although towers can hardly use traditional materials such as rammed earth or straw-bale, there is another opportunity. This involves the reinvention of one of our oldest building materials – timber. Fuelled by a growing awareness of the role embodied carbon plays in tall building sustainability, the use of timber in tall building design is gaining huge momentum, with projects built or proposed in the UK, Canada, USA, Scandinavia, Australia and more. However, these are a far stretch from the lightweight timber frames of the past. Instead, they rely on a concept known as 'mass

wood', which involves large-scale solid wood panels, engineered for strength and stability. Cross laminate timber (CLT), for example, is built up of several sheets of solid wood glued together at alternating 90-degree orientations for strength. Sheets can range upwards of 20 metres by 2.4 metres, and be 40cm thick (Green, 2012).

The use of timber as a structural material has two primary embodied carbon benefits over steel and concrete frames. Firstly, the processes needed to create structural timber through felling, sawing and manufacture typically use less energy than those needed to create steel sections or concrete. However, most significantly, timber acts as a carbon sink; during their lifetime, trees absorb CO_2 through photosynthesis, storing carbon

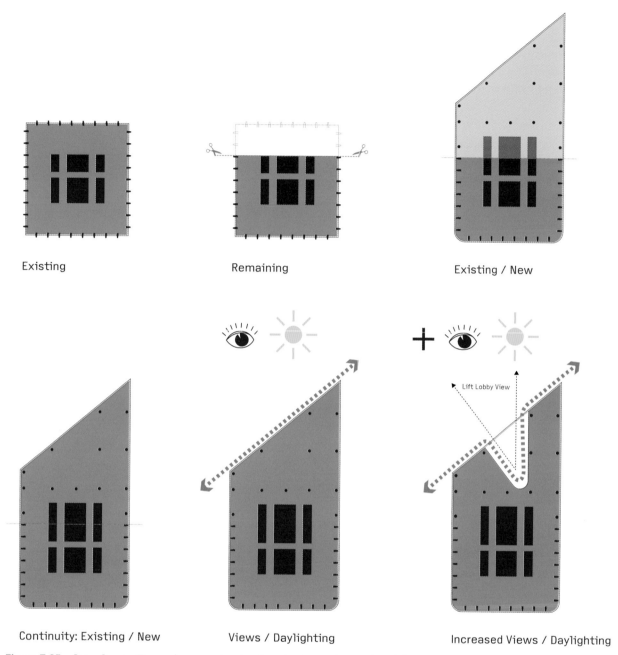

Existing	Remaining	Existing / New
Continuity: Existing / New	Views / Daylighting	Increased Views / Daylighting

Lift Lobby View

Figure 7.25   Quay Quarter Tower, diagrams showing the retention and extension of the existing AMP Tower
Source: Courtesy of 3XN

and releasing oxygen. This carbon storage is temporary; if at the end of the timber's life it decays or is burnt, the carbon will be released. However, if the original trees which were felled are replaced, these will offset this future carbon emission, rendering the process effectively carbon neutral (Skullestad *et al.*, 2016).

Research has demonstrated that these benefits can contribute to a significant reduction of embodied carbon in tall building structures. In one of the most comprehensive studies to date, Skullestad *et al.* (2016) compared the embodied carbon of a reinforced concrete frame and a mass timber structure for four different buildings – 3, 7, 12 and 21 storeys in height – using three different methodological approaches (to cater for the different mechanisms available to determine embodied carbon). Across all heights and methodologies, the timber structures had reduced embodied carbon emissions, in the range of 34% to 85% lower than reinforced concrete.

Taller towers are possible too, often using a hybrid system of timber with strategically integrated concrete and steel. Architects Skidmore Owings and Merrill studied an existing 42-storey tower with a reinforced concrete frame and compared it to an alternative structure made up of timber floors, columns and sheer walls with concrete beams and steel reinforcements. This alternative structure was made up of 70% timber and 30% concrete by volume. Overall, they found the hybrid timber structure had an embodied carbon 60–75% lower than the conventional concrete frame (Skidmore *et al.*, 2013). Just how high could a timber-hybrid structure reach? "This composite system has no theoretical height limit", suggests Benton Johnson of Skidmore, Owings and Merrill in an interview with the author. "In practice, the limiting

factor on height will be the economics of the project or municipal restrictions" (Oldfield, 2015). Research by the University of Cambridge with PLP Architecture and Smith and Wallwork engineers has shown that a 300-metre-tall, 85-storey timber-structured skyscraper would be entirely feasible. Their design for the Oakwood Timber Tower in London consists of a central tower buttressed by slender corner towers with perimeter mega-trusses (Ramage *et al.*, 2017). Such a design would require solid engineered timber columns on the order of 2.5m by 2.5m in plan, far in advance of anything currently on the market. But, it demonstrates that timber construction could become the mainstream structural material for most tall buildings, transforming the typology's planning, aesthetic and carbon footprint (Figures 7.26–7.28).

The sky may be the limit, but the tallest mass timber building in the world, as of early 2018, is the 18-storey Brock Commons Tallwood House in Vancouver. Built

Figure 7.26   Oakwood Timber Tower, London, design for a 300-metre-tall skyscraper with a primary structure of timber
Source: PLP Architecture

Figure 7.27 Oakwood Timber Tower, axonometric showing timber mega-trusses

Source: PLP Architecture

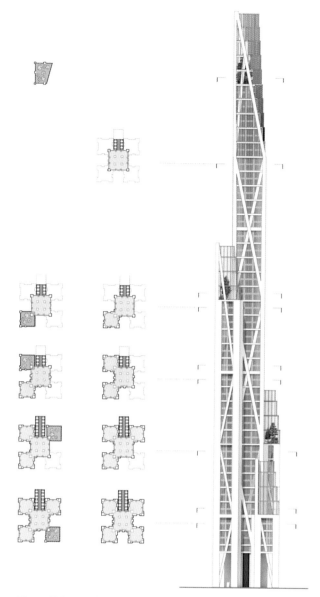

Figure 7.28 Oakwood Timber Tower, typical plans and elevation

Source: PLP Architecture

as student residences for the University of British Columbia and designed by Acton Ostry Architects, the project uses a hybrid structure of mass timber and concrete. A concrete foundation and ground floor sits below two concrete cores that rise to resist the tower's lateral loads. This works in tandem with two-way span CLT floor slabs (169 mm thick) and glulam columns (265 mm by 265 mm) with steel connection joints. Use of a two-way spanning CLT slab system eliminated the need for beams to support the edge of the CLT. Fast + Epp, the structural engineers for the project, believe

that this may be the first time that a two-way CLT slab system has been used on such a scale. The column grid is 4 by 2.85 metres, which while small, works well for a residential layout (Figures 7.29 and 7.30). The timber components are prefabricated, minimising waste through factory manufacture and increasing construction speeds (Figures 7.31, 7.32 and 7.33). Overall, the timber in the structure stores 1,753 metric tonnes of CO_2 and avoids the production of 679 metric tonnes of GHG emissions (Hill, 2018).

Figure 7.29 Brock Commons Tallwood House, Vancouver, typical timber column grid
Source: Seagate Structures. Photographer: Pollux Chung

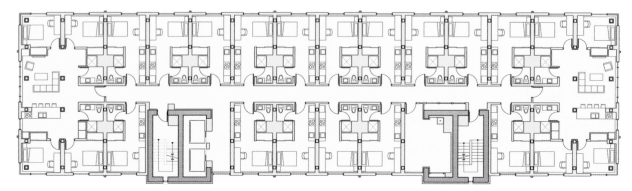

Figure 7.30 Brock Commons Tallwood House, typical plan
Source: Acton Ostry Architects Inc. and University of British Columbia

A widespread adoption of timber as a structural material in tall buildings could revolutionise the typology, providing significantly reduced embodied carbon with savings potentially far in advance of many other environmental design strategies. It is perhaps especially suited to residential towers up to 30 storeys, where long spans are unnecessary, and regular partitions allow for timber sheer walls or a dense column grid. However, there are a number of barriers to such widespread adoption. Firstly, a prerequisite for the car-

Figure 7.31   Brock Commons Tallwood House, construction from 6 June to 10 August 2016
Source: Seagate Structures. Photographer: Pollux Chung

Figure 7.32   Brock Commons Tallwood House, CLT panel installation
Source: Seagate Structures. Photographer: Pollux Chung

bon savings of timber is sustainable forestry, where any trees felled are replaced to maintain the global pool of stored carbon (Skullestad *et al.*, 2016). A rapid increase in timber construction in the tall building market would increase demand for sustainable timber products, which would need to be met by supply. Another challenge is perhaps obvious – fire. Timber is combustible, unlike conventional steel and concrete structures, which has led to questions about the safety of timber towers. Two mitigation strategies are available: *encapsulation* and *charring*.

The first, encapsulation, involves cladding timber structural components in fireproof materials, much like with steel structures (since steel loses much of its strength in low-temperature fire scenarios, it is also fire-protected). This is the strategy used in Brock Commons – the CLT and glulam components are clad in three to four layers of fire-rated gypsum board, while a sprinkler system provides active fire protection (Figure 7.34). The only problem with this strategy is that it hides the beauty of the timber from view. The warmth and natural qualities of the timber, characteristics often lacking in high-rise interiors, are encased

Figure 7.33 Brock Commons Tallwood House, prefabricated façade installation
Source: University of British Columbia

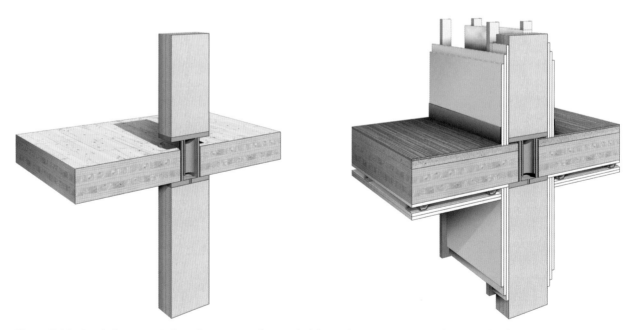

Figure 7.34 Brock Commons Tallwood House, CLT floor and glulam column connection before and after fire encapsulation
Source: Acton Ostry Architects Inc. and University of British Columbia

and entombed, never to be seen, touched or admired after construction.

An alternative method to overcome this problem is perhaps more controversial, using mass timber's inherent fire resistance. That is, to let it 'char'. "It's mother nature doing what she does best", says David Barber, a principal fire protection engineer at Arup, in an interview with the author. "In the aftermath of a forest fire you'll see trunks of trees that are black and charred. The timber inside the charcoal layer is still alive – after a fire you will see regeneration. This is the same physical property we utilise in timber towers" (Oldfield, 2015). In a fire scenario the exposed layers of a mass timber component will ignite and start to burn, forming an outer layer of char. This has a low conductivity, essentially creating a protective buffer zone to the inner layers of timber, which remain only slightly affected by increased heat, causing moisture loss, but not impacting structural capabilities. The charring method requires the inclusion of 'sacrificial' layers of timber in addition to the minimum structural requirements of the component, essentially thickening the structure. These outer layers would burn in a fire scenario but protect the structural layers inside (Green, 2012).

Conclusion

In conclusion, we can point to three main opportunities available to those involved in the creation of sustainable tall buildings:

1 Both the professional and research community should give more attention to the reduction of embodied carbon in tall buildings. Although significant effort has gone into minimising the environmental impact of high-rises, much of this has focussed on their operational energy; i.e. the energy that is consumed in heating, cooling, illuminating and running equipment and appliances in buildings. Too little has focussed on reducing embodied carbon. We can be sure that modern energy-efficient tall buildings will have a greater embodied carbon than conventional skyscrapers due to increased material requirements (additional insulation, photovoltaics, double-skin façades, etc.). As such, both the carbon benefits of design

decisions and carbon costs need to be considered within a full cradle-to-grave framework, including both operational and embodied carbon emissions. This is known as lifecycle analysis (LCA) and is an increasingly common procedure in new building design. In tall buildings LCA can be challenging given the wide variety of materials and specialised components needed for construction. However, the development of BIM integrated software and standardised methodologies[13] are making the process easier and more commonplace. Embracing LCA in future tall building design is essential to fully understand and reduce towers' total carbon impact.

2 In tall buildings, efficiency can be considered inherently sustainable, or to coin a famous line from Mies van der Rohe, "less is more". When we are able to use fewer materials in high-rise construction, we often see a triple benefit of reduced embodied carbon, reduced cost and greater available floor area for rent. This is a common theme throughout this book, but it is particularly evident in structural design. However, this should not be seen as a call to 'strip back' tall buildings to their bare essentials and to foster the repetitive efficient floorplate that has created hundreds of banal towers internationally. High-rise design should still provide urban drama, fantastic spaces and places to live, work and play. These factors cannot be measured in carbon and should not be sacrificed for a carbon saving.

3 Structural innovation in tall building design can contribute to significant reductions in lifecycle carbon emissions. Examples include the estimated 42,960 tCO_2 reduction through the optimisation of the Shanghai Tower's twisting form and the 679 tCO_2-e savings through the use of structural timber in Brock Commons Tallwood House.[14] Such strategies perhaps don't provide the visual green statement that technologies such as building integrated wind turbines or photovoltaics do, despite the fact that embodied carbon savings can be equivalent to many years of on-site energy generation. Therefore, we should aim to better disseminate and celebrate the sustainable achievements of structural design and optimisation as a vital component in high-performance tall buildings.

Notes

1 Some debate surrounds these credentials. Condit (1964) describes how in the Home Insurance Building not all the structural loads were carried by the steel frame, with a portion being carried by brick party walls. Given this, he suggests the Home Insurance Building is best considered a 'proto-skyscraper', arguing the first *mature skyscraper* in structure, utility and form was Louis Sullivan's Guaranty Building in Buffalo, completed a year later in 1896.

2 The Monadnock Building is supported by what is arguably a hybrid load-bearing wall and metal frame structural system. This consists of an interior grid of iron columns and girders supplementing a perimeter brick load-bearing wall (see Leslie, 2013).

3 For an excellent overview of different contemporary structural systems and their practical height limits, see Sarkisan (2011).

4 Some of this research was originally published as Oldfield, P. (2012). *Embodied Carbon and High-Rise*. Proceedings of the CTBUH 2012 Conference, Shanghai, pp. 614–622. It has been revised and updated for publication in this book.

5 It is worth noting that some definitions of embodied energy/carbon include the impacts associated with the building's demolition and disposal. However, within the scope of this book, demolition and disposal impacts are categorised separately. This approach is consistent with the majority of published embodied energy/carbon studies and definitions.

6 The purpose of a 'functional unit' within a lifecycle or embodied energy/carbon analysis is to present a reference to which the inputs and outputs can be related (ISO, 1997). This allows for two, or more, completely different products, services or buildings to be compared on equal footing.

7 This assumes the 80,000 tonnes of steel is split as 55,000 tonnes of rebar and 25,000 tonnes of structural steel. Embodied carbon data is considered as: steel = 1.77 $kgCO_2$/kg and reinforced concrete including rebar = 0.291 $kgCO_2$/kg (Hammond & Jones, 2008). The gross floor area of the building is 243,866 m² (Skyscrapercenter, 2018).

8 CO_2-e refers to carbon dioxide equivalent. This metric includes other greenhouse gases in addition to carbon dioxide, such as methane, nitrous oxide and chlorofluorocarbons. These are normalised to equivalent quantities of CO_2 based on the impact they have on global warming over a given timeframe (known as Global Warming Potential, or GWP).

9 Steel in China has a particularly high embodied carbon given that only a small percentage (9.8%) of the national steel production is manufactured using electric arc furnaces, which have a lower CO_2 intensity than steel created in blast furnaces/basic oxygen furnaces. Mexico, by contrast, generates 69.4% of its steel using electric arc furnaces, meaning the embodied carbon of its steel is half that of Chinese steel (Hasanbeigi *et al.*, 2015). Given the vast number of towers being built in China, structural optimisation and reduction of steel quantities in the region can have a significant and dramatic benefit to the environment.

10 Outriggers are large-scale trusses used to tie the building core to perimeter columns in order to holistically resist lateral loads. They are common in buildings over 200 metres in height.

11 Fly ash and blast furnace slag are by-products of the coal combustion and the steel-making process, respectively. They can be used as cement replacement materials, thus reducing the embodied carbon of concrete.

12 Data from Skyscrapercenter, 2018. The demolished figures do not include One, Two and Seven World Trade Center, New York, which are considered 'destroyed' rather than 'demolished'.

13 For example, in Europe the standard EN 15978 '*Sustainability of Construction Works – Assessment of Environmental Performance of Buildings – Calculation Method*' provides standardised guidance on calculating and reporting LCA results in buildings.

14 Although these may seem to be very different values, once normalised per unit floor area, they are relatively similar. The 42,960 tCO_2 saving in the Shanghai Tower over 420,000 m² equates to 102 $kgCO_2$/m²GFA. The 679 tCO_2-e saving in Brock Commons Tallwood House over 15,120 m² equates to 45 $kgCO_2$-e/m²GFA, or 161 $kgCO_2$-e/m²GFA if we include the 1,733 tonnes of carbon stored in the timber itself.

References

Aïtcin, P. (2000). Review: Cements of Yesterday and Today, Concrete of Tomorrow. *Cement and Concrete Research*, Vol. 30, pp. 1349–1359.

Ali, M. M. & Moon, K. S. (2007). Structural Developments in Tall Buildings: Current Trends and Future Prospects. In: *Architectural Science Review*, Vol. 50, No. 3, Taylor & Francis Ltd, Sydney, pp. 205–223.

Andrew, R. M. (2018). Global CO_2 Emissions from Cement Production. *Earth System Science Data*, 10, pp.195 – 217.

Baker, W., Korista, S. & Novak, L. (2008). *Engineering the World's Tallest: Burj Dubai*. Proceedings of the CTBUH 8th World Congress, "Tall & Green: Typology for a Sustainable Urban Future", Dubai, 3–5 March, pp. 43–52.

Cardno, C. (2015). Sydney Quay Quarter Upcycles Existing Tower. *Civil Engineering*, 15 December. www.asce.org/magazine/20151215-sydney-quay-quarter-upcycles-existing-tower/

Chen, T. Y., Burnett, J. & Chau, C. K. (2001). Analysis of Embodied Energy Use in the Residential Building of Hong Kong. *Energy*, Vol. 26, pp. 323–340.

Condit, C. W. (1964). *The Chicago School of Architecture*. University of Chicago Press, Chicago.

Fay, R., Treloar, G. & Iyer-Raniga, U. (2000). Life-Cycle Energy Analysis of Buildings: A Case Study. *Building Research and Information*, Vol. 28, No. 1, pp. 31–41.

Gensler. (2010). *Design Update: Shanghai Tower*. http://du.gensler.com/vol6/shanghai-tower/

Giesekam, J., Barrett, J., Taylor, P. & Owen, A. (2014). The Greenhouse Gas Emissions and Mitigation Options for Materials Used in UK construction. *Energy and Buildings*, Vol. 78, pp. 202–214.

Green, M. C. (2012). *The Case for Tall Wood Buildings: How Mass Timber Offers a Safe, Economical, and Environmentally Friendly Alternative for Tall Building Structures*. Michael Green Architecture, Vancouver.

Gu, J. P. (2014). *Shanghai Tower: Building a Green Vertical City in the Heart of Shanghai*. Proceedings of the CTBUH 2014 Conference, Shanghai, pp. 136–141.

Hammond, G. P. & Jones, C. I. (2008). *Inventory of Carbon and Energy (ICE)*, Version 1.6a. University of Bath, Bath.

Hammond, G. P. & Jones, C. I. (2011). *Inventory of Carbon and Energy (ICE)*, Version 2.0. University of Bath, Bath.

Han, J. & Fan, H. (2014). Making the World's Greenest Tall Building. In: *Shanghai Tower: In Detail*, CTBUH, Chicago, pp. 22–29.

Hasanbeigi, A., Cardenas, J. C. R., Price, L., Triolio, R. & Arens, M. (2015). *Comparison of Energy-Related Carbon Dioxide Emissions Intensity of the International Iron and Steel Industry: Case Studies from China, Germany, Mexico, and the United States*. Lawrence Berkeley National Laboratory, December, 2012.

Hill, J. (2018). Building Tall in Timber. *World Architects*, 5 January. www.world-architects.com/en/architecture-news/products/building-tall-in-timber

Irwin, P., Kilpatrick, J. & Frisque, A. (2008). *Friend or Foe, Wind at Height*. Proceedings of the CTBUH 8th World Congress, "Tall & Green: Typology for a Sustainable Urban Future", Dubai, 3–5 March, pp. 336–342.

ISO. (1997). *Environmental Management – Life Cycle Assessment – Principles and Framework*. ISO 14040, ISO, Geneva.

Jahn, H., Sobek, W. & Schuler, M. (2004). *Post Tower*. Birkhäuser, Basel.

Kestner, D. (2009). Sustainability: Thinking Beyond the Checklist. *Structure Magazine*, June, p. 5.

Kilaire, A. & Oldfield, P. (2010). Aluminium and Double Skin Facades. In: Katgerman, L. & Soetens, F. (eds.) *Proceedings of the 11th International Aluminium Conference "INALCO": "New Frontiers in Light Metals"*, 23–25 June, Einhoven University of Technology, Holland, IOS Press, Amsterdam, pp. 177–188.

Le Barron Jenney, W. (1891). The Chicago Construction, or Tall Buildings on a Compressed Soil. *Inland Architect and News Record*, November, Vol. 18, p. 41.

Leslie, T. (2013). The Monadnock Building, Technically Reconsidered. *CTBUH Journal*, No. IV, pp. 26–31.

Norman, J., Maclean, H. L. & Kennedy, C. A. (2006). Comparing High and Low Residential Density: Life-Cycle Analysis of Energy Use and Greenhouse Gas Emissions. *Journal of Urban Planning and Development*, March, pp. 10–21.

Oldfield, P. (2012). *Embodied Carbon and High-Rise*. Proceedings of the CTBUH 2012 Conference, Shanghai, pp. 614–622.

Oldfield, P. (2015). Tree Houses: Are Wooden Skyscrapers the Future of Tall Buildings? *The Guardian*, Tuesday 7 July. www.theguardian.com/artanddesign/2015/jul/07/tree-houses-are-wooden-skyscrapers-the-future-of-tall-buildings

Oldfield, P. & Wood, A. (2010). From the Orthogonal to the Irregular: The Role of Innovation in Form of High-Rise Buildings. In: *Urbanism and Architecture*, October, No. 73, Heilongjiang Science and Technology Press, Ha'erbin, China, pp. 27–31.

Patterson, M., Martinez, A., Vaglio, J. & Noble, D. (2012). *New Skins for Skyscrapers: Anticipating Façade Retrofit*. Proceedings of the CTBUH 2012 Conference, Shanghai, pp. 209–215.

Poon, D., Shaw-Song, S., Joseph, L. & Ching-Chang, C. (2004). *Structural Design of Taipei 101, the World's Tallest Building*. Proceedings of the CTBUH 2004 Conference, Seoul, pp. 271–278.

Ramage, M., Foster, R., Smith, S., Flanagan, K. & Bakker, R. (2017). Super Tall Timber: Design Research for the Next Generation of Natural Structure. *The Journal of Architecture*, Vol. 22, No. 1, pp. 104–122.

Sarkisan, M. (2011). *Designing Tall Buildings: Structure as Architecture*. Routledge, New York.

Skidmore, Owings & Merrill. (2013). *Timber Tower Research Project*. Skidmore, Owings & Merrill, Chicago.

Skullestad, J. L., Bohne, R. A. & Lohne, J. (2016). High-Rise Timber Buildings as a Climate Change Mitigation Measure – A Comparative LCA of Structural System Alternatives. *Energy Proceedia*, Vol. 96, pp. 112–123.

Skyscrapercenter. (2018). *The Skyscraper Center – The Global Tall Building Database of the CTBUH*. www.skyscrapercenter.com/

Smith, R. J. & Willford, M. R. (2007). The Damped Outrigger Concept for Tall Buildings. *The Structural Design of Tall and Special Buildings*, Vol. 16, pp. 501–517.

Sophia, M. (2014). Saudi's Tallest Tower to Consume 80,000 Tonnes of Steel. *Gulf Business*, 17 February. http://gulfbusiness.com/saudis-tallest-tower-to-consume-80-000-tonnes-of-steel/

Sturgis, S. & Roberts, G. (2010). *RICS Research – Redefining Zero: Carbon Profiling as a Solution to Whole Life Carbon Emission Measurement in Buildings*. RICS, London.

Trabucco, D., Wood, A., Vassart, O. & Popa, N. (2016). A Whole Life Cycle of the Sustainable Aspects of the Structural Systems in Tall Buildings. *International Journal of High-Rise Buildings*, Vol. 5, No. 2, pp. 71–86.

Treloar, G. J., Fay, R., Llozor, B. & Love, P. E. D. (2001). An Analysis of the Embodied Energy of Office Buildings by Height. *Facilities*, Vol. 19, No. 5–6, pp. 204–214.

Willford, M., Smith, R., Scott, D. & Jackson, M. (2008). Viscous Dampers Come of Age: A New Method for Achieving Economy in Tall Buildings. *Structure Magazine*, June, pp. 15–18.

Willis, C. (1995). *Form follows Finance: Skyscrapers and Skylines in New York and Chicago*. Princeton Architectural Press, New York.

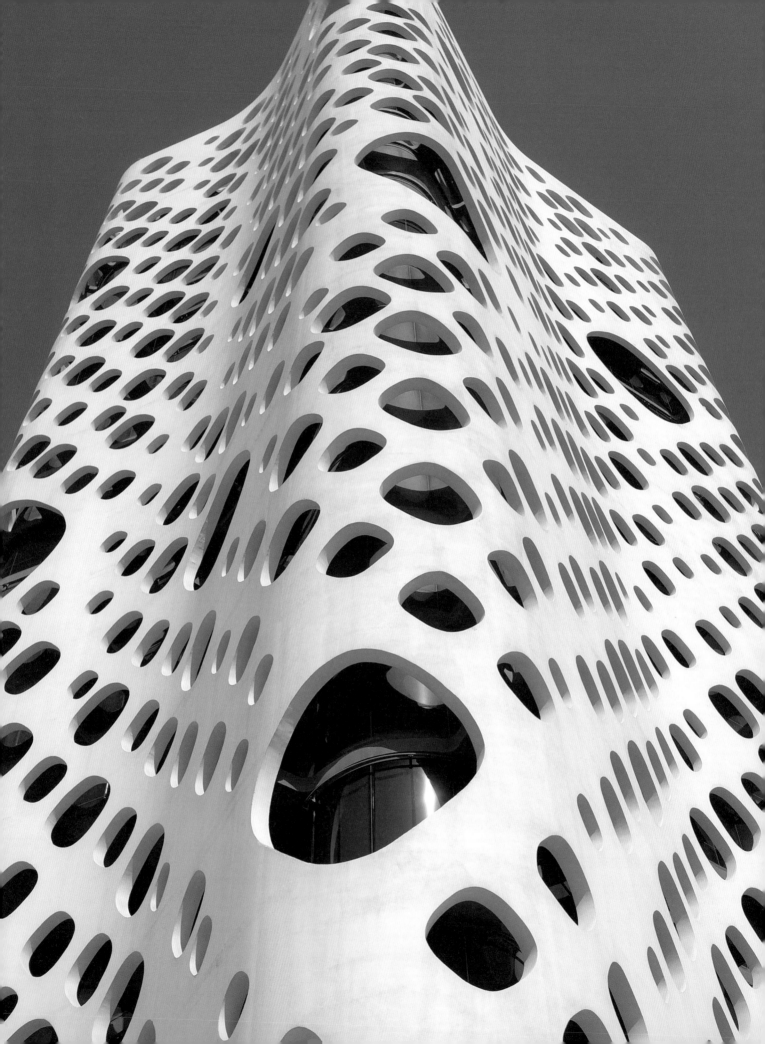

CHAPTER EIGHT

High-rise envelopes: beyond the glass wall

Introduction: from the Crystal Palace to the Shard

The first all-glass buildings were not designed for people, but instead for plants. In the early nineteenth century, horticulturalists such as Joseph Paxton used the shelter and heat-capturing properties of glasshouses to cultivate tropical plants in the otherwise temperate climates of Northern Europe (Schoenefeldt, 2008). Paxton, however, wanted to go further and use these properties to create buildings suitable for human habitat. His vision was to counter the dark, unhealthy industrial cities emerging and create civic buildings flooded with daylight, using glasshouses to create comfortable indoor temperatures at all times of the year. His ideas included removing glass partitions from glasshouses in the summer to foster natural ventilation and free cooling, while in the winter he envisioned the trapping of solar heat gain would create temperatures in the UK analogous to that of Southern Italy (Paxton, 1851).

These visions were brought to life in the first all-glass building for humans, the Crystal Palace, in 1851. Home of the Great Exhibition, the Crystal Palace was a vast prefabricated structure of iron frame, timber and plate glass (Figure 8.1). Paxman was well aware of the environmental opportunities and challenges such a large glazed building would face and incorporated a variety of mechanical and passive systems within the design. These included large textile sheets hung across the roof as a shading system, while rows of louvres could be manually operated to provide natural ventilation and cooling. Despite this, unsurprisingly, with tens of thousands of visitors daily in the summer months, the Crystal Palace often overheated. Interior air temperatures as high as 36°C were recorded (when it was 28°C in the shade outside) while newspapers at the time regularly reported on the sweltering conditions suffered by its many visitors (Schoenefeldt, 2008).

After the Great Exhibition it was decided to relocate the Crystal Palace, and proposals were sought for the redesign of the building.[1] One of the most startling ideas came from architect Charles Burton, who proposed reusing its prefabricated components to create a 300-metre-tall skyscraper in London (Figure 8.2). Burton suggested that from the upper levels of such a tower, it would be possible to view the country "for a hundred miles around London . . . without the risk of a balloon descent" (Jenkins, 1957, p. 25). This was the world's first-ever vision of an all-glass tower, over 30 years before the first completed 'skyscraper', the Home Insurance Building in Chicago in 1885, and some 70 years before the famous Mies van der Rohe drawings of glazed towers in early 1920s Berlin.[2] However, it was exactly a full century before a fully

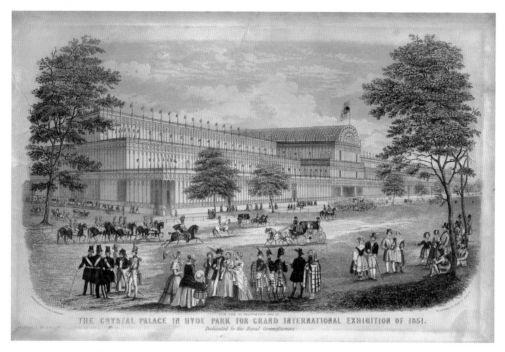

Figure 8.1   View from the Knightsbridge Road of the Crystal Palace in Hyde Park for the Grand International Exhibition of 1851
Source: Dedicated to the Royal Commissioners. London: Read & Co. Engravers & Printers, 1851

Figures 8.2   Design for the conversion of the Crystal Palace exhibition building into a supertall all-glass tower, by architect Charles Burton, 1852
Source: © Look and Learn/Peter Jackson Collection

Figure 8.3   The Shard, London, the realisation of London's first supertall all-glass tower in 2012
Source: Philip Oldfield

glazed high-rise was actually built. After World War II, technological innovations allowed the glazed curtain-wall façade to reach commercial maturity, with Mies van der Rohe's Lake Shore Drive Apartments in Chicago (1951), the first towers to truly adopt such a system (Oldfield *et al.*, 2009). By this time, widespread availability of mechanical conditioning allowed buildings to easily overcome the exterior climate and overheating challenges that Paxton faced with the Crystal Palace, ushering in the proliferation of the glazed air-conditioned skyscraper as the most common approach in tall building design (see also Chapter 3).

Yet, it wasn't until 2012, some 160 years after Charles Burton's design for the Crystal Palace Tower, that his vision was realised in London. The completion of the Shard (designed by Renzo Piano Building Workshop) finally gave the city a supertall, fully glazed skyscraper (Figure 8.3). The vision may be similar to Burton's, but the façade technology is of course far advanced. The Shard uses a triple-glazed, open cavity façade; a single-glazed outer skin protects a 250mm cavity accommodating motorised roller blinds for shade. A double-glazed unit makes up the inner leaf of the façade, providing thermal insulation and a hermetically sealed layer (Spring, 2010).

Yet despite these advances in glazing technology, is the fully glazed approach the optimum design strategy for the sustainable tall building? Should we really be embracing Charles Burton's 160-year-old vision of maximum transparency in every orientation and in every climate we build? Knowing full well the environmental challenges faced by Joseph Paxton over a century ago, just what is the sustainable impact of the fully glazed skyscraper today?

The sustainability of the all-glass façade

For me, the day of the all-glass building is finished. . . . Large glass, as lovely as it may be, requires a tremendous consumption of energy for heating and air-conditioning to combat the extremes of temperature.

[Minoru Yamasaki, architect of New York's World Trade Center Towers, in a letter to the *New York Times* architecture critic Ada Louise Huxtable in 1973. From Buchanan, 2015]

As the primary mediator between interior and exterior environment, the façade has a huge impact on user satisfaction and energy performance. Its design and characteristics impact heat loss, solar gain, thermal comfort, daylight, glare and visual comfort, noise, ventilation and views – both in and out. A significant body of evidence suggests the highly glazed skyscraper, with maximised transparent curtain walling on all façades, regardless of climate or orientation, is detrimental in terms of its impact on both the environment and the occupants.

Fundamental to understanding the energy performance of the all-glass skyscraper is acknowledging that even the most advanced glazed systems commercially available have a thermal conductive performance far inferior to a basic insulated wall. For example, a modern double-glazed curtain wall will have a U-value of around 1.6 W/m²K, with a high-performance triple-glazed system closer to 0.85 W/m²K. In comparison, a standard insulated brick wall has a U-value of 0.25 W/m²K, six times lower than double-glazing and over three times lower than a triple-glazed system. With a super-insulated wall, the comparison is starker still (Table 8.1). Put simply, in cold climates, glass walls facilitate far more conductive heat loss, and in hot climates far more conductive heat gain, than opaque walls.

There are of course thermal advantages to glazing. In cold climates, carefully positioned and designed glazing can harness passive solar heat gain from the sun. Many sustainable buildings in cold Northern European climates orientate the majority of windows to the south to capture direct solar heat gain for free heating in winter months. Far less glazing is located on the northern façade, to minimise heat losses. However, in hotter climates which are dominated by interior cooling demands, direct solar gain through glass curtain walls is detrimental, contributing to thermal discomfort or higher energy demands for mechanical cooling. It's worth emphasising the impact the all-glass curtain wall will have on our future cooling requirements. Residential energy demand for heating is expected to grow gradually in the coming decades before levelling off around 2030. However, the energy demand for air-conditioning is expected to rise rapidly in the twenty-first century, driven predominantly by increasing income in hot developing countries

(Isaac & Vuuran, 2009) (Figure 8.4). Limiting this massive increase in cooling energy through passive design and low-carbon technologies is a vital facet of reducing GHG emissions during our lifetimes.

Tall buildings are increasingly being built in hot climates, often with highly glazed and unshaded façades. Whereas the 'all-glass' skyscraper can be environmentally problematic in temperate climates, causing unwanted heat loss in the winter and unwanted heat gain in the summer, in hot desert climates such designs are senseless due to the consistently high solar radiation such regions experience (Figure 8.5). The problem these towers will face is obvious, suffering from both unwanted direct solar heat gain from the sun and indirect conductive gains through the façade. Typically, these are offset with air-conditioning at a significant energy and carbon cost. While environmentally detrimental in the short-term, the long-term resiliency of these towers is also of concern. The period 2011–2015 has been the warmest on record (World Meterological Organization, 2015), with projections suggesting this trend will increase across the coming century. The result will likely be increasing heatwaves, both in frequency and intensity, and higher temperatures in the

Façade	U-value (W/m²K)	Benefit over double-glazed system
Double-glazed curtain wall with an air-cavity and e-coating	1.6	0
Triple-glazed system with an argon-filled cavity and e-coating	0.85	188%
Standard opaque wall construction (150mm insulation)	0.25	640%
Super-insulated opaque wall construction (300mm insulation)	0.15	1067%

Table 8.1   Thermal conductive performance of transparent and opaque façade elements
Source: Philip Oldfield

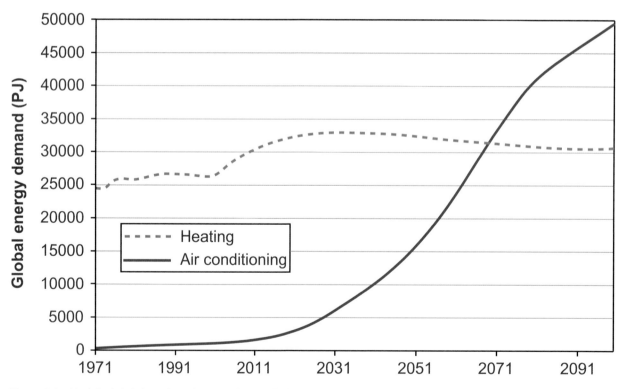

Figure 8.4   Modelled global residential energy demand for heating and air-conditioning to 2100
Source: Reprinted from Isaac & Vuuran, 2009, with permission from Elsevier

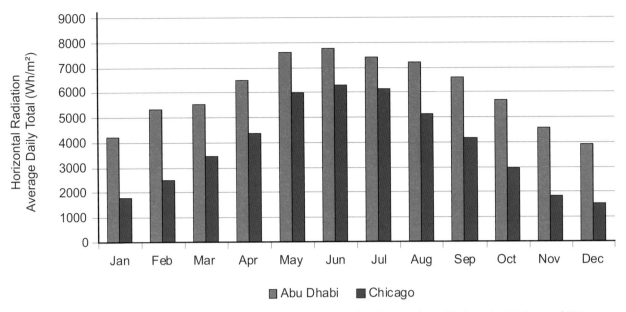

Figure 8.5   Comparison of horizontal radiation (average daily total) in the hot climate of Abu Dhabi and cold climate of Chicago
Source: Philip Oldfield, data from Climate Consultant, 2018

future. What will happen to the air-conditioning-reliant towers we are constructing today in an energy blackout, or power failure scenario, coinciding with a heatwave? The likelihood is they would very quickly become uninhabitable due to intense overheating. Such an increase in interior temperatures would carry a significant health and mortality threat to the occupants, since heatwaves can have deadly consequences. At temperatures above 25°C, there is an increase in mortality and strokes (BRE, 2016). The 2003 heatwave in Europe, for example, led to 14,947 deaths in France in two weeks alone (Poumadere *et al.*, 2005).

Glazing not only influences thermal performance but also daylighting and views. These are integral not only to energy demand but also to human health and well-being. Adequate daylight penetration can reduce the need for artificial lighting, but also plays an important role in occupant satisfaction and the circadian rhythm, impacting sleep quality. Access to a view provides a psychological link to the outside, about time, weather and place (Aries *et al.*, 2010). In high-rises, the quality of view is arguably all the more important, providing a degree of drama and 'wow factor' to any commercial development. Increasing the quantity of glazing in a tall building façade will increase daylight penetration and also offer more expansive views, but

'more' is not always 'better', as too much daylight can cause visual discomfort from glare. In addition, views also work in two directions; maximising views out, often maximises views in, which can have a negative impact on occupant privacy. In London, the extension of the Tate Modern Gallery saw the construction of a public viewing deck in close proximity to luxury high-rise apartments with floor-to-ceiling glazing. Many residents complained of being overlooked by the public, leading the Tate Director Sir Nicholas Serota to suggest residents should "get net curtains" (Brown & Ross, 2016). In fact, this is often comparable to what many occupants in fully glazed towers do. Research by the Urban Green Council (2013) studied 55 highly glazed buildings in New York, measuring and recording the fraction each window was covered by blinds, shades or curtains. They found 59% of all windows were covered, meaning the majority of glazed façades were providing neither benefits of daylight nor view. A viscious circle is created; high levels of inappropriately designed glazing can cause glare and a lack of privacy. Occupants respond by pulling the blinds down, or closing the curtains, but then having to compensate by turning artificial lighting on at a higher energy cost. Inconvenience sees the occupants leave the blinds down even in overcast conditions, meaning any benefit of transparency through daylighting or view is negated, but the envelope still has an inferior thermal performance as compared to an insulated wall (Figure 8.6).

In conclusion, we need to accept that in many tall building designs, in both hot and cold climates we are using too much glass from both an energy and human perspective. To support this, a study has been undertaken exploring the energy impact of different glazed façades in an office building in a hot climate (Miami) and cold climate (Chicago). A perimeter floor zone 6.1 by 6.1 metres in size, with a ceiling height of 2.8 metres has been modelled in COMFEN 5, a simulation tool developed by Lawrence Berkeley National Laboratory (2013) to support the systematic energy evaluation of alternative façade systems. For each climate a parametric study was undertaken, changing window-to-wall-

ratio (WWR), glazing characteristics and orientation. WWR refers to the quantity of glazing in a façade; a WWR of 40% means a façade is 40% glazed and 60% opaque. The results of the study are presented in Figure 8.7. We can see that the addition of glazing into a solid wall (WWR = 0%) coincides with a reduction in energy use, due to increased daylighting. However, as we increase the WWR further, the energy benefits of daylighting are lost to the reduced thermal performance of the façade. We can see the optimum WWR with the lowest energy demand in both Chicago and Miami is between 20% and 40% in virtually all orientations, even using high-performance triple-glazing with shading systems. This is significantly below the 50–80% common in modern tall buildings. The exception is the triple-glazed south façade in the Chicago

Figure 8.6 Blinds pulled down in an office tower, Singapore, in overcast conditions
Source: Philip Oldfield

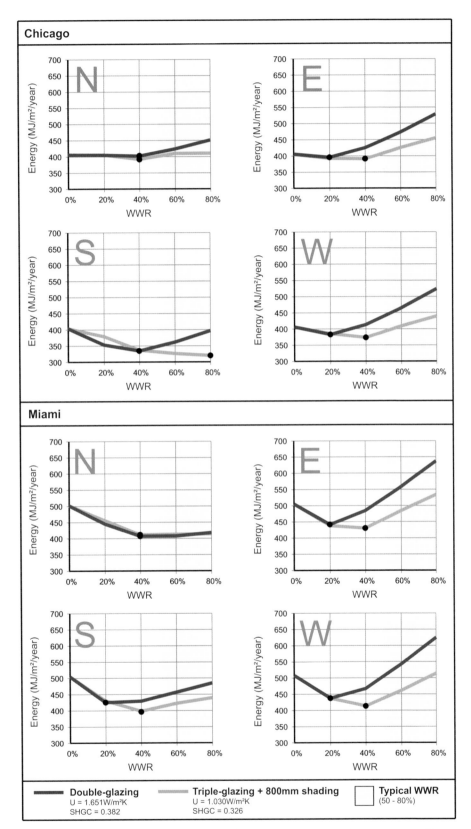

Figure 8.7   Energy requirements in different façade design scenarios for a perimeter office zone in Chicago and Miami

Source: Philip Oldfield

scenario, where a high WWR supports the lowest energy demand due to its ability to harness direct solar heat gain to offset the city's bitter winter temperatures.

Optimising transparency and opacity

You can't appreciate a vista with your shins, or see much through the glass above your head.
[Justin Davidson, *New York Magazine*, 2014]

It's clear we need to tailor skyscraper façade design to better respond to the climate, culture and context of its place, and the needs of the inhabitants within. Key to this approach is a more intelligent and imaginative use of glass in high-rise façade design and a move away from the fetishisation of transparency. Although a WWR of 20% may be optimal in terms of energy use in some climates, such a low value is often commercially unthinkable, limiting view and human contact to the outside. Arguably, WWRs in the region of 40–50% seem more sensible in many situations. However, we also need to move away from façade homogeneity in tall buildings. Different orientations benefit from different systems, WWRs and shading strategies. Too often, skyscrapers are designed with the same façade in every orientation; as designers we need to better optimise each façade for the specific environmental and human opportunities it faces, including views and sunpath. This optimisation should follow in the vertical axis too; tall buildings often specify a homogenous façade from base to peak, which is unlikely to be ideal. In a dense urban environment, lower floors may be highly shaded and benefit from an increased WWR, whereas upper floors may be more exposed and therefore benefit from a lower WWR or increased shading.

The careful use of transparency and shade is particularly vital in hotter climates, where increased tall building construction is occurring. For example, the climate in the United Arab Emirates is characterised by high temperatures for much of the year, often above the comfort zone, with high levels of solar radiation. The key challenge is to reduce solar heat gains, to keep cooling loads low. In many high-rise buildings in the region, attempts are made to combat this challenge by specifying tinted glass with internal blinds; this reduces solar heat gain and glare, but also limits visible light transmittance, increasing the reliance on artificial lighting (Armstrong *et al.*, 2013). Such an approach negates the benefits of glazing, reducing view and daylight, but still contributing to higher conductive heat gains than an opaque wall.

O-14, designed by Reiser + Umemoto RUR Architecture and completed in Dubai in 2010, provides an innovative alternative. The design consists of a central core, with undulating office floor space wrapped around. The primary structural system – a 400mm-thick concrete diagrid – is pushed one metre outside the glazing line, connected back to the floor plates by structural joints. In this sense, it plays a double role – not only structural but as integrated *brise-soleil*, shading the glazed floors within (Figures 8.8 and 8.9). Pushing the structure outside the building also creates a cavity between the concrete diagrid and glazed facade. This

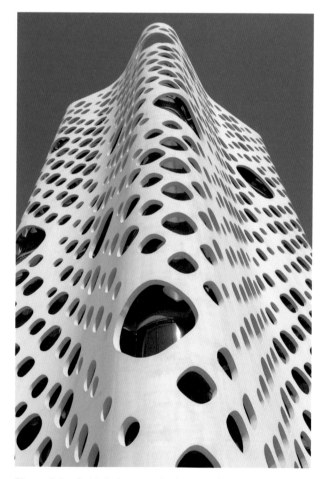

Figure 8.8 O-14, Dubai, view looking up showing the external diagrid

Source: Reiser + Umemoto, photo by Khalid Al Najjar

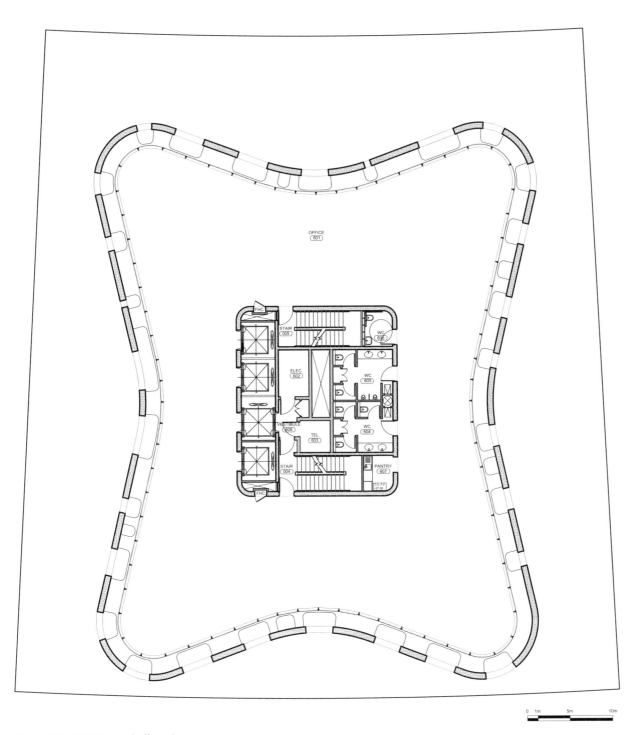

Figure 8.9 O-14, typical office plan
Source: Reiser + Umemoto

creates a thermal chimney; outside air is pulled into the cavity and rises due to the stack effect, drawing heat away and effectively cooling the surface of the glass, therefore reducing heat gains into the building (Figure 8.10). Estimates suggest this will decrease the building's cooling costs by 30% (Steele, 2012).

A total of 1,326 sinuous openings are punctured into O-14's exterior, creating an effective WWR of

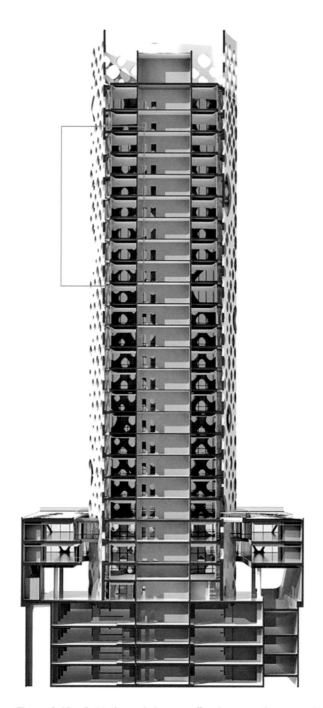
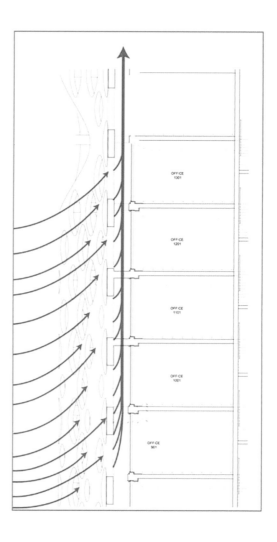

Figure 8.10 O-14, thermal chimney effect between the external structural shell and inner glass leaf
Source: Reiser + Umemoto

40%, and framing strategic views outside (Figure 8.11). The location of these openings was developed through an iterative process, balancing the structural and architectural needs of the project. Attempts were made to parametrically optimise the multiple roles of the exterior concrete shell, to balance the structural, shading and aesthetic responsibilities it takes on. However, this was abandoned in favour of a more random distribution of perforations (Steele, 2012). A parametric approach – where solidity and transparency of the

Figure 8.11   O-14, typical office interior
Source: Reiser + Umemoto

façade is optimised for environmental, aesthetic and other parameters across the surface of a tower's exterior – provides a significant opportunity for future design teams to create 'ideal' façade performance for a specific site and climate.

Although the manipulation of window-to-wall-ratio is important, we must not consider the tall building façade as a mere two-dimensional entity. Façade design is a truly three-dimensional process, and as designers, there are opportunities to tilt, twist and turn façades to improve their environmental and human performance. The Federation of Korean Industries Tower in Seoul, designed by Adrian Smith and Gordon Gill Architecture and completed in 2013, provides an excellent example. The design catalyst was the requirement to generate energy on-site from renewables, mandated by the local government. However, there were limited opportunities to manipulate the building form or orientation due to local zoning laws and the desire to contextualise with the surrounding context of mostly orthogonal blocks.

This meant adapting the building façade provided the greatest opportunity for innovation. The question was how can the façade be designed to maximise energy generation, but also multi-task the needs for shading and reduction of glare?

The design response consists of photovoltaic panels located on the spandrel areas of the south-east and south-west elevation and on the rooftop. To maximise energy generation these are tilted 10° towards the sun. Below this, transparent glass is tilted at 15° away from the sun, creating an undulating, folded façade (Figures 8.12, 8.13 and 8.14). This has the effect of shading the office spaces from the high summer sun, reducing cooling demands and some glare from the low angled sun. This also results in increased winter heating demands, although these are typically low in office buildings due to internal heat gains from computers, people and equipment. In total, the photovoltaic panels generate 824,028 kWh of electricity, which equates to 3% of the tower's total energy demand (Betancur, 2017).

Figure 8.12 Federation of Korean Industries Tower, Seoul
Source: Adrian Smith + Gordon Gill Architecture, photo by Nam-goong Sun

Adaptable and dynamic façades

The optimum façade design in any given climate or site needs to respond to a variety of different parameters, including the weather, season, sunpath and occupant use. The challenge is these parameters change across hours, days, weeks and months. A façade that can *adapt* and repeatedly change its characteristics and behaviour to respond to these dynamic conditions can bring benefits to the building in terms of reduced energy requirements, improved thermal comfort and visual delight.

In tall buildings, an increasing trend is the use of adaptable shading devices – shading systems that can dynamically adjust their position to respond to external conditions. The Al Bahr Towers in Abu Dhabi (designed by AHR, and completed in 2012) are the best example of this to date. Like O-14, the design points to an alternative to the tinted glass approach common in the hot climates of the Middle East. Instead, the Al Bahr Towers take inspiration from a vernacular shading device known as a *mashrabiya*. These traditional screens provide shade, privacy and the visual beauty of Arabic geometry in Middle Eastern architecture (Figure 8.15). Rather than a static shading device, the *mashrabiya* in the Al Bahr Towers are reinvented as a dynamic system, responding to changes in exterior weather and sunpath. The design consists of a circular plan, chosen to minimise the surface-area-to-volume ratio, and thus limit envelope area facilitating unwanted heat gains. Shading systems are provided where needed – the south, west and east – with unshaded glazing to the north, as this façade suffers little direct solar gain (Figures 8.16 and 8.17). As the sun tracks around the building, the *mashrabiya* open and close, powered by a series of actuators, to provide shade when needed, but to open up for daylighting and view once the sun has passed (Figures 8.18, 8.19 and 8.20). A building management system controls the opening and closing sequence according to the sun's position, but also allows for all *mashrabiya* to close in high wind conditions to prevent damage to the system, or all to open on overcast days for increased daylighting (Armstrong *et al.*, 2013).

While such a revolutionary strategy faced a variety of technical challenges in its realisation,[3] the environmental benefits are notable. Using a dynamic shading system allowed the project to use glass with a light transmittance of around 45%, compared to values of 15–20% that are typical in the region (Oborn, 2010). Little post-occupancy data on the Al Bahr Towers is available in the public realm, but simulated estimates prior to its construction suggest the buildings will contribute 20% less CO_2 emissions as compared to a similar tower without the shading system – a saving in the region of 1,140 tonnes of CO_2/year (Oborn, 2010). In addition, the project creates a visually striking response to both local climate and culture in a skyscraper, reflecting both the identity and environment of the region.

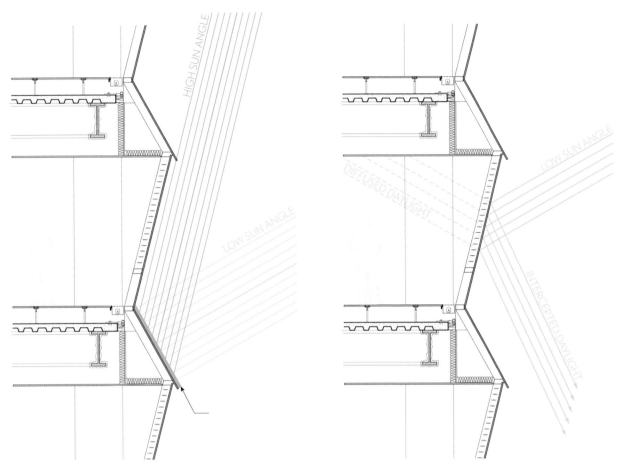

Figure 8.13   Federation of Korean Industries Tower, façade sections showing the tilt of photovoltaic panels towards the sun and vision glass towards the ground
Source: Adrian Smith + Gordon Gill Architecture

Figure 8.14   Federation of Korean Industries Tower, completed façade
Source: Adrian Smith + Gordon Gill Architecture, photo by Nam-goong Sun

Vertical greenery

A further opportunity for improving the environmental, social and aesthetic performance of high-rise façades is through the integration of vertical greenery. A variety of design opportunities exist, from living green walls (where plants are grown vertically in wall-integrated systems) to lush planted balconies.[4] Environmentally, there are several advantages (Santamouris *et al.*, 2017; Wood *et al.*, 2014; Pérez *et al.*, 2011):

- **Shading**: Locating vegetation on a high-rise façade will intercept and reflect a proportion of the incident solar radiation away from the building, shading the façade beyond. This can in turn reduce cooling demands in hot climates or summer months.

Figure 8.15 Mashrabiya façade, Dubai
Source: Philip Oldfield

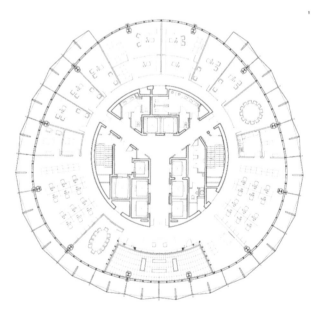

Figure 8.16 Al Bahr Tower, Abu Dhabi, thirteenth floor plan showing external dynamic shading systems on the south, west and east of the building
Source: AHR

- **Insulation**: Green walls can provide extra insulation through the addition of layers of vegetation and growing media such as soil.
- **Evaporative cooling**: The process of evapotranspiration, where water evaporates from plants' leaves, reduces ambient air temperature around vegetation, contributing to lower cooling demands (although also increasing local relative humidity).
- **Wind protection**: A green wall can protect the façade from the wind, creating a buffer zone of still air, which acts as an additional layer of insulation. Less wind hitting the façade can also reduce infiltration, and therefore unwanted heat losses and gains.
- **Urban Heat Island (UHI) mitigation**: The urban heat island effect refers to the higher temperatures experienced in urban centres as opposed to rural or suburban areas. This is caused by increased heat sources in the city (cars, air-conditioning heat extracts, etc.), but also solar energy being stored and

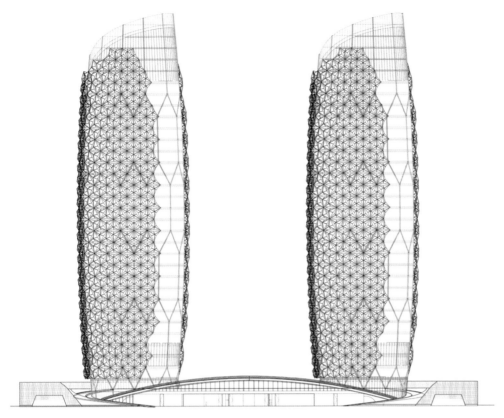

Figure 8.17   Al Bahr Towers, elevation showing shading system and exposed north-facing glazing
Source: AHR

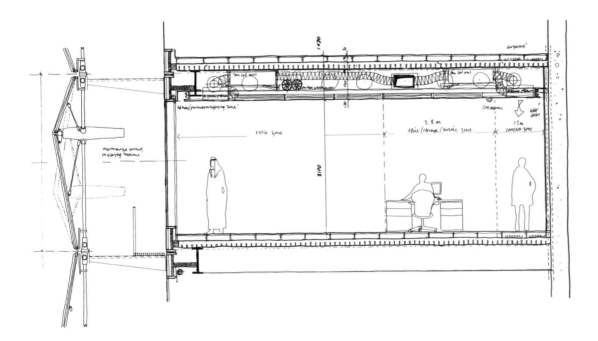

Figure 8.18   Al Bahr Towers, detailed façade section
Source: AHR

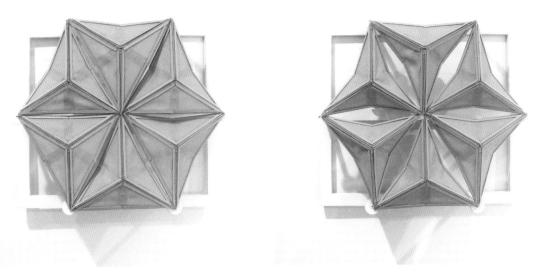

Figure 8.19   Al Bahr Towers, physical model showing the geometry of the shading system closed and partially open
Source: Oskar Carabez, Editha Supangkat, Sadina Tursunovic and Selma Tursunovic

Figure 8.20   Al Bahr Towers, view looking up
Source: Still ePsiLoN, CC BY 2.0, https://creativecommons.org/licenses/by/2.0/

re-radiated by buildings, paving and roads. The result is cities and urban areas can be up to 4–5°C hotter than adjacent rural areas, and can occasionally even exceed 7–8°C. Urban greenery can contribute to the mitigation of the UHI effect through shading and evaporative cooling as outlined earlier.

- **Air quality**: Plants absorb pollutants and particles from the atmosphere, such as heavy metals. Through photosynthesis they also absorb CO_2 and release oxygen.

However, the advantages of vertical greenery go far beyond the environmental, also bringing psychological and aesthetic benefits. Famously, Ulrich (1984) found patients in hospital with a view of a tree had shorter, less complicated recovery times than those who had a view of a brick wall. There is also evidence that exposure to nature can reduce stress, improve mood and enhance concentration (Health Council of the Netherlands, 2004). In the urban environment, vertical greenery can provide a visual beauty, vivid colours and a lushness often lacking in the built-up high-density city.

At the urban scale, no city has embraced vertical greening to such an extent as Singapore. For over 50 years Singapore has been adopting strategies to create a 'Garden City' that benefits from the visual and environmental qualities of parks, trees and greenery. In the vertical realm, this is encouraged by regulation and incentives. The Landscaping for Urban Spaces and High-Rises (LUSH) programme requires developers to provide new greenery equivalent to the site area through horizontal or vertical vegetation at ground or at height. Projects that go beyond this requirement can also benefit from floor area tax exemptions and bonus plot ratios, allowing them to construct higher towers than local zoning laws permit (URA, 2014). This progressive governance, along with a clear desire to mitigate the UHI effect in Singapore's tropical climate, has generated a built environment swathed with greenery, a fantastic experience for occupants and visitors alike (Figure 8.21).

However, perhaps the most dramatic example of vertical greenery built to date is in Milan. Bosco Verticale, designed by Stefano Boeri Architetti and

Figure 8.21 Vertical greenery in Singaporean high-rises
Source: Philip Oldfield

completed in 2014, incorporates 13,000 plants and 700 trees up to six metres tall grown on the balconies of two 27-storey towers. The technical challenges of achieving this are documented in research by Elena Giacomello (2014). Firstly, plant species were carefully selected to favour those that can tolerate higher levels of urban pollution, increased wind speeds at height and ease of maintenance. Structurally, to accommodate such lush greenery requires cantilevered concrete terraces, with rootballs anchored into their planters by textile belts, and trees tied back to the structure with steel cables for safety (Figures 8.22 and 8.23). Finally, the planting requires rigorous maintenance; ownership of the flats does not include the external plants or containers, which remain property of the building centrally. Access

to the plants is required six times a year – five times through the apartment and once via a roof-operated basket lift for external pruning. Understandably, pruning costs are estimated to be three to five times higher than pruning a tree on the ground (Giacomello, 2014).

Further research by Giacomello and Valagussa (2015) estimates the energy impact of the tree-laden façade, comparing it against more conventional envelopes using computer simulations. They found the additional shade the trees provided reduced solar gain to the towers, detrimentally increasing winter heating loads. However, the shade reduced summer cooling demands to a greater extent. Overall, it is estimated the vegetated façade of the Bosco Verticale reduces electrical energy needs by around 7.5%. Would this figure offset the increased construction and maintenance costs, both financially and in terms of embodied carbon? It's hard to tell. However, in many ways, this is beside the point. Such is the visual appeal of the towers, capturing the lushness and beauty of nature in a setting often typified by concrete and glass, that their real success is providing a vision that could make high-rise living much more appealing in the future (Figure 8.24).

The benefits of vertical greenery are clear, but we shouldn't rush out to green every facet of our built environment. Vertical greenery is a tool which needs careful and considerate application in design, especially in regards to climate. Different climates and façades will benefit from vertical greening in different ways; in consistently hot climates, vertical greenery that permanently shades glazing will be useful. Yet, in a temperate climate the use of deciduous plants that shed their leaves in the winter would still allow for some passive solar heat gain in the cooler months. Wind speed at height is a further consideration; there are many examples of vertical greenery in tall buildings, but few seem to exist above the 150-metre mark. Wind conditions at height and around tall buildings can be temperamental, and as such, specific wind studies should be undertaken to ensure that any green wall is protected from wind exposure that could be damaging to the plants or to people (Wood *et al.*, 2014).

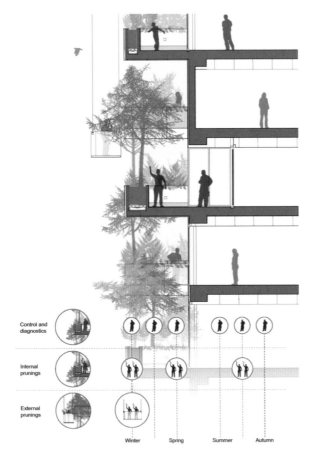

© Stefano Boeri Architetti

Figure 8.22   Bosco Verticale, Milan, section through planted balconies with the maintenance and pruning schedule per season

Source: Stefano Boeri Architetti

Conclusion

In conclusion, it is obvious that the all-glass skyscraper that dominates our cities is detrimental to

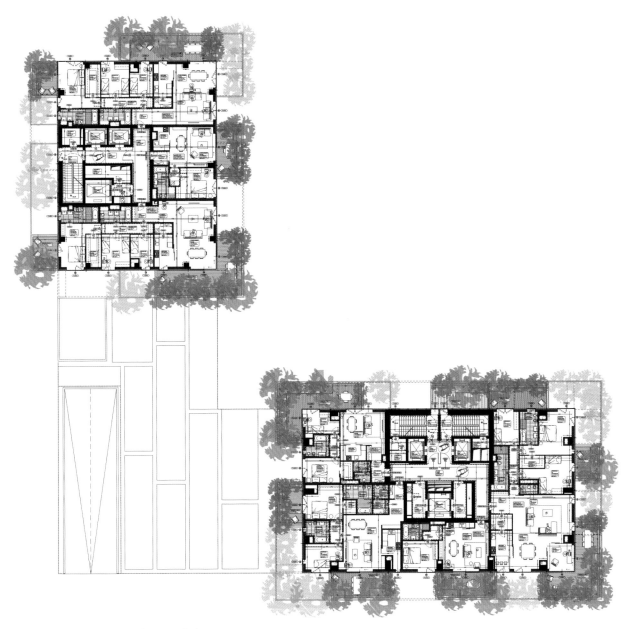

Figure 8.23 Bosco Verticale, typical plan
Source: Stefano Boeri Architetti

both the environment and its occupants. The concept, first visualised by Charles Burton in 1851, is now over 160 years old, with the problems such designs face having been widely known about (and experienced) for a similar timeframe. And yet, we still fetishise transparency in skyscrapers, an approach which is environmentally criminal given the current challenge of climate change.

Increasingly, both researchers and consultants in the field are calling for a reduced amount of glazing in tall building façades as a first step towards improved energy performance, with WWRs in the region of 30–50% often mooted (Harrington, 2016; Wood, 2015; Shuttleworth, 2008). However, there is no *one* solution. Different climates, programmes, orientations, sites and views clearly require different façade designs. Rather

Figure 8.24 Bosco Verticale, completed planted façades
Source: Stefano Boeri Architetti

than attempting to hide these differences in blanket curtain walling, with only perhaps a few glazing parameters changing, we should be celebrating these differences: framing views where spectacular, creating shade where beneficial, fostering privacy where needed. The aesthetic opportunities a balanced mix of transparency and opacity provide are far more appealing than the banality of sleek glazed repetition (Figure 8.25).

However, this chapter should not be read as an attack on glazing or transparency. No one wants to live in dark, dingy apartments, with little in the way of view and natural light. Instead, it calls for a more intelligent application of glazing to better balance the human and energetic needs of twenty-first-century skyscrapers. Achieving this balance goes way beyond

WWR, and will be helped by the commercial emergence of innovative glazing and shading technologies, including multi-layered glazing, vacuum cavities and responsive coatings such as electrochromatic glazing, as well as strategies such as dynamic shading systems and vertical greenery as outlined previously. Such technologies could allow for towers with significant levels of transparency, while maintaining low-energy needs. However, creating a transparent tower in itself should not be the aim; instead, sustainable tall building design should seek to optimise transparency, opacity, shade and technology to create façades that contribute to the lowest possible energy needs, while maintaining occupants' visual and psychological connection to the outside.

Figure 8.25 Victoria Tower, Stockholm, designed by Wingårdhs. A WWR of 50% can create more drama and frame more interesting views than continuous glazing

Source: Åke E:son Lindman

Notes

1 The Crystal Palace was eventually rebuilt at Sydenham Hill in London in 1852. It was destroyed by fire in 1936.

2 These include the 1921 Friedrichstrasse Skyscraper Project and the 1922 Glass Skyscraper.

3 The biggest challenge the system faced was maintaining reliability in conditions of high solar gain, sand storms and nearby saltwater. For example, in prototyping the shading system, a 1:1 scale *mashrabiya* was created and operated at different temperatures and with saltwater and sand sprayed onto the joints, to prove the system was durable (Armstrong, 2013).

4 For a more in-depth overview of green wall opportunities available to the tall building design team, along with several detailed case studies, see Wood *et al.* (2014).

References

Aries, M. B. C., Veitch, J. A. & Newsham, G. (2010). Windows, View, and Office Characteristics Predict Physical and Psychological Discomfort. *Journal of Environmental Psychology*, Vol. 30, pp. 533–541.

Armstrong, A., Buffoni, G., Eames, D., James, R., Lang, L., Lyle, J. & Xuereb, K. (2013). The Al Bahar Towers: Multidisciplinary Design for Middle East High-Rise. *Arup Journal*, Vol. 2, pp. 60–73.

Betancur, J. (2017). Multitasking Façade: How to Combine BIPV with Passive Solar Mitigation Strategies in a High-Rise Curtain Wall System. *International Journal of High-Rise Buildings*, December, Vol. 6, No. 4, pp. 307–313.

BRE. (2016). *Overheating in Dwellings*. BRE Trust, Watford.

Brown, M. & Ross, A. (2016). Residents Overlooked by Tate Modern Extension Should "Get Net Curtains". *The Guardian*, 21 September. www.theguardian.com/artanddesign/2016/sep/21/net-curtains-tate-modern-nick-serota

Buchanan, M. (2015). Glass, Towers. *The Awl*, 22 June. https://theawl.com/glass-towers-a229340442ae#.isl8wtmjv

Climate Consultant. (2018). *Version 6*. ©UCLA Energy Design Tools Group.

Davidson, J. (2014). Who Wants a Supertall Skyline? The Emerging Aesthetic of the 1,000-Foot Tower. *New York Magazine*, 5 December. http://nymag.com/intelligencer/2014/12/emerging-aesthetic-of-the-1000-foot-tower.html

Giacomello, E. (2014). *CTBUH Research Seed Funding Project 2013 – Green Living Façade for Tall Buildings: Bosco Verticale*. Proceedings of the CTBUH 2014 Conference, Shanghai, pp. 104–111.

Giacomello, E. & Valagussa, M. (2015). *Vertical Greenery: Evaluating the High-Rise Vegetation of the Bosco Verticale, Milan*. Council on Tall Buildings and Urban Habitat, Chicago.

Harrington, P. (2016). *Accelerating Net-Zero High-Rise Residential Buildings in Australia*. Pitt & Sherry, Sydney.

Health Council of the Netherlands. (2004). *Nature and Health: The Influence of Nature on Social, Psychological and Physical Well-Being*. Health Council of the Netherlands and Rmno, The Hague.

Isaac, M. & Vuuran, D. P. V. (2009). Modelling Global Residential Sector Energy Demand for Heating and Air Conditioning in the Context of Climate Change. *Energy Policy*, Vol. 37, pp. 507–521.

Jenkins, F. I. (1957). Harbinger's of Eiffel's Tower. *Journal of the Society of Architectural Historians*, Vol. 16, No. 4, pp. 22–29.

Lawrence Berkeley National Laboratory. (2013). *COMFEN*. https://windows.lbl.gov/software/comfen

Oborn, P. (2010). Dynamic Facades and Parametrics: Creating a New Vernacular? *CTBUH 2010 Conference, Mumbai*. www.ctbuh.org/TallBuildings/VideoLibrary/tabid/486/language/en-US/Default.aspx#/videos/watch/229

Oldfield, P., Trabucco, D. & Wood, A. (2009). Five Energy Generations of Tall Buildings: An Historical Analysis of Energy Consumption in High-Rise Buildings. *Journal of Architecture*, Vol. 14, No. 5, pp. 591–614.

Paxton, J. (1851). *What Is to Become of the Crystal Palace*. Bradbury & Evans, London.

Pérez, G., Rincón, L., Vila, A., González, J. M. & Cabeza, L. F. (2011). Green Vertical Systems for Buildings as Passive Systems for Energy Savings. *Applied Energy*, Vol. 88, pp. 4854–4859.

Poumadere, M., Mays, C., Le Mer, S. & Blong, R. (2005). The 2003 Heatwave in France: Dangerous Climate Change Here and Now. *Risk Analysis*, Vol. 25, No. 6, pp. 1483–1494.

Santamouris, M., Ding, L., Fiorito, F., Oldfield, P., Osmond, P., Paolini, R., Prasad, D. & Synnefa, A. (2017). Passive and Active Cooling for the Outdoor Built Environment – Analysis and Assessment of the Cooling Potential of Mitigation Technologies Using Performance Data from 220 Large Scale Projects. *Solar Energy*, 15 September, Vol. 154, pp. 14–33.

Schoenefeldt, H. (2008). The Crystal Palace, Environmentally Considered. *Architecture Research Quarterly*, Vol. 12, No.3–4, pp. 283–293.

Shuttleworth, K. (2008). *Form and Skin: Antidotes to Transparency in Tall Buildings*. Proceedings of the CTBUH 8th World Congress, "Tall & Green: Typology for a Sustainable Urban Future", Dubai, 3–5 March, pp. 481–484.

Spring, M. (2010). Cladding Renzo Piano's Shard. *Building Design*, 11 June.

Steele, B. (ed.) (2012). *O-14: Projection and Reception*. Architectural Association, London.

Ulrich, R. S. (1984). View through a Window May Influence Recovery from Surgery. *Science*, 27 April, Vol. 224, pp. 420–422.

URA. (2014). *Circular Package: Landscaping for Urban Spaces and High- Rises (LUSH) 2.0 Programme*. Urban Redevelopment Authority, Singapore.

Urban Green Council. (2013). *Seduced by the View*. Chapter of the U.S. Green Building Council, New York.

Wood, A. (2015). Rethinking the Skyscraper in the Ecological Age: Design Principles for a New High-Rise Vernacular. *International Journal of High-Rise Buildings*, Vol. 4, No. 2, pp. 91–101.

Wood, A., Bahrami, P. & Safarik, D. (2014). *Green Walls in High-Rise Buildings*. Images Publishing, Australia.

World Meterological Organization. (2015). *WMO: 2015 Likely to be Warmest on Record, 2011–2015 Warmest Five Year Period*. http://public.wmo.int/en/media/press-release/wmo-2015-likely-be-warmest-record-2011-2015-warmest-five-year-period

PART IV

Future concepts

CHAPTER NINE
Conclusion

Towards a high-rise sustainability revolution

Introduction

The overall theme of this book is that our current skyscraper designs are not yet realising the potential the building type offers. The design aspiration of many tall buildings seems to be limited to mainly meeting the economic needs of the developer and not the environmental needs of the planet, nor the social needs of its people. At the urban scale, there is evidence that towers can contribute to compact and sustainable cities, with efficiencies of transit and proximity (see Chapter 2). Yet, at the building scale, many high-rise designs are failing to achieve the environmental and social performance necessary to tackle the global challenges we face in the twenty-first century. Make no mistake, providing billions of new homes that are both comfortable and desirable for our burgeoning urban populations while radically reducing anthropogenic carbon emissions is a challenge of epic proportion. It is one which will require social, political and technological changes far outside the scope of discussions here. Yet, it is also a challenge that tall building design must play a role in, especially given the huge increase in the construction of towers in recent years – a trend that is more than likely to accelerate into the future. This is especially true given the long lifecycle of tall buildings and the fact that the towers we are building today will last generations, centuries even, and therefore impact the nature of our cities far beyond our lifetimes.

Throughout the previous eight chapters, the author has highlighted the many projects around the world that are using innovative architecture, technologies and engineering to challenge conventional tall building design. These includes projects using timber to create low-carbon structural systems, adaptable façades that protect against the extremes of climate, or providing dramatic spaces for the community at height through skygardens, amongst many others. However, for the potential of the skyscraper to be truly realised we need to be more ingenious still, creating radical vertical architecture that is generous to the environment, its occupants and the city.

To conclude this design primer then, the author presents here 12 tall building designs by architecture students from the University of Nottingham, Department of Architecture and Built Environment, and UNSW Sydney, Faculty of the Built Environment. The designs represent seven cities, with varying climates, cultures and contexts ranging from temperate London to tropical Singapore. They have been selected to graphically illustrate many of the suggestions the author has made to create sustainable high-rise architecture throughout this book – from embracing new functions at height for diversity of both programme and experience to the intelligent integration of skyscrapers into public transit networks to reduce transportation emissions.

These projects were created in post-graduate design studios run by the author with colleagues and practitioners from multiple disciplines, including architects, structural engineers, urban designers and MEP consultants. Students were asked to challenge the conventions that limit our current approaches and to balance creative and innovative design thinking with environmental and technical resolution. Many projects were completed in only a matter of weeks, often by a single student. The results presented here are just a snippet of often hundreds of pages of research, design process, drawing and simulation. Although they are ambitious, none are utopian, and all are tied to reality in terms of the key pragmatics of tall building design, including structural integration, planning efficiencies and building physics.

These ideas represent a new way of looking at tall buildings, transforming the typology into one which embraces sustainability and humanity, just as much as economy. Achieving these ideas in the conservative built environment will require dramatic changes; tough new building regulations and financial incentives, upskilling of design teams and dissemination of best practice, close collaborations between governmental agencies and private developers, and more. Yet, such thinking is surely necessary if we are to meet the ambitious social and environmental goals we have set for ourselves in the twenty-first century.

> [T]here is abundant evidence that our global economy is in the early stage of the Sustainability Revolution, which appears to have the scale of the Industrial Revolution and the Agricultural Revolution – and the speed of the Information Revolution. Compared to these three previous revolutions, the Sustainability Revolution is likely to be the most significant event in economic history.
>
> [The Generation Foundation, *The Transformation of Growth*, June 2017, p. 7]

Clean Air Tower

Designer: Alex Balchin, University of Nottingham
Tutors: David Nicholson-Cole, Philip Oldfield and Yan Zhu
Site: Tianjin, China
Design Themes: energy generation; stack effect; prefabrication and modular construction
(See Figures 9.1–9.5)

Air pollution in China is causing significant health and mortality problems, fuelled by increased coal burning, heavy industries, vehicle emissions and dust. In response, this design seeks to take advantage of an intrinsic environmental characteristic of height – the stack effect – to clean Tianjin's air.

The proposal consists of a slender tower with office and residential floor plates wrapped around a south-facing glazed solar chimney. External smog-filled air is drawn into the building at ground level, beneath a large glass canopy. Solar gain heats the air, causing it to rise through the solar chimney. As this occurs over a significant height, the buoyancy pressures created are large, causing the air to accelerate. This accelerating air drives wind turbines at the chimney's peak, which generates zero-carbon electricity to fuel the air-cleaning technologies. Venturi scrubbers in the atrium funnel polluted air through atomised water to remove particulates and pollution. This waste water is then filtered through a series of reed beds at the base of the building, before being re-used, creating a closed-loop system. A second system of electrostatic precipitators ionise smog particulates in the air, before collecting these at oppositely charged plates. Both of these systems are celebrated within the building's architecture by exposing their pipework and technologies within the glazed atrium.

The tower's structure consists of a braced-steel perimeter frame, creating seven-storey vertical villages with communal terraces between. The design uses modular construction and prefabricated components bolted together, allowing extra villages to be added to the structure, or removed, depending on demand and air quality changes over time. The idea is that these towers can be constructed in smog-suffering cities to improve local air quality. Once this improves, they can be disassembled and potentially moved to other cities

Figure 9.1   Clean Air Tower, Tianjin
Source: Alex Balchin

Figure 9.2   Clean Air Tower, section
Source: Alex Balchin

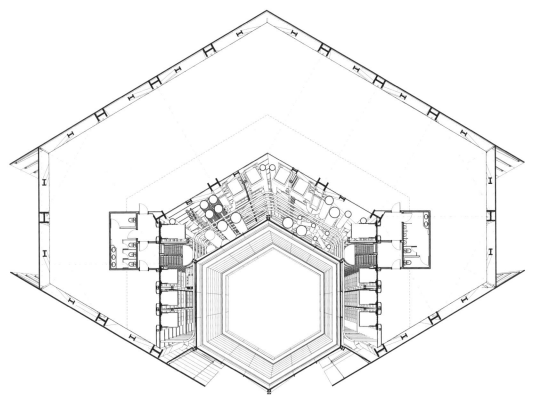

Figure 9.3 Clean Air Tower, typical office plan
Source: Alex Balchin

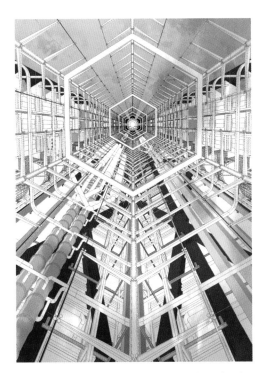

Figure 9.4 Clean Air Tower, view up the solar chimney
Source: Alex Balchin

or sites. This design for disassembly creates a reusable skyscraper, helping extend the building's lifecycle and thus reducing waste and embodied carbon (for more on this topic, see Chapter 7).

Agri + Culture

Designer: Jun Loh, UNSW
Tutors: Ivan Ip and Philip Oldfield
Site: Sydney, Australia
Design Themes: vertical farming; mixed-use; urban generosity at ground; community spaces at height
(See Figures 9.6–9.10)

This project proposes a hybrid of high-rise housing with sustainable vertical agriculture in Sydney, Australia. In doing so, it seeks to create an architecture that enhances high-rise living through intensive community growing, eating and selling of food in the city.

The site is the existing Sydney Fish Market, bounded by Blackwattle Bay to the west and a major highway

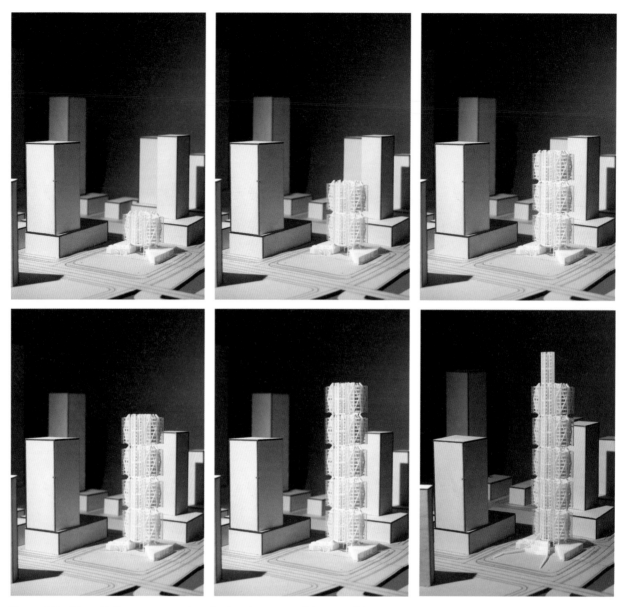

Figure 9.5 Clean Air Tower, construction phasing showing modular assembly over time
Source: Alex Balchin

to the east. At ground level, the design provides urban generosity by proposing an extension to the existing fish market, providing a new vegetable market for the region. The masterplan extends the existing street grid onto the site, reconnecting it to the city. Inspired by medieval market towns, it creates a series of narrow streets and intimate courtyards for trade and interaction, but also opens up to the water with floating markets and piers for water taxis.

Three towers rise out of the market, each made up of stacked four-storey 'vertical villages'. Cores are pushed to the south side of the plan, with façade farming integrated on the sunny north, east and west sides. The aim here is to create locally grown fruits and vegetables at a high density to be sold in the market below, thus reducing land needed for traditional agriculture and carbon-related food miles (for more on the benefits and challenges of vertical farming, see Chapter 6).

Figure 9.6   Agri + Culture, Sydney, ground-level fish and vegetable market
Source: Jun Loh

Figure 9.7   Agri + Culture, section
Source: Jun Loh

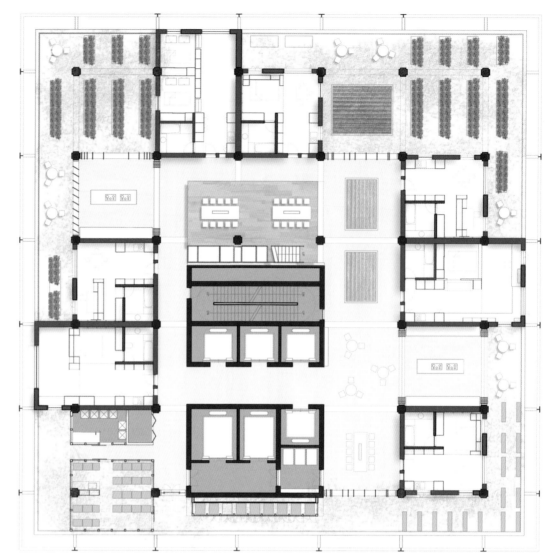

Figure 9.8   Agri + Culture, typical residential floor plan
Source: Jun Loh

Plants are grown in hydroponic beds on rotating trellises. These not only provide sustenance and income for residents but also act as a shading system for the apartments behind, dappling light through to the living spaces. The façade build-up is a mixture of mesh panels and glazing, providing permeability when needed, but also protection from increased wind speeds at height. Folded aluminium drainage channels collect rainwater for irrigation purposes and for tilapia farming.

Residential units are purposely small and simple, with minimal kitchen space. To compensate, generous shared kitchens and eating spaces are provided within each 'village' to foster neighbourly interaction and help create communities centred around group cooking and eating.

Waste food and plant cuttings are harvested and collected in a basement digestion chamber to generate biogas. This fuels a combined heating and power system, generating low-carbon electricity and heat on-site for the residents.

A New Shibam

Designers: Najla Gannur, Soha Hirbod and Fahimeh Soltani, University of Nottingham

Tutors: David Nicholson-Cole and Philip Oldfield

Figure 9.9 Agri + Culture, façade interior with vertical hydroponic beds for farming, which also act to provide solar shading
Source: Jun Loh

Site: Abu Dhabi, UAE
Design Themes: inspiration from vernacular architecture; response to desert climate; response to sunpath; community spaces at height
(See Figures 9.11–9.15)

Shibam is a walled city in Yemen, famous for its towers of mud-brick dating back to the sixteenth century.

These towers rise up to 11 storeys in height and benefit from thick walls of thermal mass, small windows and *mashrabiya* shading to respond to the harsh desert climate of consistently high temperatures and intense solar gain. What's more, these towers are closely clustered together, providing an element of self-shading, protecting a series of labyrinth-like alleyways and courtyards at ground level. Such an approach to passively

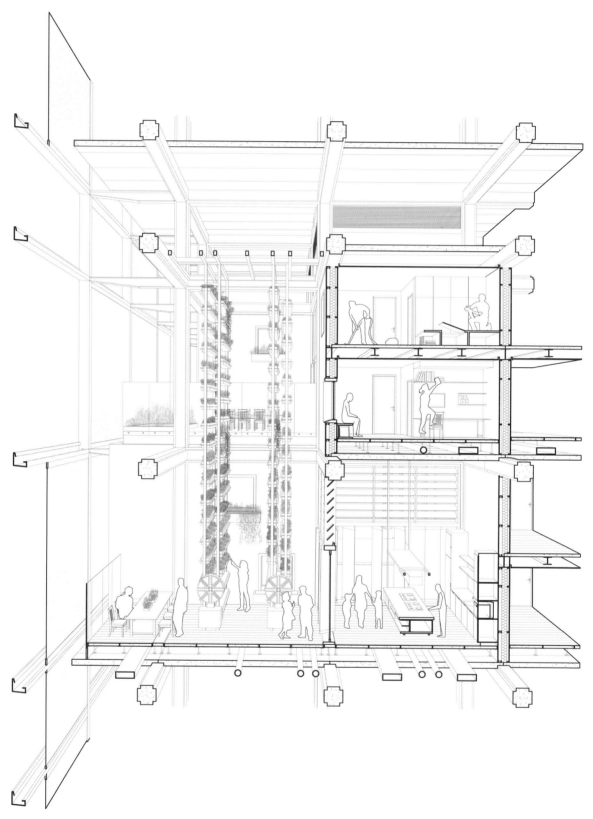

Figure 9.10 Agri + Culture, perspective section through the building's growing façade
Source: Jun Loh

Figure 9.11 Shibam – a historic city of mud-brick towers in Yemen
Source: Jialiang Gao, www.peace-on-earth.org, CC BY-SA 3.0, https://creativecommons.org/licenses/by-sa/3.0/deed.en

Figure 9.12 A New Shibam, Abu Dhabi, aerial view
Source: Najla Gannur, Soha Hirbod and Fahimeh Soltani

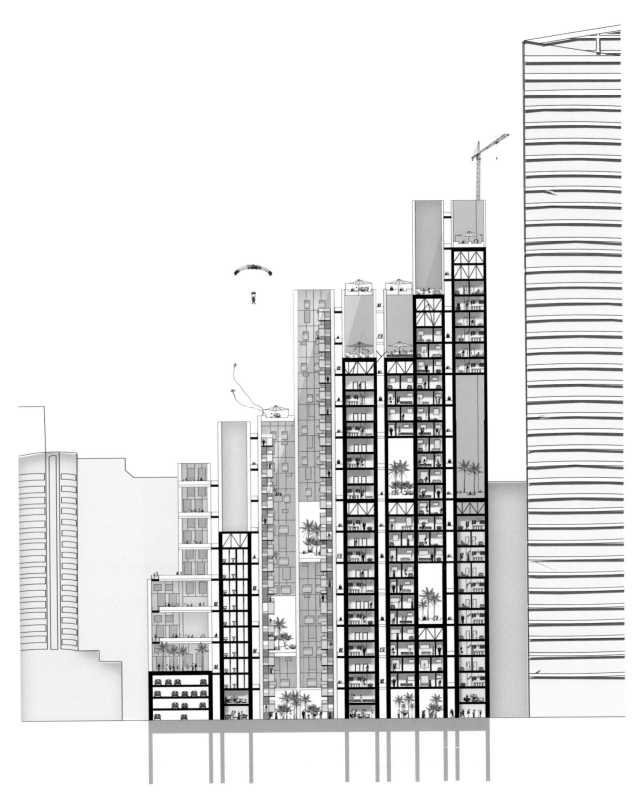

Figure 9.13 A New Shibam, section
Source: Najla Gannur, Soha Hirbod and Fahimeh Soltani

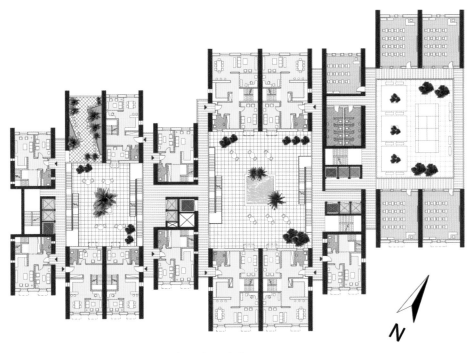

Figure 9.14 A New Shibam, typical residential plan
Source: Najla Gannur, Soha Hirbod and Fahimeh Soltani

Figure 9.15 A New Shibam, view looking up one of the central courtyards
Source: Najla Gannur, Soha Hirbod and Fahimeh Soltani

achieve thermal comfort was, of course, necessary at the time, as technologies such as air-conditioning were hundreds of years away from development. The 'New Shibam' project seeks to reinterpret this historic precedent in a contemporary manner through the design of a high-rise building in the comparable hot desert climate of Abu Dhabi.

The design consists of a series of slender residential towers tightly clustered together. These rise from 17 storeys to 33 storeys, stepping up across the site to contextually tie the skyline together, from the midrise Chamber of Commerce at the east to the taller ADIA Tower at the west. The towers are orientated facing north-south, with thick concrete sheer walls on the east and west façades. These act not only as the primary structural system for the building but also as a thermal mass buffer from the harsh desert sun on the eastern and western faces. Glazing makes up around 30% of the wall space on the north and south façades, while only a few punctured windows face east and west (for more on appropriate tall building design responses in the hot desert climate, see Chapter 4).

The towers are clustered around open, yet shaded courtyards, with passageways providing circulation from the elevator cores. Occupant privacy is maintained by ensuring passageways don't pass windows, while glazing in the courtyards is orientated to restrict views into apartments. Terraces are carved into the buildings' mass, creating large multi-storey openings orientated towards the adjacent Gulf. These channel cooling sea breezes but also create shaded spaces for social interaction at height. On the roof space, a series of stepped terraces with fabric canopies create additional places for play, social interaction and kite flying.

245 Blackfriars

Designer: Vassia Chatzikonstantinou, University of Nottingham
Tutors: Dik Jarman and Philip Oldfield

Site: London, UK
Design Themes: urban generosity at ground; mixed-use; response to sunpath; façade innovation (See Figures 9.16–9.20)

This project proposes a mixed-use office, residential and cultural programme, containing both formal and informal performance spaces in a high-rise development.

Sited on the Bankside of Blackfriars in London, the design sought to contribute to London's cultural district of arts, film and performance along the south side of the River Thames. A theatre is proposed as the primary cultural function, but rather than accommodate this in a conventional podium, which would have limited pedestrian links across the site, the theatre is

Figure 9.16 245 Blackfriars, London
Source: Vassia Chatzikonstantinou

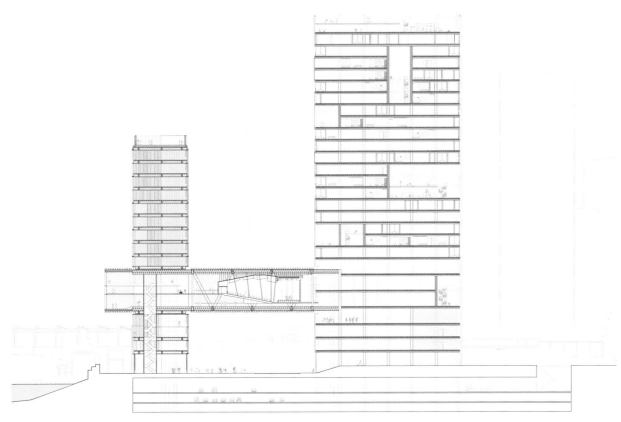

Figure 9.17   245 Blackfriars, section
Source: Vassia Chatzikonstantinou

lifted 24 metres into the sky, spanning between two towers. In doing so, it opens up a dramatic new public space in the city, reconnecting the Tate Modern with Blackfriars Road and the South Bank beyond. The ground level is slightly sunken too, creating an informal street theatre performance area, with the soffit of the theatre above acting as a place to hang scenery and props.

The two towers consist of an office building to the north and a more slender residential tower to the south – a direct response to both programme and sunpath, designed such that all residential units get access to passive solar gain. The core of the office is pushed to the south, with the occupied space to the north, to shade the office floors, since they require less solar access due to higher internal heat gains (for more on this topic, see Chapters 4 and 6).

Structurally, a concrete core with steel perimeter columns support the office. Concrete sheer walls are used in the slenderer residential tower. A hybrid steel

and concrete mega-truss spanning between them supports the floating theatre space.

The façade design uses a more tactile and climatically responsive materiality than conventional glazed curtain walling. The east and west façades of the office tower use a double-skin façade, with adjustable vertical timber louvres in the cavity, for shade. The residential tower is clad in a mixture of concrete, timber and corten steel, with punctured windows making up approximately 30% of the façade area, designed to minimise heat loss in the winter months.

Vertical Fiesta

Designers: Ankur Modi and Suruchi Modi, University of Nottingham
Tutors: David Nicholson-Cole and Philip Oldfield
Site: Singapore
Design Themes: community spaces at height; vertical greenery; inspiration from vernacular

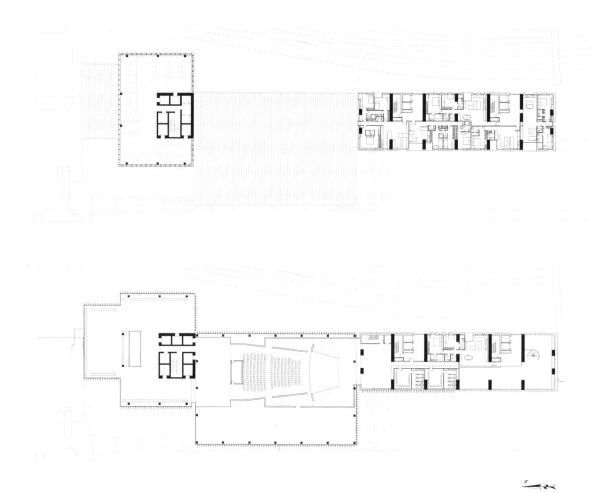

Figure 9.18 245 Blackfriars, theatre level (bottom) and typical office/residential level (top)
Source: Vassia Chatzikonstantinou

Figure 9.19 245 Blackfriars, informal street theatre at ground
Source: Vassia Chatzikonstantinou

Figure 9.20 245 Blackfriars, façade materiality
Source: Vassia Chatzikonstantinou

architecture; adaptable apartments (See Figures 9.21–9.25)

This project creates high-density residential communities with multi-cultural festival and celebration spaces at height. The site, on Beach Road in Singapore, is surrounded by a diverse mix of traditional low-rise housing and commercial high-rise towers. Site studies identified several religious and festival processional routes in the area. These have been linked and integrated into a processional ramp spiralling up the tower, to a mid-level multi-cultural performance space. The aim here was to lift the excitement, colour and vibrancy of activities that usually occur on the ground into the sky.

The residential accommodation consists of four pixelated towers of differing heights, designed to mediate between the surrounding high and low-rise setting, and maintain a strong urban axis running through the site. The towers are orientated with their longest sides facing north and south to minimise unwanted solar gain into the units, a direct response to the hot, humid climate and high tropical sunpath (for more

on appropriate tall building design responses to tropical climates, see Chapter 4). Suspended between the towers are a series of skygardens, hung in structural baskets, acting as places of community and social interaction, but also mitigating the urban heat island effect. Vegetation is embraced throughout, with the project providing 136% of the site area as green space through skygardens and vertical greenery.

Inspired by the adaptability of traditional South-East Asian housing, each apartment is given an entrance veranda and a small roof garden. These can be filled in with additional rooms over time, as families grow and children are born, or to create a home office, or sublet the upper floor for additional income. This flexibility creates apartments that can last a lifetime, adapting to occupants' changing needs and providing longevity for communities to thrive.

Unit plans are slender and carefully organised to minimise blockages, thus promoting cross ventilation to provide passive cooling. Adaptable photovoltaic shading blocks unwanted sun and provides on-site energy generation to offset the building's carbon emissions.

Figure 9.21 Vertical Fiesta, Singapore
Source: Ankur Modi and Suruchi Modi

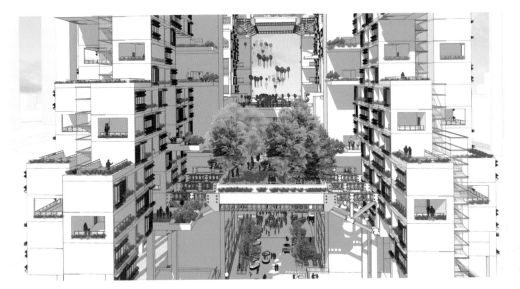

Figure 9.22 Vertical Fiesta, skygardens and view along the processional ramp
Source: Ankur Modi and Suruchi Modi

Figure 9.23 Vertical Fiesta, typical residential plan
Source: Ankur Modi and Suruchi Modi

Sustainable hyperdensity transit hub

Designer: Pansy Yau, UNSW
Tutors: Ivan Ip and Philip Oldfield
Site: Sydney, Australia
Design Themes: transit-orientated development; urban generosity at ground; connectivity at height (See Figures 9.26–9.30)

This design proposes a new high-density tall building cluster integrated into light-rail and water taxi transport networks in Pyrmont, Sydney. In doing so, it builds on the idea that the environmental performance of tall buildings is optimised when they are in proximity to public transportation networks, limiting our car dependency, promoting walkability and reducing a city's carbon footprint (for more on this topic, see Chapter 2).

The masterplan proposes a new urban vision for Pyrmont – a dense peninsular close to Sydney's Central Business District. New clusters of mixed-use towers are grouped around light-rail transit stops, providing ease of accessibility to mass rapid transit.

The design is focussed on one of these clusters, along Pyrmont's western edge. However, it seeks to go beyond a link to light-rail, by proposing a new intensive water taxi service for efficient transport east and west in Sydney. An inhabited pier is planned, acting as a water taxi stop and a cultural avenue, tying the public realm along the water's edge back into the city. At the city end of the pier, a light-rail station sits adjacent to the tower's entrance, creating a sustainable transit interchange integrating water and rail. Above this sits a mixed-use high-rise building, accommodating offices, public facilities at height, and residential apartments. The design celebrates travel further by expressing escalators and stairs within a transparent south-facing façade, providing inter-floor connectivity and encouraging walking between floors. Glazed shuttle elevators provide a direct link to a publicly accessible mid-level skygarden. Skybridges provide additional connectivity, linking to adjacent towers and allowing for greater access and interaction between residents and office workers throughout the tall building cluster.

ENTRY LEVEL PLAN

UPPER / LOWER LEVEL PLAN

Figure 9.24 Vertical Fiesta, apartment plans demonstrating adaptability

Source: Ankur Modi and Suruchi Modi

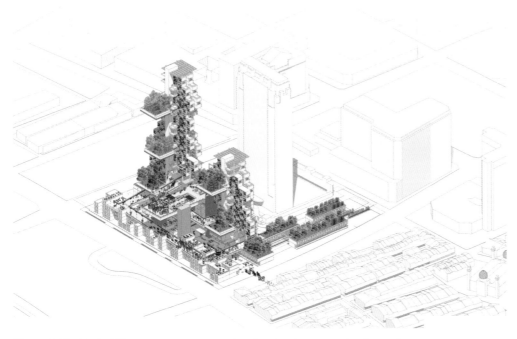

Figure 9.25   Vertical Fiesta, cut-away perspective showing the processional route in context
Source: Ankur Modi and Suruchi Modi

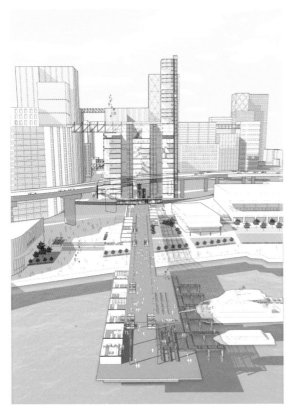

Figure 9.26   Sustainable hyperdensity transit hub, Sydney
Source: Pansy Yau

Mashrabiya Tower

Designer: Amna Shahid and Adriana
Villegas-Romero, University of Nottingham
Tutors: David Nicholson-Cole and Philip Oldfield
Site: Abu Dhabi, UAE
Design Themes: inspiration from vernacular architecture; façade innovation; community spaces at height
(See Figures 9.31–9.35)

A *mashrabiya* is a vernacular window, typically used in Arabic architecture to provide shade and privacy, but at the same time allow breezes into rooms and views out. Traditionally made up of wooden screens, they also celebrate the visual beauty of Arabic geometry through delicate latticework and patterns. The Mashrabiya Tower draws inspiration from this vernacular building element to create a climatically responsive envelope for a skyscraper design in Abu Dhabi, UAE.

The project consists of a residential tower, with a simple monolithic form. However, this hides a complexity of interior spaces and planning. Inspiration is drawn from the Arabian courtyard house through the creation of a large central atrium. This acts as the heart

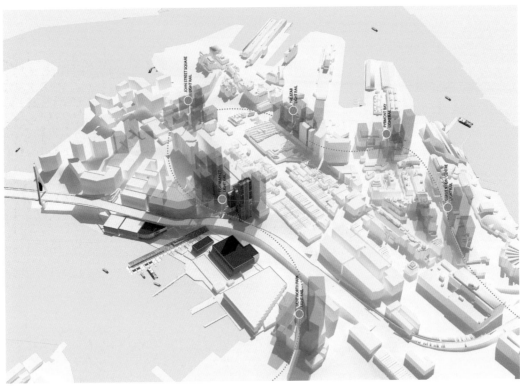

Figure 9.27 Sustainable hyperdensity transit hub, new clusters of tall buildings grouped around light-rail transit stops in Pyrmont
Source: Pansy Yau

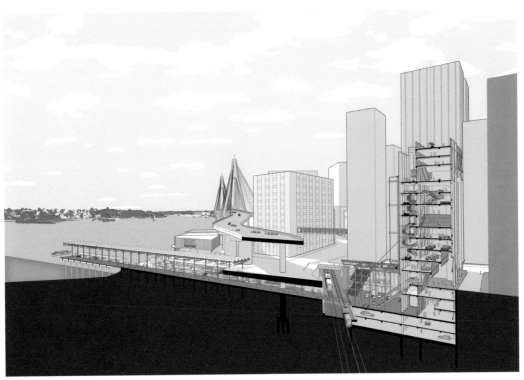

Figure 9.28 Sustainable hyperdensity transit hub, cut-away perspective highlighting the public realm horizontally and vertically
Source: Pansy Yau

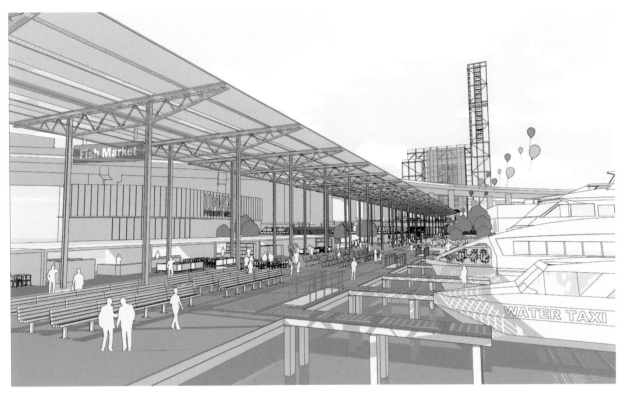

Figure 9.29   Sustainable hyperdensity transit hub, view along the water taxi pier
Source: Pansy Yau

Figure 9.30   Sustainable hyperdensity transit hub, light-rail transit stop
Source: Pansy Yau

Figure 9.31 Vernacular *mashrabiya* window
Source: Matthias Blume, CC BY-SA 4.0, https://creativecommons.
org/licenses/by-sa/4.0/

Figure 9.32 Mashrabiya Tower, Abu Dhabi
Source: Amna Shahid and Adriana Villegas-Romero

of the building and as a space for residents to gather and mingle. Each unit also has its own individual courtyard as a generous recessed balcony on the building perimeter, a place for the family to gather.

The primary design move relates to the building skin. This consists of a simple insulated inner envelope, with punctured windows and open courtyards. However, wrapping over this is a building-scale *mashrabiya* – a patterned shading system or curving aluminium profiles of different thicknesses. The density of the *mashrabiya* changes depending on programme and orientation. It is denser and more tightly woven on the east and west façade, to provide greater solar protection from the sun. Likewise, over bedrooms the density increases to enhance privacy. However, the *mashrabiya* also opens up in strategic places, to channel breezes from the adjacent Gulf and to frame views out from the central atrium and courtyards. The patterning is designed not only to improve thermal comfort but also to provide visual delight, casting evocative shadows across interior spaces.

The building programme is predominantly residential. However, this is supplemented by a library and a mosque located at the top of the tower. The mosque is set off-grid, to face towards Makkah, with the *mashrabiya* skin forming a roof to cast beautiful shadow effects below.

Terraced Tower

Designer: Xin Pei Chong, UNSW
Tutors: Ivan Ip and Philip Oldfield
Site: Sydney, Australia
Design Themes: inspiration from vernacular architecture; adaptable apartments; prefabrication; thermal mass
(See Figures 9.36–9.40)

The terraced house is a common typology in Sydney's inner suburbs. Built predominantly in the nineteenth century to house a growing worker population, such buildings still demonstrate a variety of environmental and social benefits over one hundred years later. They provide living at high densities while their compact form minimises winter heat loss in Sydney's cooler months. Verandas provide external space and shade from the summer sun, while their construction

Figure 9.33 Mashrabiya Tower, detail of the façade with the high-rise mosque beyond
Source: Amna Shahid and Adriana Villegas-Romero

Figure 9.34 Mashrabiya Tower, residential atrium
Source: Amna Shahid and Adriana Villegas-Romero

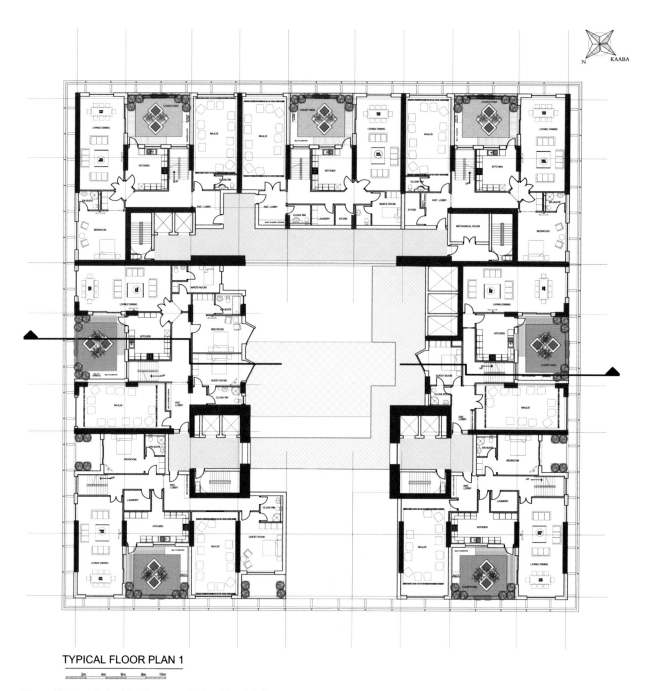

TYPICAL FLOOR PLAN 1

Figure 9.35   Mashrabiya Tower, typical residential plan
Source: Amna Shahid and Adriana Villegas-Romero

is standardised, yet easy to adapt or personalise over time. Given this wealth of qualities, this project aims to reinterpret the principles of the terraced house into contemporary high-rise housing in Sydney.

The design consists of three blocks of accommodation, organised within a well-defined existing street pattern. A low-rise four-storey block sits on Harris

Street, to maintain the existing street scale, while behind two slender towers rise to 41 storeys at their peak, but step down at the site edge, to tie into the surroundings. At ground level a series of community facilities are provided, including retail, cafes, a crèche and a library providing an active street frontage. Overall, the project provides a residential density of 500 units/

Figure 9.36 Terraced Tower, Sydney
Source: Xin Pei Chong

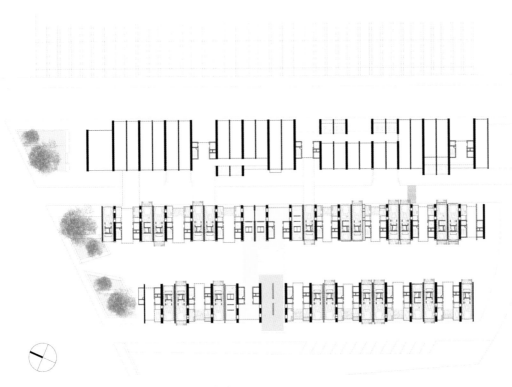

Figure 9.37 Terraced Tower, typical mid-level plan
Source: Xin Pei Chong

Figure 9.38 Terraced Tower, skygarden bridge
Source: Xin Pei Chong

hectare, a figure far above traditional terraced housing (for more on this topic, see Chapter 2).

Structural sheer walls at regular centres provide gravity and lateral stability, echoing the party walls of terraced homes. These are insulated externally, with the concrete expressed within the interior, thus providing exposed thermal mass to dampen the extremes of the hot summers and cool winters. Apartments are long and thin, but like terraces, have access to daylight and ventilation from both sides. The units are arranged in a 'hit and miss' fashion, providing permeability to enhance cross ventilation, but also reducing over-looking between the two blocks.

Apartments can be extended over time, through the addition of extra balcony space on either side or by infilling a small terrace provided to each unit. This creates extendibility and the option of adding rooms to apartments as families grow – a rarity in high-rise housing. The façade is prefabricated and standardised, yet can be individualised. Residents can choose from a variety of different façade packages when moving in, each providing different aesthetics and functionality. These include window seats, an office space, balconies,

winter gardens and more. The façade can easily be changed over time, by deconstructing and recycling older components and upgrading these, reducing waste and embodied carbon (for more on this issue, see Chapter 7). Each façade panel is 1.2 metres wide, meaning these can be easily transported via the elevator, rather than relying on cranes, providing ease of installation and adaptability.

Tanjong Pagar Vertical School

Designer: Michael Photiou, University of Nottingham
Tutors: David Nicholson-Cole and Philip Oldfield
Site: Singapore
Design Themes: vertical education; vertical greenery; response to tropical climate; community spaces at height
(See Figures 9.41–9.45)

Set against the reduced availability and increasing price of inner-city land, this project explores how educational facilities can compete with lucrative high-rise

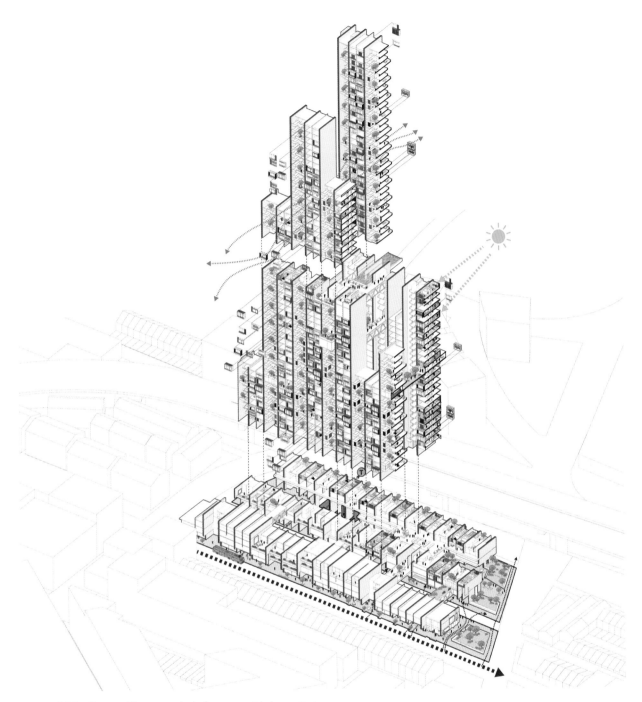

Figure 9.39 Terraced Tower, exploded axonometric in context

Source: Xin Pei Chong

residential and commercial towers (for more on this topic, see also Chapter 6). In response, a vertical school is proposed with a programme of underground transit station, public lecture theatre and performance spaces, primary school, secondary school, and student and staff residential accommodation in a single tower. In this way, the project efficiently stacks several functions on a small site, with direct access to public transit.

The building footprint consists of two wings of accommodation, with the long sides orientated towards the north and south, minimising direct solar heat gain from the east and west. The two wings are

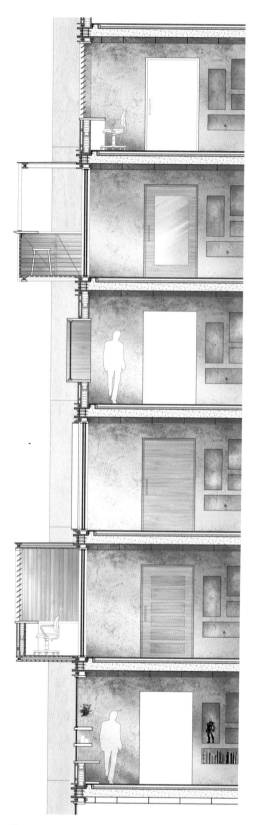

Figure 9.40 Terraced Tower, façade details with exposed concrete sheer wall internally
Source: Xin Pei Chong

Figure 9.41 Tanjong Pagar Vertical School, Singapore
Source: Michael Photiou

pulled apart, opening up a central atrium. This accommodates the social areas for the schools including sports facilities, a swimming pools and playgrounds, all spanning between the two towers and shaded by their form. Open-air terraces and skybridges provide generous outdoor areas and act as informal teaching spaces, supplementing the learning landscape vertically. This arrangement also creates a permeable building form, channelling breezes onto the playgrounds, but also facilitating cross ventilation through classrooms to provide thermal comfort in the humid tropical climate (see also Chapter 4). Aesthetically, this permeability is celebrated by breaking the mass of the tower into smaller villages expressed in the façade. This provides an identity for different school classes and years, but also acts as a transition between the adjacent low-rise

context to the north and the larger commercial towers to the south.

The design embraces greenery and vegetation throughout, to provide psychological relief from the glass and concrete surroundings, but also to mitigate against the urban heat island effect. The building creates a 'green link', connecting previously separated parks with a new landscaped route across the site. This is extended vertically through a series of green walls and landscaped terraces in the atrium, providing continuous greenery both horizontally and vertically, creating natural migration routes for butterflies and insects.

In terms of vertical circulation, shuttle elevators transfer occupants from the ground to the two main playgrounds, which act as the drop-off points for

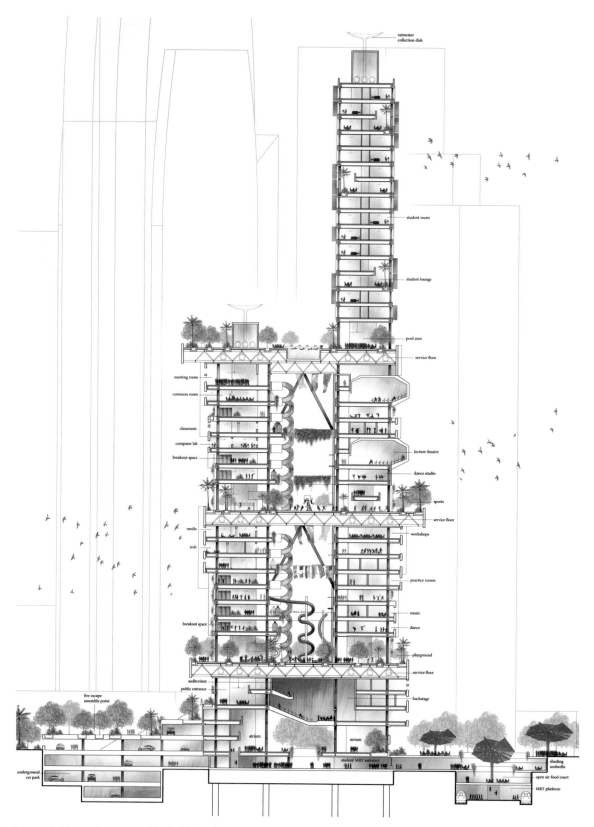

Figure 9.42   Tanjong Pagar Vertical School, section

Source: Michael Photiou

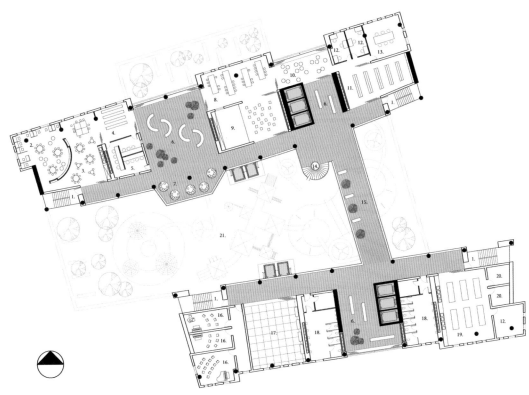

Figure 9.43 Tanjong Pagar Vertical School, typical school-level plan
Source: Michael Photiou

Figure 9.44 Tanjong Pagar Vertical School, children's playground
Source: Michael Photiou

Figure 9.45   Tanjong Pagar Vertical School, children's sport centre
Source: Michael Photiou

parents to safely leave children. From here, local elevators, stairs and slides act as secondary circulation within the schools.

Tea Haven Tower

Designer: Helen McGhee, University of Nottingham
Tutors: Dik Jarman and Philip Oldfield
Site: Hong Kong, China
Design Themes: façade innovation; response to sunpath; urban generosity at ground; community spaces at height
(See Figures 9.46–9.50)

The building envelope is perhaps the most important design element influencing tall building energy performance, thermal comfort, aesthetics and privacy. Throughout this book, the author emphasises that a failing of contemporary high-rise architecture is its over-reliance on the highly transparent curtain glass wall. Often this is the same on every façade, despite these offering different views and environmental conditions. Even more common still, façade design changes little with height, despite variations in environmental factors occurring vertically too (see also Chapter 8).

This project seeks to challenge this failing by creating a façade that better responds to its place and programme. The design consists of a residential tower, on a tight site in Mong Kok, Hong Kong. Vertical fins made of corten steel are used as the primary façade shading system. However, the density, depth and location of these fins is optimised to respond to three different factors:

- providing most solar shading on the east and west façade – the two 'hottest' sides of the building in the Hong Kong climate
- framing strategic views, but also providing privacy where needed

Figure 9.46   Tea Haven Tower, Hong Kong
Source: Helen McGhee

Figure 9.47 Tea Haven Tower, physical model in context
Source: Helen McGhee

- defining the site boundary and protecting a public courtyard at the base from the busy adjacent street-scape

So, for example, the density of fins on the east and west façade increases with height, since over-shading from surrounding buildings means less direct sunlight reaches lower levels (and thus, less shading is needed). Fins on the south are shallower and supplemented with recessed balconies to provide horizontal shading to limit solar penetration from the high-angled sun. At a unit level, the density of fins adjacent to bedrooms is greater than at balconies and living spaces, to provide additional privacy. The result is a façade that is consistent aesthetically, but which changes subtly with height and elevation, to respond to the surrounding environment.

At ground level, the fins provide a permeable barrier to an intimate public courtyard, set against the hustle and bustle of Nathan Road. A south-facing 'box' projects out of the building form to capture the sun, creating a naturally lit shadow puppet theatre as a cultural attraction. Small teahouses are located at different heights across the building, providing a communal space for resident interaction. Tea drinking was chosen because it is a mutual tradition, shared by many of Hong Kong's multi-cultural residents.

Sky Podium

Designers: Samuel Holt, Shreela Sharan and Willie Yogatama, University of Nottingham
Tutors: David Nicholson-Cole and Philip Oldfield
Site: New York, USA
Design Themes: Passivhaus performance; community spaces at height; response to sunpath
(See Figures 9.51–9.55)

This project seeks to create a Passivhaus skyscraper design and new urban gateway for Lower Manhattan, New York.

The site consists of three isolated plots of land at the entrance to the Brooklyn-Battery Tunnel off-ramp – a major artery into Manhattan and a route travelled by some 50,000 cars a day. The design seeks to reconnect these parcels of land into the urban fabric, but also to create a generous new urban space for the city. Given the challenge of creating large open spaces at ground in such a dense environment, it instead lifts this into the sky, envisioning a one-hectare 'sky podium' linking together three towers. This hosts a variety of public facilities typically found on the ground, but here, with the added benefit of spectacular views over the Statue of Liberty and the bay beyond. Public access is provided by shuttle elevators from the ground, but also a series of dramatic escalators stepping off surrounding roofs, which have been landscaped to create green terraces and roofgardens. The occupation of the Sky Podium changes throughout the year, even accommodating an ice-skating rink in the winter – a nod to New York's heritage of generous public space at the Rockefeller Center.

Programmes inside the tower are organised as per their optimum requirements for Passivhaus. As noted in Chapter 4, a Passivhaus design achieves thermal comfort to a maximum extent through a high-performance building façade, including the use of super-insulation to minimise heat loss and strategically located windows to harness solar free heating. In the Sky Podium, office accommodation is on the lower floors, shaded by the surrounding urban fabric as it benefits from high internal heat gains. Contained within the horizontal podium is a five-storey hotel, which benefits from south and east-facing rooms and a large atrium for daylight penetration deep into the circulation

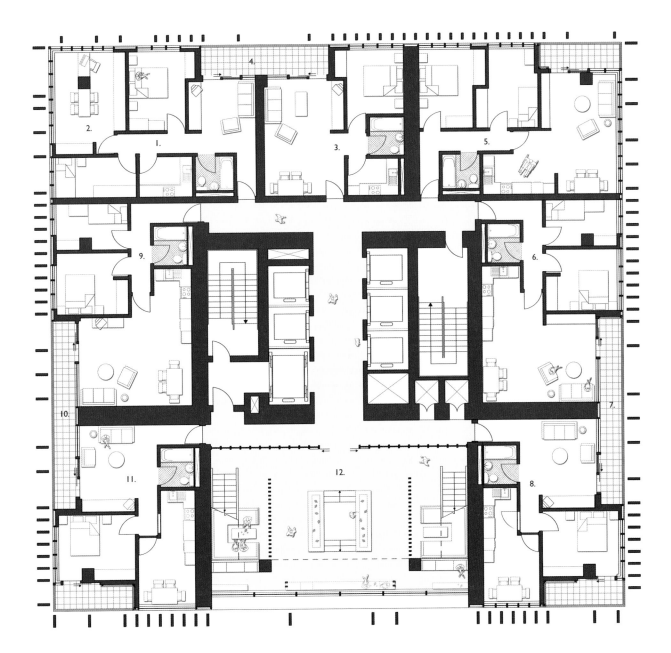

Figure 9.48 Tea Haven Tower, typical residential plan
Source: Helen McGhee

Figure 9.49 Tea Haven Tower, ground floor plan in context
Source: Helen McGhee

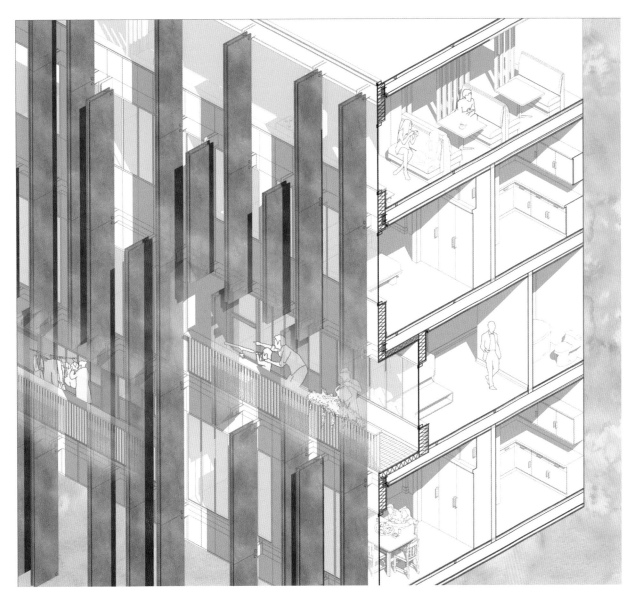

Figure 9.50   Tea Haven Tower, façade cut-away isometric
Source: Helen McGhee

spaces. Above is perched a slender residential tower facing south, designed to maximise passive solar gain. Apartments are single-loaded off a north-facing corridor, meaning almost every living space and bedroom is south-facing, benefitting from free heating. The façade is super-insulated, with thermal bridges minimised in the detailing and a typical opaque U-value of 0.14 W/m²K. Adjustable solar shading provides protection from overheating in the summer months. Mechanical Ventilation and Heat Recovery (MVHR) pre-heats incoming air, while an energy-sharing system captures

waste heat from the offices for use in the hotel and residential areas. Excess heat is stored underground via geothermal piles.

The complexity of the building form also responds to an additional layer of urban generosity for the surrounding context. Recognising that the creation of a new skyscraper on the site would block spectacular southern views from '88 Greenwich' – an existing art-deco residential tower to the north – the design removes building mass at lower levels, instead lifting the Sky Podium on two vast structural legs. While

Figure 9.51 Sky Podium, New York
Source: Samuel Holt, Shreela Sharan and Willie Yogatama

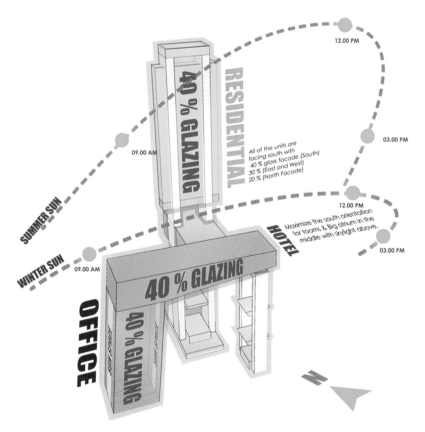

Figure 9.52 Sky Podium, arrangement of programme and glazing to achieve Passivhaus performance
Source: Samuel Holt, Shreela Sharan and Willie Yogatama

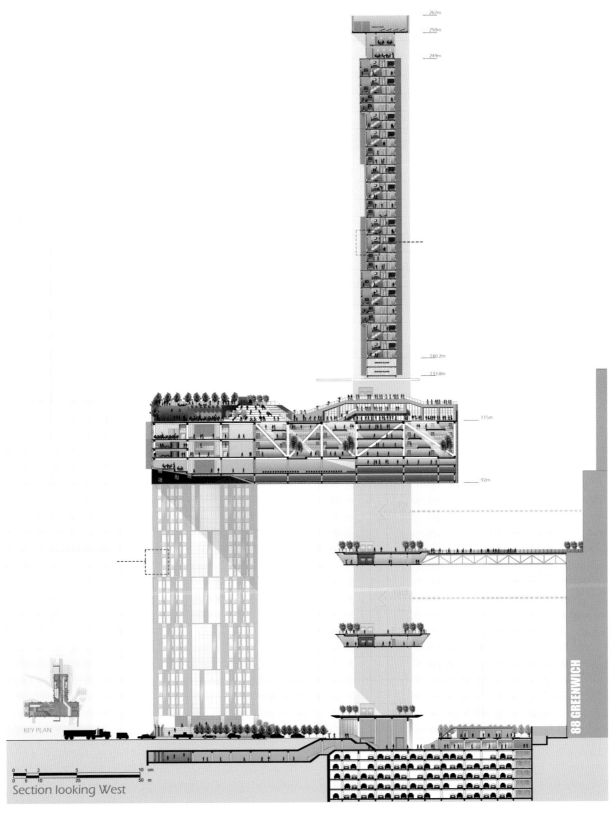

Figure 9.53 Sky Podium, section
Source: Samuel Holt, Shreela Sharan and Willie Yogatama

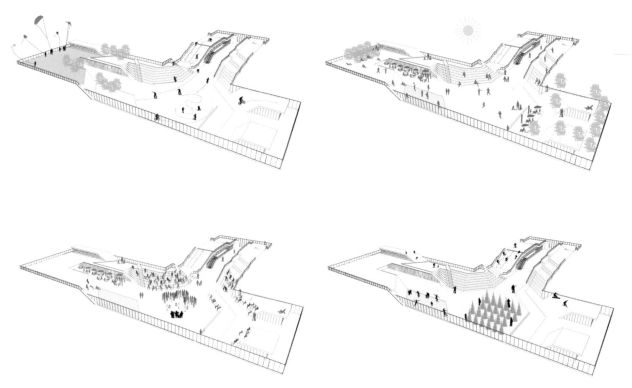

Figure 9.54 Sky Podium, occupation of the Sky Podium deck at different times of the year
Source: Samuel Holt, Shreela Sharan and Willie Yogatama

massive, these maintain vistas through the site, and thus, access to views for surrounding residents.

Solar Tower

Designer: Porus Vakshoor, UNSW
Tutors: Ivan Ip and Philip Oldfield
Site: Sydney, Australia
Design Themes: response to sunpath; façade innovation; on-site energy generation
(See Figures 9.56–9.60)

Sunpath and solar access has played a significant role in the design of high-rise buildings for over a century now. As far back as 1916, the New York Zoning Law stipulated towers should have set-backs to allow light and air to penetrate onto the streets below, creating the famous 'wedding-cake' skyscraper style of the time (see also Chapter 3). Today, a similar strategy is used in the City of Sydney, where a 'solar envelope' prescribing building heights and form is a major component of local planning legislation, designed to make sure

new towers don't cast shadows onto important public spaces in the city. Inspired by this history, this project aims to create vertical architecture shaped by the sun at three different scales – urban massing, building form, and energy generation technologies.

The design consists of three towers, accommodating a mix of commercial, residential, hotel and public facilities at Circular Quay, at the northern most edge of the city's central business district. Given this location, high-rise forms could cast significant shadows onto streets and public spaces to the south. To mitigate this effect, the mass of the three towers has been generated with computational design tools and algorithmic modelling to create a form that allows sunlight to penetrate onto specific public spaces beneath the towers, and to their south, at key times of the day, such as lunchtime. At the building scale, staggered atria are carved out of the towers' interior, allowing sunlight to penetrate deep into floor plates and through the northern-most tower onto the buildings behind.

In terms of technologies, a double-skin façade is used in the northern-most tower; sunlight hitting the

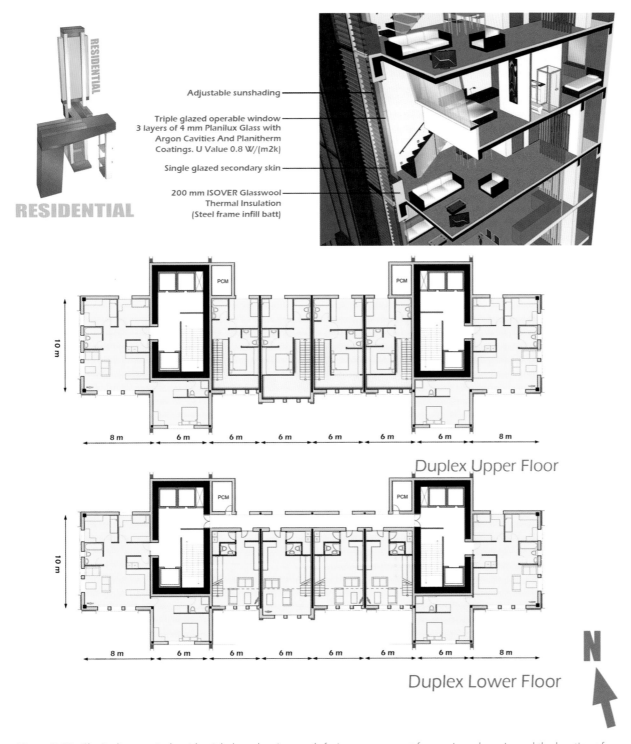

Adjustable sunshading

Triple glazed operable window
3 layers of 4 mm Planilux Glass with
Argon Cavities And Planitherm
Coatings. U Value 0.8 W/(m2k)

Single glazed secondary skin

200 mm ISOVER Glasswool
Thermal Insulation
(Steel frame infill batt)

RESIDENTIAL

10 m

8 m   6 m   6 m   6 m   6 m   6 m   6 m   8 m

Duplex Upper Floor

10 m

8 m   6 m   6 m   6 m   6 m   6 m   6 m   8 m

N

Duplex Lower Floor

Figure 9.55 Sky Podium, typical residential plans showing south-facing arrangement for passive solar gain, and the location of super-insulation to minimise heat loss

Source: Samuel Holt, Shreela Sharan and Willie Yogatama

Figure 9.56   Solar Tower, Sydney
Source: Porus Vakshoor

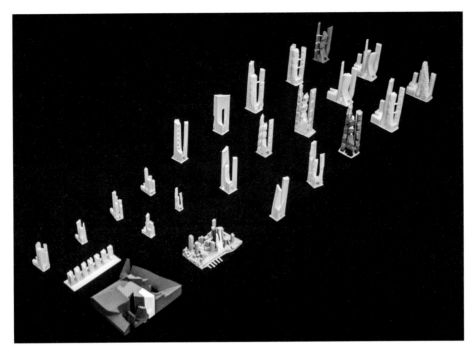

Figure 9.57 Solar Tower, evolution of building mass and form shaped by solar angles
Source: Porus Vakshoor

Figure 9.58 Solar Tower, public plaza at the tower's base facing north
Source: Porus Vakshoor

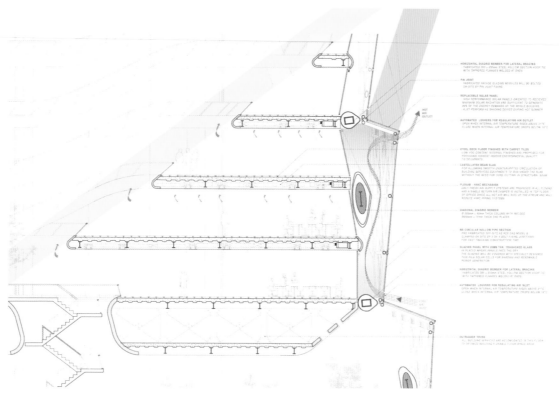

Figure 9.59 Solar Tower, section through north-facing, double-skin façade
Source: Porus Vakshoor

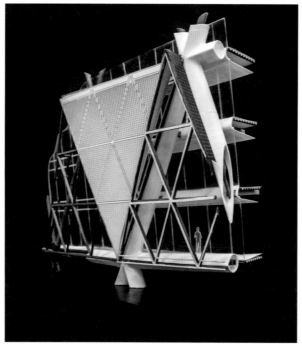

Figure 9.60 Solar Tower, 1:50 model through north-facing, double-skin façade
Source: Porus Vakshoor

façade drives the stack effect, which in turn removes heat from the void, drawing cool air in, and reducing conductive heat gains into the office spaces. The external layer of the double-skin façade has an undulating form, optimised such that transparent glazing is tilted down, to limit direct solar gain, while photovoltaic panels are tilted up to maximise energy output and provide shade. By doing this, the tower is estimated to be 'carbon positive' in operations; that is, the building will save 508 tonnes more CO_2 per year than it needs for the entirety of its annual operation of lighting, heating and cooling (for more on this definition, see Chapter 4).

Index